Research and
Practice in Education

Research and Practice in Education

Building Alliances, Bridging the Divide

Edited by Cynthia E. Coburn and Mary Kay Stein

ROWMAN & LITTLEFIELD PUBLISHERS, INC.
Lanham • Boulder • New York • Toronto • Plymouth, UK

KH

Published by Rowman & Littlefield Publishers, Inc.
A wholly owned subsidiary of The Rowman & Littlefield Publishing Group, Inc.
4501 Forbes Boulevard, Suite 200, Lanham, Maryland 20706
http://www.rowmanlittlefield.com

Estover Road, Plymouth PL6 7PY, United Kingdom

British Library Cataloguing in Publication Information Available

Library of Congress Cataloging-in-Publication Data

Research and practice in education : building alliances, bridging the divide / [edited by] Cynthia E. Coburn and Mary Kay Stein.
    p. cm.
  Includes bibliographical references and index.
  ISBN 978-0-7425-6406-0 (cloth : alk. paper) — ISBN 978-0-7425-6407-7 (pbk. : alk. paper) — ISBN 978-1-4422-0364-8 (electronic)
  1. Education—Research—United States. 2. School improvement programs—United States. I. Coburn, Cynthia E., 1967– II. Stein, Mary Kay.
  LB1028.25.U6.R46 2010
  370.7′2—dc22   2009050221

Printed in the United States of America

3/23/11

Contents

Figures

Tables

Foreword

Deborah Stipek

Why is so much that is known about how to help U.S. students reach high levels of achievement not applied in most school settings? How can research be more useful and usable to promote changes in educational practices that will improve student success? These two questions guided the work of the MacArthur Network on Teaching and Learning, which inspired this careful study of promising solutions to the research–practice disconnect.[1]

The U.S. education system faces profound challenges. The movement to a global economy requires an educated workforce possessing skills far beyond those we sought even thirty years ago. Ambitious academic learning for all—what historically was asked of only a modest portion of our students—has become a universal goal. Meanwhile, the changing demography and increased cultural and language diversity of many school systems poses new challenges. Because of these demands and challenges, political and educational leaders and the public are calling for dramatic efforts to improve the performance of our schools.

In other sectors of our society, efforts to deal with such challenges and demands rely on substantial guidance from their research-and-development communities. Consider medicine, for example. It is unimaginable that efforts to improve patient outcomes in the field of medicine would be based predominantly on trial and error at the local level or the dictates of fads or charismatic personalities. Yet this is a fair description of education reform. Despite calls for "evidence-based practice" and "data-driven decision making" in education, research and development play a minor role in current educational improvement efforts.

The studies described here provide much needed guidance for working smarter in education reform. They describe the lessons learned from successful efforts to improve practice by reconfiguring the relationship between researchers and practitioners. The authors point out that partnerships between research and practice are challenging because of differences between practitioners and researchers in incentive structures, cultures, goals, status, and more. But the initiatives profiled in this book have achieved productive partnerships that bring research and practice together. The strategies vary; they include researchers and practitioners working collaboratively to build, test, and refine instructional curricula, professional development programs, and tools that range from fairly scripted instruction to general principles designed to inspire reflection and new frames for thinking about practice. Also described are efforts that build infrastructures to disseminate knowledge developed out of practice and others that develop processes and protocols or involve intermediaries to render districts and schools more fertile environments for research-based ideas.

The book analyzes the pros and cons of these different approaches. It prepares readers for the challenges of each, and it provides helpful suggestions for overcoming those challenges, including ways to establish overlapping goals that sustain ongoing commitment; draw on practitioners' and researchers' different kinds of expertise effectively; help participants forge the new professional identities that are needed to engage in the collaborative work successfully; and establish trust, norms to overcome status differences, and shared mental frameworks for interpreting joint work.

Contrary to the linear notion of research being conducted and subsequently disseminated to practitioners who apply the findings, the case studies reported here reveal variable, complex, and shifting roles of researchers, practitioners, and intermediaries and the multiple pathways through which researchers and practitioners can interact productively. In some cases, research guides the development of tools, which are then refined by practitioners. In others, researchers and practitioners work side by side from the beginning, or researchers' primary role is to help codify the experience and wisdom of practitioners. All cases illustrate the value of reciprocal relationships, with researchers learning from practice as much as practitioners learn from research.

The book moves us one giant step forward from simplistic models of employing research to improve practice—models that have failed miserably—to complex, dynamic, and realistic ways to conceptualize connections between research and practice. By applying the lessons learned from the pioneers of these more productive strategies described so well in this book, we may very well begin to see education reform based on systematic knowledge about teaching and learning.

NOTE

1. The MacArthur Network on Teaching and Learning was a network of scholars and practitioners brought together with generous funding from the John D. and Catherine T. MacArthur Foundation to investigate the relationship between research and practice in school improvement. Network members included Tony Bryk, John Bransford, Cynthia Coburn, Tom Corcoran, Tom Glennan, Louis Gomez, Diana Lam, Fritz Mosher, Nancy Owen, Charla Rolland, Mary Kay Stein, Deborah Stipek (chair), and Janet Weiss.

Acknowledgments

This work was done under the auspices of the MacArthur Network on Teaching and Learning. We are grateful to the members of the Network for helping conceptualize the study, providing feedback on the individual chapters and our emerging cross-case analysis, and providing assistance crafting the final implications. We thank the researchers, practitioners, and designers involved in the ten initiatives we studied for being so open and honest and allowing us to learn from their experiences. We thank the Pittsburgh-based team of Carolina Belalcázar, Judith Touré, and Mika Yamashita for their research assistance. We especially thank project director Judith Touré for the complex work of coordinating the ten teams of researchers involved in the case studies. We thank the Berkeley-based team of Soung Bae, Lori Hurwitz, and Erica Turner for research assistance and Corrie Park for assistance in preparing the manuscript. We thank Randi Engle, Teresa McCaffrey, and Kim Powell for their contributions during the case selection phase of the project. Finally, we thank the John D. and Catherine T. MacArthur Foundation and the Spencer Foundation for generous funding to support this ambitious endeavor.

1

Reframing the Problem of Research and Practice

Mary Kay Stein and Cynthia E. Coburn

More than ever before in the history of education, talk is abundant and expectations are high about the role of research in improving educational practice. Just as research and development play key roles in medical advances and technological improvement, educational research, it is argued, must inform how we instruct our youth, prepare our teachers, and organize and manage our educational system. Because of increased technological capacity as well as theoretical and methodological advances, our ability to collect, analyze, and synthesize evidence has grown by leaps and bounds over the past decades. Even more important, educational research has begun to tackle meaningful, practice-based questions and increasingly focuses on the problems facing schools and districts.

At the same time, educators are facing a host of challenges. The number of students in special education continues to climb. Teachers feel increasingly pressured to prepare students for high-stakes tests. School leaders are expected to provide for the ongoing education of their teaching staff as well as engage in data-based decision making, communicate with parents, and, even, market their schools in an increasingly choice-driven environment.

Daunting as these problems are, there are also educational success stories worthy of celebration. For example, more than 1,000 schools are successfully teaching traditionally underserved children how to read by the third grade. Teachers in thousands of schools are regularly devoting time and energy to develop (and share with their colleagues nationwide) sound, practical knowledge for how to teach writing that brings research and practice together. Over a dozen project-based, technology-enhanced science units have been created for middle school teachers in high-poverty, urban districts and have been continuously used to foster improvements in students' science achievement.

These three successes have a common ingredient: each came to fruition because of a strong partnership between educational research and efforts to improve practice. The first, Success for All, is based on knowledge gained from a twenty-five-year union of research on the teaching of reading and careful monitoring of on-the-ground implementations of a schoolwide reading program based on that research. The second, the National Writing Project, is a nationwide organization that for thirty years has been facilitating the exchange of information between university-based researchers and classroom teachers and the development of new writing practices. And, finally, the Learning Technologies in Urban Schools project brought researchers, teachers, and district personnel together to develop new instructional approaches to improve science instruction in two urban districts, an activity that continues to this day.

Although the names Success for All (SFA), National Writing Project (NWP), and Learning Technologies in Urban Schools (LeTUS) are well known within the education community, little is known about their inner workings. How was SFA first developed? How do teachers in the NWP develop knowledge for writing instruction in dialogue with relevant research? What role did teachers and researchers play in the development of LeTUS science units?

The answers to these and other questions are sorely needed if we are to uncover the ways in which research joins with practice to spur productive reform. To date, however, few researchers actually study the ways in which researchers and practitioners go about their work in projects such as these. What knowledge is brought to the table by the researchers? by the practitioners? How is that knowledge integrated and used in the creation of educational tools and in their implementation? What conditions support or hinder researchers' and practitioners' work together? How do developers scale up approaches beyond the initial sites and bring these research-based approaches to more schools and students?

This book provides answers to these questions and more. We do so by reporting on empirical studies of SFA, the NWP, LeTUS, and seven other successful, nationally known research-and-development projects. Because the participants in each of these projects were too busy doing their work to document how they were doing it, we received permission from them to investigate how researchers and practitioners interacted in each project. We interviewed the projects' founders, early adopters, and present-day participants; we studied their internal paperwork, their research papers, and their educational projects; and (whenever possible) we observed their current work in action. By investigating the roles played by research and practice in these educational improvement efforts, we have uncovered lessons for those who seek to do this kind of work in the future.

We have learned, for example, that the early phases of SFA were characterized by research findings being applied to practice, but that, over time, SFA developed mechanisms to incorporate the wisdom of practice into ongoing refinement of the program. These mechanisms enabled SFA to help schools continue to improve after initial achievement gains reached a plateau. It also enabled the Success for All Foundation as an organization to be more responsive to unique or changing local needs. We came to appreciate that one of the NWP's most important accomplishments is the infrastructure it has created to link the national organization to local sites across the country. This infrastructure creates opportunities for knowledge development and spread among teachers across the country. And we learned about the shifting roles played by researchers and practitioners as the tasks of the LeTUS project changed from curriculum design to professional development to institutionalization in the districts. Contained within these findings are important lessons for future work—about the timing, efficacy, and process of incorporating site-based adaptations, about the need for infrastructure to support research–practice interactions, and about the characteristics of teacher–researcher partnerships that successfully design and use tools for practice.

In this book, we draw on studies of these and seven other carefully selected research-and-development projects to identify lessons heretofore untold. We argue that when conditions are right, research and practice influence each other in productive and wide-ranging ways: through relationships that are sown, tools that are designed, and pathways and infrastructures that are developed to support current and future research-based improvement initiatives. We conclude by discussing implications of these findings for designers, funders, school and district leaders, and universities.

HISTORICAL CONTEXT

It is clear to even the most casual observer of educational policy that concerns about the quality and influence of educational research have become a central part of the debate about the future of educational reform. The landmark legislation No Child Left Behind mentions "scientifically based research" more than 100 times and includes new requirements for districts and schools across the country to adopt only programs for which there is scientific evidence. In the past decade, there have been at least two major task force reports on the quality of educational research and the relationship between research and practice (National Academy of Education 1999; Shavelson and Towne 2002) that have generated vociferous debate within the academy (see, e.g., Berliner 2002; Erickson and Gutierrez 2002; Feuer, Towne, and Shavelson 2002a, 2002b). There are also efforts in some cities to create new mechanisms for more continuous and more productive exchange between research and practice for school improvement (see, e.g., the Strategic Educational Research Partnership in Boston and San Francisco [http://www.serpinstitute.org] and the Consortium on Chicago School Research [http://ccsr.uchicago.edu/content/index.php]).

Amid the current flurry of activity surrounding research-based practice, it may be hard to recall that discussions about the relationship between research and practice in education have a long history. The issue has been a central topic of debate almost since the dawn of formalized approaches to educational research in the early twentieth century (Clifford 1973). But it became a central concern for researchers, practitioners, and policymakers during the 1960s and 1970s in the wake of new federal investments in education research. At that time, the debate assumed a linear relationship in which research precedes and informs practice. In this model, basic research is conducted in the research laboratory, and its insights flow unidirectionally into practice settings. In its most unembellished form (Havelock 1969), this linear model views basic research as leading to applied research, which then leads to the development of products or codified professional practices that are then disseminated to educational practitioners and systems (see figure 1.1).

The underlying conceptualization of the relationship between research and practice is important because it influences the way we view the problem and the policy solutions that we offer. Envisioning the relationship between research and practice as linear suggests that the so-called research–practice gap is the major challenge to overcome. This has led to policy solutions that focus mostly on *bolstering* the quality of basic and applied research, *translating* research findings into forms usable in practice, and *disseminating* research-certified programs and practices to

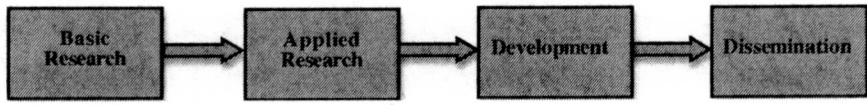

Figure 1.1. The Linear Model

practitioners. For example, concern about the research–practice gap in the 1970s led to attention to the role of "linking agents" (Hood 1982)—organizations or individuals who translate research findings for people in public schools—and federal funding of a series of regional education laboratories to fulfill the translational role (Clifford 1973). Concerns with diffusion of research findings and research-based approaches led to the development of the National Diffusion Network (NDN) (Hood 1982). Along with other federal efforts (e.g., the Educational Research and Improvement Clearinghouse), the NDN utilized the most up-to-date technology to gather, store, and widely distribute educational research findings.

The linear view of the relationship between research and practice has continued to hold sway in the resurgence of the debate in the early twenty-first century. For example, the Institute for Education Sciences, the arm of the U.S. Department of Education that funds education research, has implicitly drawn on the linear model to structure its *Requests for Proposals* since 2002. Funding is organized by phases of research for the improvement of practice, beginning with basic research studies that are intended to uncover new principles of learning, followed by studies that aim to design interventions based on those principles, and leading, finally, to larger-scale studies of the effectiveness of those interventions.

Contemporary debates have also focused on how to improve the quality of basic and applied research in education as a way to improve public schools (e.g., Kaestle 1993; Lagemann and Shulman 1999; Slavin 2002; Sloane 2008; Mostellar and Boruch 2002). This concern has resulted in the development of the What Works Clearinghouse, a federally funded agency the goal of which is to certify programs and approaches that are rooted in scientifically based research. As in the 1960s and 1970s, there are also increased efforts to translate research findings into practitioner-ready practices and programs, ranging from research briefs and Internet sources to organizations known as research intermediaries (see, e.g., the American Education Research Association's *Research Points* and the National Council of Teachers of Mathematics' *Abstracts, Briefs, and Clips*).

The problem with the linear model is that existing research on the relationship between research and practice suggests that, even in successful instances where research influences practice, things work quite differently. Research does not follow a linear path from research lab to the classroom. Rather, its influence is manifested via a complex system of processes and people, including the work of product developers, consultants, and service providers who are located in the space between researchers and practitioners (Clifford 1973; Nelson, Peck, and Kalachek 1987; D. Stokes 1997). These actors shape the substance of the information that is exchanged between researchers and practitioners and influence the pathways by which research reaches practice and practice influences research (Coburn 2005; Clifford 1973; Cohen and Barnes 1999). Moreover, studies of policy and reform implementation provide strong evidence that practitioners should not be expected to "take up and use research" through a process of dissemination or information transfer. Rather, implementation of research-based ideas necessarily involves learning (Kennedy 1997; Spillane, Reiser, and Reimer 2002); "handing off" research findings to practitioners is likely not a robust-enough strategy to ensure the uptake of research in the classroom. Finally, the linear model gives too narrow an account of the sources of innovation (Stokes 1997). In particular, it ignores practice, practitioners, and developers as a source of ideas and approaches. Yet many promising approaches historically have emerged from innovative practitioners and their partners involved in local development and experimentation (Clifford 1973). For example, under the leadership of Superintendent Anthony Alvarado, Community School District #2 in New York City became an existence proof of how to organize an entire urban school district for instructional improvement and improved student learning in literacy. The work of the superintendent, his assistants, school principals, staff developers, and teachers was subsequently captured, analyzed, and spread by researchers (Elmore and Burney 1999; Fink and Resnick 2001; Stein and D'Amico 2002), a clear example of researchers learning from practice.

While current policy solutions based in the linear model may hold promise in improving the quality of and access of practitioners to research, they are likely to miss the mark if they are rooted in assumptions that do not attend to the reality and complexity of how research and practice interact with one another. Fortunately, at the same time that there is increased concern about the relationship between research and practice, there is also a surge of initiatives designed to address this issue. For example, federal and foundation support for comprehensive school reform in the 1990s provided seed money for the development of research-based school reform designs (Datnow, Hubbard, and Mehan 2002), resulting in a raft of new school-improvement models rooted in research. Educational researchers were also developing new ways to do more practice-focused and practice-relevant research. For example, the new field of learning sciences, which places collaborative, research-based design at its core, was developing at this time as well (Brown 1992; Cobb et al. 2003; Collins

1992). Researchers from this tradition are forging new ways to work with practitioners to develop and study innovative instructional approaches.

The advent of new and promising initiatives that are bringing research and practice together for school improvement provides an ideal opportunity to investigate how research and practice *actually* interact. But to do so, we need a conceptual framework to guide the study that enables us to capture the multiple pathways through which research and practice interact as well as the various mechanisms—beyond transmission—by which each exerts an influence on the other.

OUR FRAMEWORK

To avoid the limitations of the linear model, we developed an alternative framework for understanding the relationship between research and practice for school improvement. We draw on research by Donald Stokes (1997) on the relationship between science and technology as a basis for our work. Through careful historical analysis, Stokes shows that the linear model—and the separation of basic research, applied research, and technological development it implies—is an artifact of the postwar conditions that gave rise to this conceptualization. He provides evidence that rather than being linear, the paths between research and technological development are multiple, reciprocal, and unevenly paced. Innovation arises from multiple places in the research–technology enterprise. Technological development influences research as much as, if not more than, the other way around. Furthermore, Stokes characterizes the relationship between research and technical development as "dual but semiautonomous trajectories" (48) that often are only loosely coupled with one another. That is, each enterprise moves along at its own pace in its own cycle, only occasionally intersecting and influencing the other.

Just as Stokes describes scientific research and technological development as semiautonomous enterprises, it can be argued that educational research and instructional improvement follow semiautonomous trajectories as well. It is not unusual, for example, for major school improvement initiatives to proceed with little or no input from research; similarly, it is possible to attend the annual meeting of an educational research conference and not hear from a single practitioner. Yet there are improvement efforts—like those profiled in this book—that have constructed sets of relationships that both pull from and feed back into research and improvement, bringing these semiautonomous streams into contact in productive ways. Our goal here is to explicate the nature of these linkages and the factors that facilitate productive interaction.

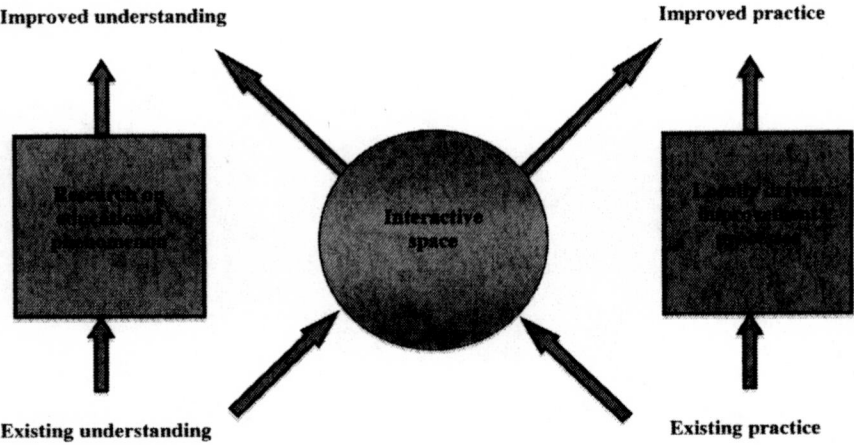

Figure 1.2.   An Alternative Model

Figure 1.2 depicts these semiautonomous streams of research and practice and the possibility of their linkage. The left side of the diagram depicts the world of research, where new efforts, building on the fruits of past work, contribute to new understandings. The right side depicts the world of practice, where iterative experimentation often leads to new practices and approaches. This book seeks to understand the ways in which these two semiautonomous trajectories interact in intentional efforts to bring research and practice together. Thus, we are interested in the activity that happens in the center of the diagram, which we call the "interactive space."

By drawing our attention to this interactive space, this framework enables us to elucidate the people, activities, and mechanisms that the linear model left shrouded. The framework also helps us to more clearly see the contributions of both research and practice to innovation. As shown in figure 1.2, the interactive space is potentially fed by information that comes from extant research knowledge and from existing practice. In addition, the figure shows that innovations created in the interactive space can enrich not only educational practice but also research understandings. Overall, the new framing provides a more balanced picture of how the worlds of both research and practice can afford and constrain a more productive research–practice relationship.

THE STUDY

Given our model's emphasis on multiple pathways for research–practice interaction, we focused on selecting projects to study that portrayed a range of possible ways that research and practice might interact. We also identified projects that were established, had existed for five years or more, had a track record, and were viewed as successful. (Details of the case selection can be found in the appendix.) Ultimately, we selected the following eight projects for investigation:

- Bay Area Lesson Study: a locally grown lesson study project in one San Francisco Bay Area school district
- Boston Public Schools, Boston Plan for Excellence, and Education Matters: a unique three-way partnership that brought educational research to bear on policy decisions in the Boston public schools
- Institute for Learning: a university-based design center that creates and supports innovative professional development systems in schools and districts
- LeTUS: a collaboration between researchers at Northwestern University and the University of Michigan with educators from the Chicago and Detroit public schools, respectively, to improve teaching and learning in middle school science through the use of learning technologies to support inquiry-based instructional methods
- Middle School Mathematics Applications Project (MMAP): a curriculum development and research project aimed at developing materials that would help middle school students learn mathematics in an inquiry-based fashion
- NWP: a national professional development network devoted to improving the teaching of writing in public schools
- QUASAR: an educational reform project aimed at fostering and studying the development and implementation of enhanced mathematics instructional programs for students attending middle schools in economically disadvantaged communities
- SFA: a schoolwide reading/writing/language arts program for prekindergarten to grade 5.

We then purposely selected two additional cases that were just starting out at the beginning of our study so that we could study research–practice interaction in more detail. The two projects were the following:

- Information Infrastructure Systems (IIS): a collaboration between researchers from the University of Chicago and Northwestern University and education professionals in Chicago schools to design technological systems and social practices for continuous school improvement
- Partnership for District Reform (PDR):[1] a collaboration between an external research organization and a major urban school district to promote evidence-based decision making at the district level

Whereas the eight established cases provided insight into larger patterns over time, the two emergent cases created the opportunity to gain microlevel understandings of the nature of research–practice interactions as they unfolded in real time. Together, the two kinds of cases enabled us to gain a more comprehensive understanding of the challenges and opportunities of rethinking the relationship between research and practice for school improvement.

Given the scant prior research and limited degree of theoretical development in this area, we used qualitative cases to create in-depth portraits of the nature of the research–practice phenomenon and to generate theoretical development. Each of the eight retrospective cases was studied over the course of a calendar year through interviews, observations, and the collection of project artifacts. To understand how projects evolved over time, we identified and interviewed individuals who played important roles at different stages of the initiative, including former project leadership, developers, and site liaisons or professional developers. The two longitudinal cases—IIS and PDR—were studied through iterative interviews with key participants and sustained observations of key events as the work was actually unfolding over the course of four years. (Further details about methodology can be found in the appendix.)

KEY THEMES

Taken together, the case studies identify a set of fundamental challenges to connecting research and practice and offer concrete suggestions about how to overcome them. First, we know from past research that establishing and maintaining cross-institutional partnerships—a frequently used mechanism for bridging research and practice—is difficult (Grossman, Wineburg, and Woolworth 2001). The obstacles to smooth, meaningful collaboration between researchers and practitioners include different incentive systems, asynchronous work practices, and the different statuses of researchers and practitioners. However, three of our case studies—MMAP (chapter 2), LeTUS (chapter 3), and IIS (chapter 4)—provide insight into ways to address these difficulties.

One of the key dilemmas successful partnerships must resolve is how to establish overlapping goals that sustain ongoing commitment. Often, partnerships begin by bringing together individuals chosen precisely for the variety of their viewpoints and expertise without acknowledging the complications that may surface as the result of different underlying goals, identities, and incentive structures. The cases in chapters 2 to 4 suggest that long-lasting collaborative work can require participants to forge new professional identities, sometimes forsaking earlier career pathways for something more novel and uncertain.

These chapters also reinforce and extend earlier research findings on the importance of trust and shared mental frameworks. In particular, chapters 2 and 3 show how the establishment of trust in the initial phases of a partnership can pay long-lasting dividends. Chapter 4 illustrates how lack of trust early on can haunt future work and how the trust becomes more difficult to establish with each additional partner, especially when those partners have different institutional homes (in this case, in the commercial sector). Closely related is the establishment of shared mental frameworks for interpreting joint work across researchers and practitioners. Often partners assume that they share goals and strategies for reaching them based solely on general discussion. Sometimes work proceeds quite far before they realize that they have different, sometimes irreconcilable conceptualizations of what the work will accomplish and how. Our cases offer clear suggestions for developing shared frameworks, such as engaging in the construction of concrete artifacts (e.g., a curriculum unit) in which partners are invested and that can—early on—reveal differences.

Second, as interveners have faced demands to scale up their practices, tools (e.g., curriculum materials, observation protocols, and rubrics) have become an increasingly popular way of bridging research and practice. Although often cited as a way to influence large numbers of teachers and classrooms, the opportunities and challenges presented by tools as carriers of research have not been carefully scrutinized. Chapters 5 to 7 address this issue. Taken together, the cases of SFA (chapter 5), the Institute for Learning (chapter 6), and QUASAR (chapter 7) demonstrate the importance of how tools are designed, how they are actually used in practice, and the relationship between the two.

When creating tools intended to change instructional or school-based practice to be more aligned with research, designers face an important question: is their tool meant to carry research directly into practice by identifying what practitioners should do, or is it meant to catalyze practitioners' thinking, encouraging them to become more aligned with research-based understandings and thereby supporting their ability to create, implement, and reflect on practices in ways that research suggests is effective? Tools designed in these different ways make different assumptions about teacher learning. When tools are meant to guide practice to align with empirically proven methods, the goal is for teachers to learn how to use the tool correctly; when tools are designed to develop research-aligned understandings, the goal is to develop new conceptual frameworks through which teachers can reflect on and reinvent their practice.

Tool designers also must determine how specific versus how adaptable their tools should be. Too much specificity restricts the range of contexts in which the tool can be used, while too much adaptability risks implementations that are unmoored from the deeper meaning and structure of the approach the tool intends to foster. The cases discussed in chapters 5 to 7 placed their bets at different points along the specificity–adaptability continuum; we show the pros and cons of each.

Third, past research suggests that the conditions in schools often work against opportunities for teachers to learn new approaches, sustain research-based interventions, and use research in their decision making in meaningful ways (Hargreaves and Stone-Johnson 2009; Kennedy 1997, 2005; Lortie 1975). This suggests that research—no matter how high quality or relevant—may miss its mark absent attention to the conditions for ongoing professional learning and decision making in public schools. Our case studies illustrate the importance of paying attention to the practice side of the research–practice equation. In particular, chapters 8 and 9—Lesson Study in a San Francisco Bay Area school district and the NWP, respectively—show that the introduction of processes and protocols to support knowledge-development activities for teachers, when coupled with pathways that bring research ideas and approaches into schools, can create fertile environments for research-based ideas in schools. More specifically, activities where teachers work with one another on problems that are central to their practice, use a process of iterative experimentation, and use measures of student learning to systematically verify the fruits of experimentation can help bring research into classrooms by helping teachers connect research to specific classroom moves and environments. This, in turn, enables smoother and deeper implementation of research-based ideas. The development of intentional pathways to bring research and research-based ideas into schools introduces new ideas and perspectives. These new ideas—when coupled with opportunities to critically evaluate and structures for experimentation—can prompt teachers to question their assumptions, clarify their understandings, and move toward deeper forms of practice. It can also increase the demand among teachers for research-based knowledge to support their work.

Finally, school district central offices are increasingly seen as a locus for bringing research and practice together for school improvement. Because district leaders make key decisions about textbooks, intervention programs, assessment, and professional development, they can play an important role in the degree to which instructional improvement efforts in schools are rooted in research and evidence (Coburn, Touré, and Yamashita 2009; Honig and Coburn 2008). Most efforts to increase district policymakers' use of research focus on increasing access to research and research-based approaches (Curriculum Review Panel 2004; Weiss,

Murphy-Graham, and Birkeland 2005; What Works Clearinghouse 2007). However, two of our case studies—the PDR (chapter 10) and an innovative partnership between the Boston public schools, an intermediary organization, and a research organization (chapter 11)—provide evidence that access is a necessary but not sufficient condition for substantive use of research by central office administrators. Even when district administrators have access to high-quality research on pressing topics, they often fail to use it in substantive ways in the decision-making process. Our case studies show, instead, that it is crucial to pay attention to the social processes that surround the research as a way to leverage research use. Frequent communication across diverse sectors of the district office, opportunities to engage deeply with research ideas outside the decision context, relations of trust, and shared understandings about instruction all promote more substantive engagement with research as part of decision making. Finally, these cases show that district capacity is crucial—not only the capacity to access, interpret, and bring research to bear on local problems but the capacity to orchestrate systemic responses as well.

All the foregoing suggests that forging linkages between research and practice is neither easy nor straightforward, but it is possible. And it helps to learn from those who have done it. The cases in this book teach us how to overcome obstacles: how to negotiate the different worlds of research and practice, how to use tools to spread reform beyond small-scale implementations, and how to move beyond naive ideas regarding the ease with which practitioners can be expected to engage with research in meaningful ways. Armed with lessons from these ten cases of successful research–practice interactions, researchers and practitioners can plan for future collaborative work with a more realistic road map of what to expect and prepare to successfully meet potential challenges. And policymakers, funders, and universities can take steps to create conditions that are more conducive to productive research–practice exchange.

NOTE

1. PDR is a pseudonym.

I

FOSTERING PARTNERSHIPS
FOR EDUCATIONAL
INNOVATION

The chapters in this part focus on the interactive processes that occur between individuals who are engaged in efforts that span research and practice. Because these individuals typically hail from separate institutional homes that have different incentive systems, asynchronous work practices, and different statuses, creating arrangements that foster productive exchanges between them is not trivial. When the goal is educational improvement at scale, collaborative work becomes even more complex.

We know from past research that partnerships can be challenging (Grossman, Wineburg, and Woolworth 2001). Lack of shared goals (Cochran-Smith and Lytle 1999; Wood 2007); the establishment of trust (Bryk and Schneider 2002); varying expectations regarding roles, responsibilities, and group norms (Lieberman and Grolnick 1996; Little 1990); and resentments over perceived status differentials and different work rhythms (Grossman et al. 2001) have plagued researcher–practitioner partnerships. Moreover, when researchers and practitioners have found ways to work together successfully at a small scale, they often face new hurdles when expanding to include greater numbers of practitioners (D'Amico 2005).

Over the past decade, a new form of research–practice collaboration has emerged: design research. Working shoulder to shoulder with practitioners, researchers build, test, and refine interventions in an effort to both improve practice and test and elaborate theoretical principles (Collins, Joseph, and Bielaczyc 2004). Typically, design researchers begin their work in specific contexts working on local problems of practice and then seek to move their interventions to new contexts (i.e., entire districts or national implementations). We know little, however, about the collaborative processes that unfold within these design research projects. Are they plagued by the typical problems cited in the literature on collaboration? How do the collaborations change when the projects expand to include new sites? Have they found specific ways of overcoming challenges? If so, what lessons do they hold for others?

In this part, we examine three design research projects, all of which established productive collaborations among groups of individuals representing diverse backgrounds, forms of expertise, and institutions. These projects demonstrate different approaches to building collaboration. The first project involved primarily researchers and teachers who together created curricular materials that were meant for publication and large-scale use; the second project (also a curriculum development effort) involved district-level practitioners in addition to researchers and school-level practitioners in an effort to push toward transformative system-level goals. The third project enlarged its circle of collaborators to an even more diverse group, including commercial vendors—along with researchers and clinical practitioners (individuals housed at the university who work primarily with teachers)—in order to design, test, and spread a technology-based professional development system. Thus, the three projects represent increasingly ambitious efforts to involve an expanding array of diversity within their collaborations.

In chapter 2, Randi Engle analyzes the evolution of work processes as the Middle-School Mathematics through Applications Project progressed from curriculum design work with a small set of practitioners to efforts to build a comprehensive curriculum for use by teachers nationally. The initial curriculum design phase teaches us how leaders can lay the groundwork for productive joint work among diverse participants (i.e., teachers, researchers, curriculum developers, and math-using professionals) and build norms to overcome status differentials. The second phase demonstrates how the development of trust and knowledge of others' expertise in the earlier phase allowed researchers' and practitioners' roles to diverge in the later phase without destroying the integrity of the collaboration.

In chapter 3, Laura D'Amico examines researcher–practitioner collaboration in two urban districts involved in Learning Technologies in Urban Schools, also in two distinct phases. The first phase yields insight into how researchers' and teachers' differential expertise was optimally drawn on in two very different contexts. The second phase demonstrates how the focus of design work shifted to professional development leading to new roles for teachers (from curriculum designers to lead teachers) and new foci for researchers (from researchers of science learning to researchers of professional development).

In chapter 4, Lisa Rosen examines a novel, cross-institutional partnership to create, implement, and study the effectiveness of a Web-based Professional Development Support System for video case-based professional learning by literacy coaches and teachers. Because this project spanned three separate organizations (a university, a university-based nonprofit, and a commercial business), the establishment of relational trust and the building of shared mental models were critical yet difficult to achieve. Similarly, communication among all three partners was challenging but critically important at all phases of the work. The case helps us to see the importance of these supports by showing us what can happen when they develop unevenly across the three partners.

2

The Middle-School Mathematics through Applications Project: Supporting Productive Collaborations during Two Different Phases of Curriculum Design

Randi A. Engle

A growing literature on teacher networks, teacher learning communities, teacher–researcher collaborations, and similar groups illuminates the challenges in establishing, supporting, and sustaining productive collaborations involving teachers and other educational stakeholders like researchers and curriculum designers (e.g., Grossman, Wineburg, and Woolworth 2001; Hindin, Morocco, Mott, and Aguilar 2007; Wood 2007). Collaboration is not a primary feature of most participants' workplaces, so establishing norms for collaborating effectively is a major undertaking for such projects (e.g., Grossman et al. 2001; Lieberman and Grolnick 1996; Little 1990). It is often a balancing act to make progress on joint goals while also addressing those of individual participants (e.g., Cochran-Smith and Lytle 1999; Grossman et al. 2001; Wood 2007). Such groups regularly struggle to create environments in which disagreements can be publicly voiced let alone addressed effectively (e.g., Borko 2004; Cochran-Smith and Lytle 1999; Grossman et al. 2001; Hindin et al. 2007; Pfeiffer and Featherstone 1997; Thomas et al. 1998). These and other challenges are magnified to the degree that participants differ in their goals, values, status, backgrounds, and accountabilities (Grossman et al. 2001). Finally, if groups are to be sustained, they need to make regular adjustments in how they address these challenges amidst continual changes in both the groups themselves and the larger contexts in which they and their participants are embedded (Stein, Silver, and Smith 1998; Wood 2007).

This chapter summarizes selected findings from a larger study of how collaborations between a diverse group of teachers, researchers, curriculum developers, and other educational stakeholders were supported over a decade within the Middle-School Mathematics through Applications Project (MMAP; see Engle 2006). On the whole, the project was very successful at managing many of these challenges and did so despite significant changes in the project as well as in the various policy, funding, and institutional contexts in which it and its members worked. Given that, the purpose of this chapter is to provide a summary of some key lessons learned by the project. In particular, I focus on how MMAP supported the collaborations that led to the codesign of an innovative middle school mathematics curriculum that consisted of technology-supported, project-based units that engaged a broader range of students in mathematics by situating their learning within workplace scenarios in which mathematics is regularly used (e.g., architects designing buildings or biologists modeling animal populations; see Goldman 2002; Greeno et al. 1999).[1]

In the rest of this chapter, I first briefly share evidence for the existence of productive collaborations in the MMAP project. Then I introduce four principles (problematizing, authority, accountability, and resources) that provide the theoretical framework for analyzing how MMAP supported productive collaborations. In the core of the chapter, I then compare how the project embodied these principles during two key phases of its curriculum design work:

1. During the height of the mathematics reform movement in California (where MMAP was based) from 1992 to 1995 when the National Science Foundation (NSF) provided MMAP funding to design and research replacement units to engage a wider range of students in learning mathematics by having it be embedded within real-world technology-based scenarios in which math is used
2. During its second NSF grant (1995–1998) when the project became responsible for building on its past work to construct a full comprehensive middle school mathematics curriculum that would be responsive to emerging standards for reform-based mathematics curricula while also being commercially publishable just as a backlash against mathematics reform was heating up in California and across the country

I compare these phases of MMAP's work in order to understand how projects like MMAP shift their means for supporting productive collaborations as their goals, capabilities, and embedding contexts change over time.

EVIDENCE OF PRODUCTIVE COLLABORATIONS IN MMAP

Three lines of evidence suggest that MMAP fostered productive collaborations between teachers, researchers, and curriculum developers:

Perspectives of Teachers. Although interviewees disagreed about many things, they were unanimous on the high quality of the collaborations they had experienced during the project. Teachers talked about there being a lot of "buy-in" and "really feeling valued in a professional sense," something most did not experience in the rest of their careers. They appreciated exposure to innovative ideas, developing instructional skills, discussing curriculum issues, and learning to design curricula for their own and others' use. Two of seven teachers even spontaneously reported that MMAP was the best professional development they had ever participated in. These results were corroborated in an evaluation report of MMAP that concluded that "teachers felt professionally respected in MMAP in ways some had never before experienced. Those who participated consistently spoke of MMAP not merely enthusiastically, but with a fervor that bordered on the evangelical" (Lichtenstein, Weissglass, and Ercikan-Alper 1998, 50).

Perspectives of Staff Researchers and Curriculum Developers. Staff members had similar perspectives on collaborations in the project. For instance, one MMAP programmer noted, "This was truly a place where I felt like the whole was better than the sum of the parts, like the team worked as a team." Similarly, one graduate student who became a longtime staff member commented, "For me, I always felt unbelievably fortunate to have stumbled in there, and once I was there I never wanted to leave . . . I was in heaven." The quotes could go on and on.

Concrete Achievements of the Project. In addition to these self-reports, the quality of MMAP's collaborations can be assessed by the products that resulted from them. In six years, MMAP's team created a full middle school mathematics curriculum that was later designated as a "promising" curriculum by two separate Department of Education panels, one on mathematics and the other on technology curricula.

An outside evaluation found that MMAP met its primary equity goal of having "a broad range of students (regardless of gender, ethnicity, or ability level) [be] motivated by MMAP materials" (Lichtenstein et al. 1998, iv). At the same time, the project produced more than fifty publications for a wide range of audiences (see Project CV in Engle 2006), with six being cited more than twenty times. Finally, the project lasted more than a decade, from 1990 to 2002, and people kept participating long after their initial commitments were over.

THEORETICAL FRAMEWORK FOR EXPLAINING HOW MMAP'S COLLABORATIONS WERE SUPPORTED

I explain how MMAP supported productive collaborations among its diverse stakeholders by adapting a set of principles my colleagues and I developed to explain productive engagement in classrooms (Engle and Conant 2002; Engle and Faux 2006). These four principles, which appear in various forms within research on professional collaborations, can be summarized as follows:

1. *Problematizing* together: The group finds joint problems to work on that all members of the collaboration are committed to working on together, as they are considered to be sufficiently unsolved, important, and accessible to all (e.g., Cobb, Wood, and Yackel 1990; Greeno et al. 1999; Lieberman and Grolnick 1996; Stein et al. 1998).
2. Respecting everyone's *authority*: Participants are truly given the *agency* to contribute their own perspectives on the joint problems (e.g., Cobb et al. 1990; Lieberman and Grolnick 1996). In doing so they become true *contributors* (e.g., Grossman et al. 2001; Palincsar et al. 2001; Thomas et al. 1998) and in some cases even *authors* of joint products (e.g., Hindin et al. 2007; Lieberman and Grolnick 1996); and through ongoing participation may even become *local authorities* about particular aspects of the work (e.g., Greeno et al. 1999; Stein et al. 1998).
3. Engendering a dynamic internal *accountability* to others and to shared norms and goals: Specifically, in the process of working together, participants are held responsible for accounting for how they are addressing both what others have done (e.g., Greeno et al. 1999; Grossman et al. 2001; Lieberman and Grolnick 1996) and agreed-on norms and goals for the enterprise (e.g., Palincsar et al. 2001; Wood 2007).[2]
4. Having access to sufficient *resources* to make all of the above possible: Resources may be as straightforward as having sufficient time

or money to do something (e.g., Hindin et al. 2007) to having access to specialists who can share relevant tools for addressing problems (e.g., Cobb et al. 1990; Stein et al. 1998). Some resources, like those mentioned previously, support productive collaboration directly, while others support the embodiment of the other three principles, as when one assembles a team with different perspectives on an issue in order to encourage it to be problematized (e.g., Grossman et al. 2001).

Although originally derived from classroom learning communities research, as the previous citations indicate, these principles incorporate findings from prior research on factors found to support productive engagement in teacher and teacher–researcher learning communities as well.

The basic idea behind the principles is that problematizing provides appropriate joint productive activities for groups to collaborate on (Stein et al. 1998). Supporting authority provides opportunities for everyone to become engaged in increasingly deep ways (Cobb et al. 1990; Palincsar et al. 2001; Stein et al. 1998), while accountability provides a check on untrammeled authority (Cobb et al. 1990; Grossman et al. 2001; Wood 2007). A dynamic balance between authority and accountability helps form collaborative communities that are supportive but challenging, in which relationships are built while productive work gets done, and that incorporate ideas from both inside and outside the community (e.g., Borko 2004; Grossman et al. 2001; McDonald and Klein 2003). Finally, resources make productive engagement possible while supporting the development of the many new group norms that problematizing, authority, and accountability require (e.g., Lieberman and Grolnick 1996; Grossman et al. 2001).

SUPPORTING PRODUCTIVE COLLABORATIONS WHILE DESIGNING REPLACEMENT UNITS (1992–1995)

I now begin using the four principles to explain how MMAP supported productive collaborations, starting with the first phase of its work. This is when the NSF provided MMAP with its first major grant to design replacement units that embodied its vision of applications-based mathematics and to study their impact on student engagement. As with other examples of design-based research (e.g., Cobb et al. 2003; Collins, Joseph, and Bielaczyc 2004; D'Amico, chapter 3 in this volume), units were designed and redesigned over numerous iterations involving extensive pilot testing and data collection. Teachers and MMAP staff together did curriculum design during monthly teacher workdays and multiweek summer institutes, by MMAP staff between these meetings, and during piloting when new activities were made up on the fly to address emergent problems or learning opportunities. How were problematizing, authority, accountability, and resources embodied by the project to support its collaborative work around this kind of curriculum design?

Problematizing by Recruiting Diverse Participants with Partially Overlapping Goals

In recruiting teachers as well as staff researchers and curriculum developers, MMAP simultaneously made sure there was some overlap in goals between the project and them while emphasizing the importance of otherwise having a diverse pool of expertise and perspectives to draw on. Having some overlap in place from the start helped make it easier for the project to find relevant problems that participants would want to engage in, a resource for problematizing (cf. Lieberman and Grolnick 1996; Stein et al. 1998). However, the overlap between the goals of potential participants and those of the project did not need to be extensive, nor did anyone's full set of goals need to be the same as those of anyone else. Instead, each person had to have at least one goal that overlapped enough with others to suggest problems to engage in with them.

Beyond that, MMAP sought to recruit staff and teachers who were as different as possible from each other to provide further expertise to the project while also making it more likely that important issues would be problematized among the group. Most MMAP teachers were not at all "like some researcher's dream of reform" (Knudsen interview), and they did not have identical perspectives on effective mathematics instruction, which sometimes led to discussions among them about why they had different perspectives. Similarly, MMAP staff were drawn not only from the field of education but also from former Stanford undergraduates who had pursued a wide range of majors and extracurricular activities and had lived in the dorm in which principal investigator (PI) Goldman and co-PI Raymond McDermott served as faculty fellows. Among other things, this led to the inclusion of gifted writers on the project who challenged standard ideas about how to write math curricula, suggesting new ways to organize and write MMAP's units so that they were much more engaging and accessible to both kids and teachers. Because many of these people were not typically focused on mathematics education or even education, they provided perspectives to the project that it might not have had were it to have recruited more narrowly. In general, diversity in perspectives among MMAP's participants tended to lead to productive problematizing of issues, as it was expected that people would not immediately understand or agree with each other, thus providing a safe platform for differences to get hashed out. In addition, this diversity was a factor in people's continued participation in MMAP, with numerous interviewees commenting on how cool, friendly, talented, and creative the other people at MMAP were and how getting to interact with these people was a key element that they found attractive about the project.

Problematizing Current Practices to Motivate the Need for New Designs

The project then engendered commitment to designing new forms of mathematics teaching and learning by engaging participants in problematizing current practices (Cobb et al. 1990). For example, during its first orientation, the project had participants experience the problems with the demonstrate-then-practice methods of learning mathematical procedures that are rampant in U.S. mathematics classrooms by putting them in the position of students learning an unfamiliar procedure in another domain using these same methods. In the ensuing discussion, the group reflected on their and others' experiences in such lessons, leading to ideas about why lessons like these do not support students' productive engagement in learning. Thus, by having participants problematize the typical ways in which mathematics is taught, the orientation provided concrete reasons that deepened everyone's commitment to create new kinds of mathematics instruction.

Problematizing through Multipurpose Design Tasks

Having helped participants personally appreciate the importance of project goals, MMAP then further supported problematizing by anchoring its collaborations around multipurpose curriculum design tasks that also addressed practical problems or dilemmas in which teachers, researchers, and curriculum developers all had a stake. Design tasks were a particularly effective anchor for collaborations because of their relatively open-ended nature (Goldman 2002; Greeno et al. 1999). To complete them, the group needed to create what did not already fully exist, providing space for multiple people to make contributions (Stein et al. 1998). At the same time, such tasks created concrete artifacts that helped prompt and ground conversations about larger issues of teaching and learning (Hindin et al. 2007). MMAP staff reported that they typically provided at the most a broad "map" of a proposed unit along with "some sample activities" or "prototypes of the software" that everyone would then try out at meetings, presenting them as unfinished "working hypotheses" to be improved on (Greeno et al. 1999; cf. Lieberman and Grolnick 1996). Teachers were then asked for their feedback on what changes should be made. As a result, new versions of the unit's design would be created that would then provide concrete anchors for subsequent revisions of that unit and others designed in parallel or subsequently.

MMAP further promoted problematizing by using design tasks that accomplished multiple goals, each of which was important to different MMAP participants (Greeno et al. 1999). For example, the same design activity of developing a teachers' guide for a unit allowed 1) the project as a whole to better disseminate its curriculum, 2) teachers to use their professional expertise to engage in the valued work of helping other teachers, and 3) researchers to learn more about what was pedagogically important to their collaborating teachers. Thus, one way to foster problematizing across a diverse group is working on joint problems that simultaneously satisfy the sometimes differing goals of participants from different communities.

Fostering Teachers' Authority by Making Sure Other Project Members Respected It

Fostering teachers' authority was especially important to MMAP, as teachers commonly have lower status than researchers. This was compounded by the fact that many of its staff were drawn from a very high status university: Stanford. MMAP began to support teachers' authority by hiring staff who already demonstrated respect for teachers. As PI Goldman explained,

> We didn't want anyone on the project ever who wasn't going to be collaborative with the teachers or had put-down attitudes about teachers or kids. You could not be thinking the problem with education was either the teachers or the kids and hope to get a job on the project.

For example, one programmer hired on the project described an interview process in which he was being carefully screened for his ability to be respectful of other people, especially teachers. He was asked to meet many different people involved in the project and felt that he was being watched for the extent to which he could listen as well as talk, to make sure that "I wasn't, for lack of better words, one of those kind of arrogant engineers." Thus, in endeavoring to select staff who already knew how to respect teachers, MMAP stacked the deck with people who would be more likely to treat teachers as having authority, thus using the resource of MMAP's staff to promote the principle of authority in regard to the teachers.

However, it was not always possible to prevent all problems around respecting teachers' agency and authority. When lack of respect was shown, say, by someone trying to use an academic degree as a basis for deciding an issue, that person was informed privately that this was unacceptable and was encouraged to do better next time. However, this did not work with the collaborating scientists with whom MMAP's PIs had originally written their NSF grant. Even after efforts to address the situation privately, the scientists still tended to put the teachers into recipient rather than contributor roles, tried to unilaterally make decisions for the whole group, and sometimes even showed clear disrespect for teachers' expertise, as in one occasion in which a scientist made a point of demonstrating that his daughter knew more about one math topic than a particular teacher. As a result, the project decided to end its collaboration with these scientists.

Subsequently, the project was careful to mediate its relationships with other high-status math-using professionals so that their expertise could be drawn on without its impinging on the authority of the teachers and other potentially lower-status participants. For example, rather than asking math-using professionals for their curriculum ideas, the project had teachers shadow these professionals while they worked in order to identify the interesting applied problems and relevant middle school mathematics embedded in their work that could then be turned into curriculum units. Later, the project informally consulted with various math-using professionals in an effort to make sure that the units were as authentic as possible. In so doing, MMAP addressed the potentially overwhelming authority of such high-status professionals by allowing their ideas to be considered but without giving them the power to make decisions. This in fact increased the quality of the ideas used from the math-using professionals, as teachers and MMAP staff could identify flaws in the ideas that were based on ignorance of school realities and then adapt the promising aspects to better account for them.

Fostering Teachers' Authority by Treating Them as True Agents and Contributors to Joint Work

Beyond making sure that other participants did not disrespect teachers, MMAP greatly supported teachers' authority on the project by providing them with agency and treating them as true contributors to joint work. With respect to agency, MMAP allowed teachers to decide exactly how they wished to participate in the project, and this fit with the overall working environment at MMAP's home, the Institute for Research on Learning (IRL), a research-and-development nonprofit that focused on developing and embodying practice-based theories of learning. In addition, teachers always had the agency to make the final decisions about which aspects of the MMAP curriculum to use in their classrooms and how exactly they would be used. As one teacher summarized it, "There were a lot of ways of participating and contributing to [MMAP]. . . . They didn't come in trying to tell people what to do. That made a huge impact, and a high level of trust was developed quickly out of that."

Treating them as true contributors to MMAP's curriculum designs solidified teachers' authority on the project. As mentioned earlier, teachers were presented with partially worked out curricula and asked for their feedback. However, crucial for making teachers actually *be* contributors was that their feedback was regularly reflected in the next iteration of the curriculum, something that many teachers noted as an essential feature of the project. Several teachers mentioned specific things that they had authored that became part of the MMAP curriculum, with staff also regularly crediting teachers with authorship of particular MMAP products. A few teachers also noted that this practice of regularly incorporating teachers' ideas made such a difference in their participation, as it contrasted markedly with standard practices in schools and other projects of asking for teachers' feedback and then doing nothing with it.

Fostering Accountability by Asking Participants to Account for Their Own Ideas and Practices while Being Responsive to Those of Others

If teachers' and others' engagement in the project was to be truly productive, however, much more had to be done than to find tasks to engage everyone in and make sure that everyone's ideas would be heard. MMAP had a vision to realize and deadlines to meet, and there were differing views among participants that needed to get negotiated (at least to some extent) for the project to do its work. The project managed this by gradually fostering participants' sense of accountability to each other and to a small set of crucial project norms while relaxing accountability in other ways to support teachers' authority.

At core, accountability was fostered in the project through regular encouragement for developing well-grounded accounts (or explanations) for instructional and design decisions. For example, when staff members saw teachers doing something that seemed antithetical to core MMAP values, rather than object they would ask them to explain the basis for their decisions. Sometimes the process of responding to such inquiries caused teachers to reexamine their practices and change them, while in other cases inquiries elicited an understandable reason that staff members would then accept. No matter the outcome, through this process MMAP staff would learn what underlay teachers' choices and then (in the words of one teacher-turned-staff-member) would be "in a great position to deal with people's worries" and persuade them indirectly by gently "suggesting things or giving them something to try."

Through similar processes, staff encouraged teachers to be responsive to staff ideas. For example, on one occasion the teachers initially rejected the first version of one unit because it did not seem to include much mathematics. However, rather than simply accepting this judgment, director Goldman acknowledged their skepticism but asked them to try it out anyway. The group did a partial run-through of the unit, with MMAP staff querying teachers on what mathematics, if any, arose. As a result, teachers left the session amazed at all the mathematics that could be drawn out of the unit and provided the project with suggestions for how to make it more explicit.

Similarly, persistence was demonstrated around the creation of accountability to the core notion of what made a curriculum unit "applications-based." In a process that took more than a year, staff provided nascent explanations of what such a unit is, teachers attempted to create examples that fit with them, staff noted ways in which they did not fit, and staff reexplained their ideas while teachers looked for mathematics in workplace contexts. Eventually, both groups were explicit enough about what it meant for a unit to be applications-based[3] that it became possible for everyone to hold themselves accountable to this vision during curriculum design.

Thus, in general, MMAP staff did not try to directly convince teachers to change their minds or follow particular guidelines but instead presented teachers with new ideas, encouraged them to "experiment" with them while incorporating their own ideas, and then saw "if they took to them or not."[4] In the end, the authority to use (or not) any ideas or materials shared by MMAP staff remained with teachers. However, this process provided many opportunities for teachers to "account for" their decisions. Thus, the teachers' accountability was fostered without impinging on their authority, a key challenge in promoting productive engagement (Engle and Faux 2006).

Additional Resources Facilitating MMAP's Collaborations

A wide variety of resources supported MMAP's work during this phase. Already mentioned several times was the key resource of which staff and teachers were included in the project. Money from the NSF and other funders as well as the time that it bought were also essential for allowing teachers to meet with researchers and curriculum developers monthly during the school year and for three to six weeks during the summer and to have regular e-mail contact at other times. MMAP participants also highlighted the importance of times and places to socialize and talk informally over meals, in hallways, while carpooling, and in shared offices as being important for supporting collaboration by facilitating the sharing of new ideas, providing nonthreatening ways to get feedback, enhancing awareness of what others were doing, and helping develop the close personal relationships that kept everyone working well together on challenging tasks.

The location of the project within the IRL facilitated MMAP's collaboration, as the organization encouraged the concrete embodiment of innovative theoretical ideas within practice, was run as a "flat organization" that made purposeful efforts to reduce hierarchical power relations, brought in a steady stream of visiting researchers who would share their own ideas while providing feedback on MMAP's ongoing work, had an open office plan that encouraged the sharing of ideas, and in general provided a "third space" (Wenger 1998) that was partially sheltered from MMAP participants' originating school and university contexts so that they could experiment with ideas and practices in ways that they might not have been able to do otherwise. Finally, the fact that MMAP was initiated during the dawn of the reform-oriented mathematics movement in California and the rest of the nation meant that there was a real demand for a mathematics curriculum that could support new kinds of teaching along with an openness for projects to experiment with different possibilities for what that curriculum could look like. Thus, the project's designs and its processes of collaboration were facilitated internally while not being constrained negatively externally.

SUPPORTING PRODUCTIVE COLLABORATION WHILE DESIGNING A COMPREHENSIVE CURRICULUM (1995–1998)

How MMAP supported collaborations between teachers, researchers, and curriculum developers during the next phases of its work changed in several significant ways because of changes in the project itself as well as in the larger contexts in which it and its participants lived. With respect to larger contexts, MMAP's funder, the NSF, was impressed by the quality of the units that MMAP had created so far and, as a condition of continued funding, required it to build and then commercially publish a comprehensive and reform-oriented middle school curriculum. However, what counted as "reform oriented" became more clearly and narrowly defined through the publication of the first National Council of Teachers of Mathematics (NCTM) standards and the creation of a tight community of reform-oriented mathematics educators (Wilson 2003). At the same time, a backlash against reform-oriented mathematics instruction, now known as the "Math Wars," began in California and started spreading across the nation (Schoenfeld 2004; Wilson 2003), making it increasingly difficult for MMAP's curriculum to both avoid controversy and be fully used by its collaborating teachers.

Because of these and other factors, MMAP made some changes in how it supported its collaborations. New kinds of work needed to get done in this phase, so its collaborative processes needed to be adjusted to accommodate them. However, MMAP had the advantage of being able to make use of what it had learned from the first phase about designing curricula as well as supporting collaborations. At the same time, challenging constraints from the larger contexts made these tasks more difficult than they had been during the first phase. Next, I summarize the resultant changes the project made with respect to each of the four principles.

Narrowing of Problematizing around Most Aspects of Curriculum Design except Assessment

During the comprehensive curriculum phase, problematizing around most aspects of curriculum design was significantly narrowed, while new problems around assessing student learning were increasingly opened up for investigation. The problem space for curriculum design was narrower, as new units needed to be designed primarily with an eye to how they could be coordinated with MMAP's already existing units and address the NCTM standards. This meant that there was not as much space for creativity or for using the richest applications-based contexts to anchor the new units. In addition, because the project had learned which elements were crucial for applications-based units to work, it did not have to figure out nearly as much during the second grant's design process, reducing problematizing further. Thus, although the overall design problem of creating the full curriculum package was challenging and engaged experienced participants, the day-to-day work of designing units was more straightforward, as the overall content and structure of the full curriculum and its component units was set, reducing the problematizing of specific curriculum design tasks significantly.

However, during this phase, problematizing was widened around issues of assessment, which ended up engaging almost everyone in the project. Improved assessments were needed, MMAP teachers argued, to provide better information for supporting student learning and, with the Math Wars heating up, to justify this unfamiliar approach to mathematics instruction to parents, administrators, and other stakeholders. This dovetailed well with MMAP researchers' historical interest in alternative assessment. As a result, the project experimented with many alternative assessment methods, which it then incorporated into a series of research papers, suggestions for assessment in the curriculum, and a professional development CD illustrating different methods.

Movement toward More Asymmetric
and Distributed Models of Authority

In part because of the constraints of building a comprehensive curriculum, MMAP increased the speed of an already existing trend in the project from relatively symmetrical models of authority, in which everyone seemingly did everything together at the same time, to more asymmetrical and distributed models, in which work was divided among smaller teams, with individuals specializing in particular functions and contributions sometimes made in sequence rather than simultaneously. Examples of the increasingly asymmetric and distributed nature of MMAP's collaboration included 1) the division of the project into many more and smaller design teams, 2) the hiring of selected teachers with unique skills to join MMAP's staff, and 3) the hiring of professional writers to implement curricular decisions made by design teams.

The shift toward more asymmetric distributions of authority resulted in part from the project's realization that fully symmetric collaborations between researchers, teachers, and curriculum developers did not take into account the most essential skills each brought to the table. For example, most teachers and graduate students found writing curricula difficult and uninteresting, so the project shifted from having almost everyone write curricula to having this task be done by professional writers plus the select few who had shown interest and facility with it. This allowed most teachers, for instance, to focus on what MMAP most crucially needed them for, which was "giving us the initial ideas, setting parameters for things, trying them out in their classrooms for us, and having lots . . . to suggest in the way of changes or features they want or specific kinds of math they want to see" (Goldman/Knudsen interview).

Second, another important reason for the shift to more asymmetric roles occurred because of expertise that the project and its participants had developed from working collaboratively in the larger group during the first phase. The project as a whole had developed enough shared understanding of goals, definitions, and processes to make it feasible for it to be organized into parallel design teams. In addition, over time, particular people developed expertise in particular areas and became recognized as authorities about them, so it made sense to distribute the workload so that people worked on those tasks for which they were most suited. From a management standpoint, having longtime participants lead work groups was a sensible next step in their participation.

Finally, the shift to a coordinated set of distributed work teams made it easier to get the work of the comprehensive curriculum phase done in time, as it allowed for simultaneous but coordinated work on many subprojects at once.

Fostering Accountability to Deadlines

Because more units needed to be created than had been created in the first phase of MMAP's work, fostering accountability to deadlines was a stronger focus during this phase of MMAP work. Although the IRL's setting made this challenging because of its relatively social and free environment, accountability to deadlines was fostered by the modeling done by a prominent staff member who could be seen to be regularly "pumping out deliverables." At the same time, a lot of important additional work was completed because project leaders allowed people to work on anything that interested them about the project whenever their assigned tasks were done. In addition, MMAP sped up development time by strategically making use of already existing materials and lessons learned. Finally, if someone was being seriously unproductive, they were talked to privately, or new organizational models were created around them, and if neither worked, they were let go.

Other Accountabilities Began to Diverge

However, reductions in the depth of participants' engagement in the project occurred when the project as a whole became accountable to goals that were less personally meaningful to both teachers and staff members. For their part, MMAP's collaborating teachers had no need for a comprehensive curriculum from MMAP, as they continued to use MMAP materials as replacement units. Thus, although the project needed to develop additional materials, its collaborating teachers had no compelling interest in them for themselves. At the same time, several MMAP staff became of increasingly mixed minds about the comprehensive curriculum strategy. On the one hand, they saw the potential of such a curriculum for allowing more students, especially in poorer districts, access to more engaging, high-demand mathematics. On the other hand, they became increasingly uncomfortable with the compromises on design principles and teacher collaborations that were involved in creating a sellable package and having districts adopt it for use by all their teachers. Thus, increasingly there were disconnects between what others held the project accountable for doing and what participants wished to do themselves, reducing the strength of participants' engagement even as the project's work did get done.

SUMMARY AND IMPLICATIONS

The findings from the case of MMAP have implications for understanding the dynamics of collaboration. First, it suggests that it is indeed possible to develop productive collaborations across groups of individuals with different knowledge, work practices, occupational cultures, and levels of status. The case suggests that such collaborations are fostered by collectively realizing the principles of problematizing, authority, accountability, and resources. In both phases of MMAP's work, participants' degree of engagement was influenced by the degree to which there was joint problematizing around issues important to its diverse community, something found in other successful projects as well (Cobb et al. 1990; Lieberman and Grolnick 1996; Stein et al. 1998). Because of teachers' traditionally low status, fostering teachers' authority and preventing others from inappropriately disrespecting it is particularly challenging. However, these challenges can be met by carefully selecting participants inclined to respect teachers, structuring tasks to depend on and benefit from diverse points of view, regularly incorporating teacher feedback into the next versions of designs, and establishing and enforcing norms around respect for diverse points of view. At the same time, accountability can be fostered without impinging on the authority of lower-status participants by regularly asking participants to explain their ideas and practices and by encouraging everyone else to deeply listen to these accounts to find the sense within them. Finally, key resources, such as sufficient time and money, are crucial. In collectively realizing these principles, one can avoid the all-too-common extremes of creating either a contrived community in which everyone pretends to agree with one another or one in which hurtful disagreements are rampant (Grossman et al. 2001).

Second, the case of MMAP suggests that conditions in the larger contexts in which projects are embedded can provide strong affordances and challenges to such collaborations. For example, during MMAP's second phase, pressure from its funder to rapidly produce a comprehensive curriculum worked against collaboration, as this direction was not a high priority for some MMAP staff and many teachers, and being able to complete this task required more differentiated work roles. Fortunately, MMAP had not been under such pressure during its first phase, so when it came, MMAP had already built trust, shared understandings, and knowledge of how various participants could best contribute that allowed role differentiation to be successful. Had such pressure been placed on the project earlier, the quality of its collaborations and collaborative products would have suffered.

Similarly, it is clear from the case of MMAP that collaborations in such projects are not immune from the winds of change in the broader policy environment, although projects can create institutional structures to help shelter participants from their most negative effects. Because MMAP was founded during the height of experimentation with mathematics instruction in California in the early 1990s and at an institution like the IRL that encouraged innovative ideas and attention to practice, this greatly facilitated its initial ability to support problematizing and teacher authority. This was then made more difficult during the Math Wars and the push for scale-up that followed. However, MMAP adapted quickly, embracing aspects of the push in the environment that they felt could strengthen the project (like an increased focus on assessment) while using the institution of IRL to partially shield teachers and others from the controversy and provide them space to make progress on those parts of the project they found most compelling. Thus, it is important for projects to consider ways to create new institutional contexts or else reshape existing ones to provide spaces partially sheltered from the larger policy environment for teachers and other members of collaborations to create, test, and improve on innovative educational designs.

NOTES

1. Because of space considerations, in this chapter I focus on the successful models for supporting collaboration among diverse stakeholders that were the outcomes of the project's experimentation with a variety of models as it learned to do its work (for more about that process, see Engle 2006). These findings are based primarily on interviews, both those I conducted with twenty longtime participants between 2003 and 2006 and those the project conducted with teachers midway through the project in 1996 for a paper that several members of the project and some local colleagues (including myself) wrote about MMAP's collaborative processes (Greeno et al. 1999). My interviews included seven with former MMAP teachers of different levels of teaching background and who joined the project in different years, eight with former MMAP staff who served in a wide range of roles, and a long series of interviews, phone conversations, and e-mail exchanges with MMAP's principal investigator Shelley Goldman and project manager Jennifer Knudsen. In order to glean participants' perspectives, most interviews were organized in the form of extended narratives of personal experience on the project (Linde 1993). I then supplemented these interviews by examining a wide range of archival documents shared by project participants along with a project videotape of the first orientation for teachers. For more details about methods and additional examples that support the findings, see Engle (2006).

2. Here I expand Engle and Conant's (2002) original language about "disciplinary norms" to encompass enterprises like MMAP that are focused on other kinds of goals. What matters is not that "disciplinary" or any other kind of norms are being oriented to but rather that participants are holding themselves accountable to those shared norms important for their type of enterprise.

3. That is, it began with a rich problem from a workplace and used it to draw out the mathematics.

4. These methods also appear consistent with the kinds of activities often recommended for promoting conceptual change, which have been primarily studied in science, but also apply to the difficult process of teachers changing their ideas and practices.

3

⚜

The Center for Learning Technologies in Urban Schools: Evolving Relationships in Design-Based Research

Laura D'Amico

Educators, policymakers, and reformers alike express despair over the fragile and one-dimensional nature of many innovations when attempts are made to scale them beyond a few carefully nurtured classrooms. These concerns become particularly acute in urban settings, where such innovations may not be "sufficiently sensitive to the actual context in which the innovation is to be used, and do not attend to the many problems associated with school restructuring, all of which need to be addressed for lasting change" (Gomez et al. 1997, 2).

The members of the Center for Learning Technologies in Urban Schools (LeTUS)—researchers at Northwestern University (NWU) and the University of Michigan (UM) and educators within the Chicago and Detroit public schools—proposed to tackle this problem by using a client-focused research-and-development effort in which the contexts of teaching and learning in the two school districts would shape LeTUS's work. Their aim was to improve teaching and learning in middle school science through the use of learning technologies to support inquiry-based instructional methods. To achieve this goal, they felt it was important that researchers and district educators work together closely to create designs informed by their differing knowledge and expertise and localized to the contexts in which they would be used.

The legacy of LeTUS, at least in the short term, is an impressive one. The number of papers, follow-up grants, and real changes to teaching and learning in the two districts are a considerable achievement. During the six years that LeTUS was in existence (1997–2003), somewhere between 20 and 30 percent of middle school science teachers along with key district staff in the two school systems participated in the work. Together, the LeTUS participants created fourteen curricular units, built a cadre of teachers with expertise in inquiry-based science, fostered improvements in science achievement for the middle school students who experienced the work of these teachers (e.g., Grier et al. 2004), and crafted enduring relationships between educators and researchers that lasted beyond the end of the grant.

To achieve these ends, the participants in LeTUS strategically built on and expanded a cross-institutional network of collaborative relationships that would enable them to meet their collective goals. At the core of this network was a strong and productive relationship between researchers and educators in each location (Chicago and Detroit). The strength of these relationships was due in part to a history of collaboration between key players but also to thoughtful strategies for supporting and moving beyond these initial working relationships. As a result, they built a significant population of teachers, district leaders, and researchers engaged in and capable of doing work of this kind in both locations.

At the core of the cross-institutional network were two collaborative tasks: the design of curriculum and the design and provision of professional development. Design was, in some sense, the medium of collaboration for LeTUS. Decisions about what to design and how to design it became a task space that brought people together, drew on their various expertises, and anchored their negotiations for how to proceed. The design of curriculum was the initial task that brought the researchers and educators together to exchange expertise and deepen their collective knowledge and capacity with respect to science instruction. Once created, the curriculum itself became an integral feature of the cross-institutional network, acting as a common referent around which the relationships revolved as well as a mechanism for supporting new teachers joining the work. Professional development anchored in the curriculum then became the next design task that connected educators and researchers. Eventually, it too became a feature of the network. Professional development provided not only an opportunity for both new and continuing teachers to learn about technology-enriched, inquiry-based science instruction but also a space in which teachers and researchers could exchange information about improving the curriculum and the professional development itself.

LeTUS participants endeavored to craft designs responsive to both standards for science education and the conditions of teaching and learning in real urban contexts. To this end, their efforts were anchored in the needs of the participating districts, and their resulting designs were localized to meet the different structures, challenges, and strengths of each school system. This localization, in turn, led to different working procedures in the two sites as well as different curriculum and professional development designs. It also led to the development of unique cross-institutional partnerships at each site.

A comparison between the two sites and a review of shifts in participants' roles and work patterns over time in both locations demonstrate the usefulness of building on and extending past collaborations and anchoring collaborative work in the needs of the local community. After discussing how both the Chicago and the Detroit sites took into account local needs and resources, the two primary collaborative design tasks that held together the evolving network of relationships are described and analyzed.[1]

COLLABORATIVE CONTEXT

There were a number of preconditions that paved the way for the network's genesis. The standards and accountability movement, in conjunction with the explosion of the Internet, created a political and social context welcoming of the inquiry-based, technology-supported science learning championed by LeTUS. Moreover, some of the LeTUS participants were already enmeshed in a network of relationships that were both congenial and productive. The researchers at NWU and UM had similar though not identical theoretical commitments and practical experiences with respect to the use of technological tools to support science learning, and both research teams had developed working relationships of some kind with the local urban district—NWU with Chicago Public Schools (CPS) and UM with Detroit Public Schools (DPS)—through prior related research. Each of the two districts had received grants for Urban Systemic Initiatives from the National Science Foundation (NSF) (1994–1999) that were used to improve scientific and mathematics literacy, thereby setting the stage for LeTUS's proposed work. This nascent network of collaborative relationships paved the way for them to create a productive working relationship among the four institutions. However, the differing district contexts required unique strategies of implementation in each city, a topic to which we now turn.

DPS is a centralized system serving over 160,000 students. District offices in each subject area provide both curricular direction and professional development support. Michigan has state-mandated tests in science tied to their educational standards, called the *Michigan Bench-marks*. In addition, the district administers its own yearly tests in science. Both have strong currency within the system as a whole (e-mail and phone conversation with DPS professional developer, August 27, 2003).

As part of their Urban Systemic Initiative, Detroit's central office sup-ported teachers' efforts to provide instruction that would help their students meet the *Michigan Benchmarks*. They created a curriculum frame-work—topical guidelines along with suggested activities and resources, including a city-adopted textbook—that laid out which of the bench-marks that teachers should focus on throughout the year (interview with DPS professional developer, June 4, 2003). This structure meant that all (or most) science teachers in a given grade were covering the same topics simultaneously and with many of the same resources.

In contrast, CPS is a highly decentralized system serving nearly three times as many students (435,000). Although the district did establish a set of Chicago Academic Standards and Frameworks just prior to the incep-tion of LeTUS, in the end all curriculum choices were under local control, and school choices varied greatly. Across the district, teachers might not be covering the same topics in a given year, much less in the same order or using the same resources to do so. Moreover, Chicago considered its pressing needs to be basic literacy and numeracy, a fact reflected in its accountability system. District and state tests in reading and mathematics were "the ones CPS [cared] about the most" (e-mail from Northwestern professional developer, August 7, 2003). Science achievement thus re-ceived far less scrutiny.

Chicago's Urban Systemic Initiative was shaped accordingly. The initiative did not adopt a particular curriculum or even make recom-mendations to schools about which curriculum to adopt. Instead, the program focused on providing schools and teachers with professional development, but that professional development was largely divorced from curriculum.

Interestingly, the two research teams were also organized differently and in ways parallel to the district differences with the UM team orga-nized in a more centralized fashion than the NWU team. The UM re-searchers had been working together for a decade; LeTUS was just one of many projects they were working on together. Over time, the researchers had each carved out a fairly established role based on their expertise and experience. Thus, the group tended to divide up the territory of work by tasks related to these areas of expertise: curriculum development, profes-sional development, assessment, classroom research, and so on.

In contrast, while the NWU team had collaborated together in the past, this was the first time so many of them were collaborating in such an in-tensive fashion. LeTUS was their unifying umbrella. In general, the NWU team functioned more as a loosely federated group of projects. Division of labor was not along the lines of roles or expertise but rather was tied to particular funding streams and the research agendas of the individual researchers. This structure was a deliberate choice as each of the research projects joining LeTUS wanted to maintain their individual identities. Thus, they tended to divide up the work by curriculum topic, with each team taking care of curriculum, professional development, and research related to their topic.

These differences in district accountability context and the researchers' history of work roles at each site led the cross-institutional collaborative networks in each city to evolve in slightly different ways. While their basic goals remained the same, the processes of collaboration and the curriculum and professional development systems designed at each site were structured differently.

ANCHORING LETUS IN EDUCATORS' NEEDS

From the outset, project participants were determined to build "multi-tiered trust relationships across the levels of [the university] organization as a project and the levels of the school system in both cities" (interview with Northwestern codirector, June 6, 2003). As a basic strategy, they began by meeting on the educators' ground. This entailed physically holding their meetings in the educators' offices or schools but also, more important, starting each discussion from the educators' framework—with their problems and their expertise as the point of reference. This meant that the university participants needed to remain flexible regarding their focus, to the point of even changing directions after the initial set of meetings. As stated by one NWU researcher, "We didn't propose LeTUS as a curriculum project to the NSF, and I don't think we knew how central a role curriculum was going to play" (interview with NWU researcher, June 5, 2003).

They did know early on, however, that they were going to work in problem-solving teams or "work circles" and needed to anchor their relationship in productive tasks. It was the educators involved in the work who made it clear what that task should be:

> In some of our first meetings, the administrators and teachers both in Chicago and in Detroit said, "You want us to use technology in our teaching to help kids learn? Then we need to have curriculum that embeds the technology, otherwise, we can't do it. . . . You want us to do inquiry. You want us to use technology. We need examples. We need the materials." (UM researcher focus group, June 14, 2004)

Although not proposed or anticipated by the researchers, this idea resonated well with them. They knew that project-based science was challenging for many teachers to implement. The creation of curriculum materials
might help scaffold teachers into the use of inquiry techniques. Moreover,
to design those materials effectively, the curriculum teams would need
people with knowledge of each district's standards and accountability
framework as well as those with knowledge and expertise related to inquiry-based teaching and learning technologies. Curriculum design was a
natural vehicle for pulling the practitioners and researchers together.

DESIGNING CURRICULUM

Using curriculum "seeds" in the form of either specific tools or activities
created in earlier research projects, the researchers and educators worked
closely to build curricula that scaffolded students' development of inquiry
skills in the context of each district's priorities, structures, and needs. The
two sites (Detroit and Chicago) designed their curricula separately, leading, not surprisingly, to different designs and design processes. Specifically, Detroit's design work was more centrally coordinated, the district
leadership played a more active role, and local standards had a stronger
impact on design choices than in Chicago's design efforts.

Design Teams and Detroit Curricula

The Detroit branch of LeTUS had a centralized curriculum design team,[2]
led by one of the researchers who was trained as a science educator. Initially, this team consisted of three UM researchers, a DPS administrator,
a teacher-cum-professional developer in science, and two other Detroit
teachers with project-based science experience. This group selected the
topics that each project would explore and constructed an outline or overview for the projects. They then would pass the project to a point person
(usually a graduate student) who would do the detailed design work in
consultation with one or two teachers.

The district administrator helped the team choose topics that corre-
sponded with the Detroit's curriculum time line. For the first few projects
they created, the central design team leveraged their efforts with prior
work. They reviewed the technologies and/or nascent curricula that
UM researchers had already developed. Then, among the topics or driving questions that these resources could support, they chose those that
seemed to fit reasonably with their state's benchmarks.

Once the point person and collaborators had created a detailed project
framework and sequence of activities, the district leaders involved in

the central design team identified teachers to pilot the nascent projects. Generally, the point person would be present in the classroom during the early piloting, serving as a participant observer/assistant, coteaching, or in some cases running particular lessons. The following summer, they tore apart the pilot curriculum and rebuilt it. Every summer afterward, they would do some tinkering based on what they had seen in classrooms or heard back from teachers.

By the end of LeTUS's grant cycle, the researchers at UM did most of the writing and revision of the curriculum. The teachers valued the effort the researchers put into revising and improving the curriculum, an activity that they didn't feel they had the time to do on their own. "We have our students that we're taking care of, that's our main responsibility" (DPS teachers focus group, June 15, 2004). As a result, curriculum improvement was one of the reasons they saw the researchers as a necessary part of LeTUS, "I don't think the curriculum would be the same. I don't think it would be updated. I don't think it would be improved upon if they went away" (DPS teachers focus group, June 15, 2004).

Nonetheless, the teachers interviewed still felt real ownership of the LeTUS curriculum. The concerns and suggestions of teachers, teacher leaders, and district leaders were regularly sought and incorporated into the designs. "This is more of a collaboration between the teachers and the university. Because of that, I think we have a lot more ownership, and we don't hesitate to say, 'Hey look, this doesn't work and we need something else.' They don't hesitate to say, 'Well if you don't think this works, do you have something to offer?'" (DPS teacher leaders focus group, June 15, 2004).

Work Circles and Chicago Curricula

In contrast with Detroit, there was no centralized design team at NWU but, rather, independently functioning work circles. In the fall of 1997, the researchers at NWU collaborated with the Chicago district leaders to identify schools to participate in LeTUS. Members of the research team met with the principals of those schools to discuss LeTUS's plans, see if they were willing to participate, and discuss which teachers might be good candidates for becoming involved. Then, in the winter of 1998, they held a daylong meeting with all the interested educators in which the researchers described the goals of LeTUS. At the end of this meeting, they broke into small groups based on areas of curriculum interest. Those groups eventually became the work circles that designed the projects.

As in Detroit, the initial choice of topics to be explored in the work circles tended to be informed by activities already generated in previous research projects and/or core pieces of technology that were available.

However, interest, rather than district priorities or state standards, drove the selection among which of the possible project topics to pursue from these resources. As in Detroit, each project had an advocate who was in charge of the work circle for a given project. The advocates for each work circle were usually members of the research team, such as graduate students or postdoctoral researchers. The advocate generally facilitated the work circle design meetings and collected, tracked, and maintained the design work as it was completed. The projects were designed collaboratively; however, the advocates often did the initial "write-up" of the designs. After pilot testing, teachers frequently took over the task of cleaning up, rewriting, and refining them while working at NWU over the summer for that purpose.

The work circle design teams differed greatly in composition. They varied in size from three to sixteen people. Most included both teachers and researchers, though some teams were researcher heavy and others teacher heavy. Universally, there were some tensions around researcher and teacher definitions of the structure of curriculum, and several groups struggled initially to create a working relationship in which all members of the work circle felt equally valued. Each group handled these tensions in different ways, but nearly all came to have a productive working relationship (phone conversation with NWU graduate student, December 15, 2004).

Indeed, many researchers and educators described their involvement in the work circles as a worthwhile learning experience. As one CPS teacher noted, "Things we wouldn't have thought about before, or maybe thought at some buried level . . . got pushed to the front. How much do I really know about where my kids are? Do I really take the time to think about what they're bringing into the classroom and what their prior knowledge is? What do I do with kids who are going off and all of that? . . . To provide teachers with that opportunity is huge" (interview with CPS teacher, June 6, 2003). At the same time, researchers had the opportunity to test their broad design ideas against teacher and classroom realities and have them tempered and refined by practice (Shrader et al. 2003).

Comparison between Detroit and Chicago

There are many similarities to the collaborative design work done in the two sites. Both educators and researchers were deeply involved in the initial design and piloting stages. District leadership helped coordinate the process of finding teachers and schools who would be good collaborators in the work, while researchers usually took on the role of coordinating and tracking the curriculum development. And, finally, curriculum seeds from prior research were used to leverage the design of at least the first few initial projects.

However, there are also a few critical differences. In Detroit, the district leadership played a strong role in selecting curriculum topics to be explored and outlining the projects to be designed. In Chicago, they did not. Moreover, while local standards for science education were used in both locations to guide design work, they were a strong factor in the selection of which topics to pursue only in Detroit. In Chicago, areas of interest to the teachers and researchers were a stronger determinant of the topics to pursue. Finally, the number of teachers involved in the design process in Chicago was larger than in Detroit, with some work circles including four or more teachers, in contrast to the one or two who generally worked on piloting curriculum in Detroit. Moreover, a subset of the Chicago teachers did a lot of the "cleanup" of the first set of projects during the summer. In Detroit, however, such curriculum refinement was handled by the researchers.

These differences are linked, in part, to differences in accountability in the two districts and the extent of centralization in the districts and university research teams. The lack of a centralized curriculum and limited accountability in science gave the Chicago work circles a great deal of flexibility in the topics they chose to pursue. With its centralized curriculum and strong accountability in science, the Detroit team needed to negotiate between areas of interest, resources available, and the state and district standards and curriculum when making design choices. While the deep involvement of the district leadership was in part due to personal interest on the part of the leadership, it also made sense given the centralized system. In Chicago, the site-based management system led the district leadership in science to generally take a hands-off approach to curriculum. All these choices, in combination with the working history of each research team, led the Chicago branch of LeTUS to develop their federated work circles model and Detroit a centralized design team approach.

The structure of the curricula created at the two locations also differed. The Chicago curricula tended to be structured around a core open-ended project or investigation that was front-ended with introductory activities and materials to supply background information, scientific concepts, basic skills, and motivation. Concerned about teachers' time, the written format was text lean, with use of terse bullet points that could be skimmed quickly. The Detroit curricula were more like units, with a driving question broken down into subquestions, each of which focused on core concepts related to the driving question. The activities and materials in each subsection included inquiry activities, labs, readings, discussions, and so on. Interwoven throughout might be a long-term investigation.

The written format tended to be text rich with lots of detail and support-ive commentary, including sidebars with information about teaching and pedagogy.

The teachers interviewed in both sites were enthusiastic about the cur-riculum. They universally found it motivating for their students and were delighted with the depth of learning in which their students engaged. Indeed, research on student achievement as measured by pre- and post-tests conducted by LeTUS as well as state tests in science indicated that students involved in LeTUS classrooms made significant learning gains (e.g., Grier et al. 2004; Herman, Mackenzie, Reiser, and Sherin 2003; Her-man, Mackenzie, Sherin, and Reiser, 2002; Marx et al. 2004). However, the teachers also found the curriculum challenging to implement. The teach-ers believed that the payoff of the curriculum made it worth managing the challenges, but high-quality professional development was critical to expanding the work beyond the initial pilot teachers in each district.

The university researchers and school-based participants proceeded into this expansion phase, having developed a trusting collaboration that formed the nucleus of what was to become a lasting cross-institutional network. Teachers not only were keen fans of the new curricula they had helped to create but also knowledgeable partners who felt respected and able to "talk back" to the researchers. District leaders felt heard and supported in their efforts to improve student learning in the district. The researchers went forward with the confidence that they had curricular materials that were suited to the contexts into which they were being inserted and a strong partnership with the teachers and district leaders who had participated in the design work.

CREATING A PROFESSIONAL DEVELOPMENT SYSTEM

The creation of a professional development system provided the oppor-tunity for additional design work. This work was shared among teachers, district leaders, and researchers and led to further solidifying the relation-ships of the initial participants as well as to an expansion of the network of collaborators.

Once again, the context shaped what transpired. Although there were similarities to the professional development provided in both sites (for-mer science teachers serving as LeTUS liaisons, summer institutes or conferences, and an increasingly central role played by a cadre of core teachers in the provision of professional development), the core of their professional development structures was quite different. The differences, which are explored next, are at least partially connected to the centralized versus decentralized nature of improvement efforts in each district and the different procedures for curriculum design at each site.

Professional Development in Chicago

From the beginning of the expansion phase (summer 1998), Chicago teachers took the lead in designing and running most of their professional development sessions. Although NWU researchers collaborated in the design and provision of professional development, they were able to pull teachers from the rather large pool of those who participated in the design of curriculum to actually run the three main types of professional development: summer conferences, kickoff meetings (curriculum previews held right before the time when most teachers "did" projects during the school year), and graduate courses. All these professional development offerings had a project-by-project focus—each kickoff meeting was for a particular project, as were the graduate courses. Likewise, the summer conferences were structured as a way for teachers to sample the various project curricula and make decisions about which to pursue in the following year.

In order to provide the teachers with the opportunity to delve into the ideas of technology-enriched project-based science deeply, NWU offered teachers semester courses (ten weeks) for graduate credit. These courses were usually taught by a LeTUS teacher but organized and planned in collaboration with NWU faculty. In a few cases, particularly with very new curricula, the researcher took the lead role. Each course explored one of the LeTUS projects in depth. The participating teachers did the curriculum in their classrooms as they were learning about it in the course. The classes tended to be fairly small, with about fifteen teachers, and met once a week. During that time, the course instructors reviewed the curriculum and scientific concepts related to it for the lessons in the coming week. They also did some of the lessons during the session and discussed a range of topics related to pedagogy, content, and practical issues of implementation.

This professional development structure made sense given the decentralized and curriculum-focused nature of the LeTUS's design work in Chicago. However, it had implications for the ability to foster an expanded teacher network at that site. NWU researchers estimated that approximately 200 teachers participated in the various LeTUS professional development offerings. Although a substantial cohort regularly attended these offerings—forming a core network of deeply involved teachers—most of the teachers did not come regularly, and many fell off LeTUS's radar screen after about eighteen months. Thus, this organization of professional development enabled them to reach many teachers but made the creation of a sustained professional network challenging.

Professional Development in Detroit

Provision of professional development in Detroit was handled somewhat differently. Initially, professional development planning was done by district leadership along with the researchers but largely led by the researchers. The major components were a weeklong summer institute and monthly Saturday meetings during the school year run as part of the district's professional development system in science. As the work expanded to include more project curricula and more teachers, however, this arrangement was no longer meeting the needs of either the teachers or researchers. The researchers could no longer afford the time to provide professional development for all the teachers who needed it in addition to doing research and curriculum design and refinement. In addition, the researchers' knowledge base, while respected by the participating teachers, was not sufficiently localized or attuned to daily classroom realities to meet their professional development needs.

As a result, they began to shift the provision of professional development to LeTUS teacher leaders within the district.[3] In the course of this shift, they realized that the teacher leaders' knowledge base needed expansion beyond their own personal experience if they were to be able to meet the wide range of needs of their fellow teachers and expand the work beyond the specific LeTUS projects. Thus, researchers from UM met with the teacher leaders a week before each Saturday session to help design the sessions. The researchers brought teacher survey results from the previous year's professional development related to the curricula that they were about to cover and the results of the prior year's pre- and post-test measures of student achievement for the project to be covered. They also brought summaries from the research literature about the design and provision of high-quality professional development and findings from LeTUS's research on teacher learning and classroom practice. In this way, they expanded on the information base from which the teacher leaders could do their session designs (Fishman et al. 2003).

Placing the core of LeTUS professional development within the district's formal organizational support structure (the Saturday morning sessions) and having the sessions run by district teachers had a positive impact in several ways. First, the teacher leaders were aware of the different instructional initiatives within the district and could incorporate these within their professional development offerings. For example, word walls were one strategy for vocabulary development being adopted throughout the district as part of their literacy initiative, so the teacher leaders incorporated word walls into LeTUS professional development. Later, when there was a big push for students to do concept mapping, teachers incorporated that as well, using the word walls as a way to support students' concept map work in science. Second, they expanded the monthly meetings to cover both LeTUS and non-LeTUS topics. This change led to inquiry-based strategies spreading beyond the LeTUS projects. Finally, a network of teachers developed who knew one another well and could turn to each other for advice and support. "The community thing is fabulous . . . you always feel that you can communicate with someone," and the exchange of ideas and strategies among the teachers often led to "these huge aha moments in the workshops" (DPS teacher leaders focus group, June 15, 2004).

The researchers, however, continued to play an integral role in the professional development offerings in Detroit by helping the teacher leaders design the sessions and providing support, particularly with regard to subject-matter knowledge. Moreover, as new projects were introduced, the sessions for those units tended to be led or co-led by the researchers/curriculum developers until some number of teachers gained sufficient expertise with them to feel comfortable providing leadership. Thus, rather than a simple handover of power, the leadership of professional development in Detroit became a shifting shared space to which both researchers and practitioners contributed knowledge, expertise, and time.

Comparison between Detroit and Chicago

As we have seen, both the Chicago and the Detroit branches of LeTUS involved a large number of teachers in the professional development, created capacity for the provision of inquiry-based forms of teaching and learning, and developed strong leadership in middle school science in each district. Moreover, the kind of knowledge and experiences the teachers were receiving at both sites was similar. However, the structure and integration of the deepest professional development offering at each site—the Saturday sessions in Detroit and the graduate courses in Chicago—differed dramatically, and these differences were rooted in the district contexts. With its centralized structure and history of strong professional development in science, it made sense to incorporate LeTUS professional development under the district's umbrella in Detroit. By so doing, they were able to integrate LeTUS into the organizational fabric of DPS, both shaping and being shaped by larger organizational initiatives. This strategy of curriculum-driven, centrally organized professional development would have been difficult—if not impossible—to mount within the site-based management context of Chicago. Thus, although a large number of teachers were "touched" by the professional development in Chicago, their development did not congeal into a broader organizational force for districtwide change, at least not during the time frame of the LeTUS grant itself.

The two structures had implications for access, participation, and network building. The monthly Saturday sessions required significant commitment on the part of teachers, not all of whom were willing to give up their personal time for this kind of work, even when paid. About half as many teachers participated in Detroit as did in Chicago, but those who did attend regularly formed a strong professional network. In contrast, the NWU graduate courses required only a short, intense commitment, but they were limited in their ability to foster ongoing professional interaction and to build a lasting network. Thus, while both approaches were effective in creating a strong core of inquiry-based science teachers, each reveals issues related to scale. The Detroit model may be limited in the number of teachers it affects, thus limiting the size of the network overall, while the Chicago model may be limited in its ability to create a sustained professional community, potentially affecting the stability of the network.

Those concerned about bringing work of this kind to scale might also note that researchers remained involved in at least planning and often attending, supporting, or codelivering professional development even when the teachers led it. The researchers provided a conduit to big ideas with respect to pedagogy from the scholarly literature. Teachers noted that many of the instructional strategies they employed in LeTUS classrooms originally came from the researchers. They saw their job as both identifying which of these strategies were promising in real classrooms and then adapting them to work in a variety of classroom contexts. Professional development opportunities that allowed them to discuss such adaptations with their fellow teachers were critical to that work and fed into the continual redesign of both the curriculum and professional development. Having researchers involved in the professional development offerings also provided an easy path back to curriculum redesign.

Likewise, the researchers were considered important sources of science content knowledge, a critical issue given the demanding nature of the science content in the units and the sometimes fragile knowledge base some teachers had with respect to that content. Providing teachers with access to this knowledge from sources other than the researchers then becomes a critical issue when scaling this work beyond the LeTUS configuration of two districts and two research teams. Likewise, alternate routes for feedback into the curriculum redesign or, at the very least, to local adaptations of the curriculum become an issue if researchers are no longer in regular contact with practitioners.

CONCLUSION

Design-based research typically requires a broad knowledge base spread across several individuals and institutions. LeTUS was no exception. In this case, the knowledge base was spread across teachers, researchers, and district administrations. The knowledge and expertise they brought to the problems facing them ranged from theories of learning and instruction to knowledge of district policy and classroom realities to knowledge of science content and skill with technological infrastructure. Effective use of this vast array of knowledge and expertise required understanding whose knowledge was strongest in what areas. While some decisions were matters of making compromises between differing perspectives, most were a process of deciding the most relevant knowledge for solving a given problem. Moreover, the way the teams in each site marshaled that expertise and organized their work was influenced strongly not only by the district contexts but also by the historical working patterns of both the educators and the researchers. Thus, Detroit's model for both curriculum development and the provision of professional development was a centralized one, while Chicago's was not.

The organization of work also needed to change over time in reaction to shifting knowledge capacity and needs as well as the press for scale. As the number of teachers involved increased, the researchers could no longer work with them each individually, develop and revise curriculum, and continue to conduct research. Fortunately, as the teachers gained more confidence and expertise with the materials, they were able to take over more and more of the professional development work. However, they could not do that work, be deeply involved in curriculum design, and continue to have time to prepare for and provide effective instruction for their students. Eventually, curriculum design and redesign became the responsibility largely of the researchers.

It is arguable that these more divided roles (researchers doing the bulk of curriculum design while educators provide the bulk of professional development) were possible only because of the close working relationships researchers and educators had during their early design work. The early collaboration around curriculum design seeded each district with a small cadre of teacher leaders capable of providing the professional development necessary to grow a professional community. It also built the researchers' curriculum development capacity by exposing them to the critical conditions and constraints educators face. Finally, it resulted in a set of materials that embodied their collective understanding and could be used to leverage the participation of others in the work.

Likewise, the collaborative design of professional development led to the creation of a set of models for supporting teacher learning as well as a professional network for providing that support in each site. Finally, the cross-institutional partnerships formed a space in which continued research and development to further their collective goals was possible. Indeed, many of the LeTUS participants continue to be involved in related research and development, including the creation of a full inquiry-based middle school curriculum aimed at a national audience (Krajcik 2001).

The LeTUS example provides us with a couple heuristics to consider when trying to develop cross-institutional collaborative networks elsewhere. The first of these entails being attuned to and basing one's designs on local conditions. The localization of each site's curriculum and professional development designs gave them a palpable power with the educators. However, localization of these designs also made them less amenable to use in other contexts and was part of the reason materials were rarely used across the two sites. Nonetheless, the knowledge gained from the separate design efforts in each site provides insights into the range of design challenges that might be faced in other contexts. This knowledge can, in turn, be used to support designs meant to be usable in a broader set of districts. It will be interesting to see how this issue of localization is handled by those collaborators from LeTUS now engaged in the development of a full middle school curriculum. Will the intent be to create a curriculum robust within many contexts? Or will it be to suggest that each district or school create its own organizational structures capable of adapting that curriculum and an associated professional development system to its local needs and contexts? If the latter, to what extent are researchers a critical component to successful implementation?

The second heuristic is to start small and use prior work and relationships to bootstrap the process. Collaborative work prior to LeTUS provided the seeds for crafting the beginnings of an infrastructure to support improvements in science teaching and learning. These seeds, in the form of technologies, protocurricula, and collegial relationships and understandings, gave the LeTUS participants a launching point. Deliberate work on their part to deepen relationships, create tools collaboratively, and use those tools to increase the scope of their work and those involved within it enabled them to "grow" a cross-institutional collaborative network and to shift the roles of individuals within that network to meet changing needs. Whether that network is sustainable in the long term is still an open question, but the prospects thus far look good.

NOTES

1. The data collected for this case study came largely in the form of individual and focus group interviews conducted with university researchers, graduate

students, teachers, and district leaders associated with the project. The interviews were conducted in two waves. In 2003, eight individual interviews were conducted with the codirectors for each university team, two other researchers from each university, and one teacher from each site who was deeply involved in the professional development offerings and worked closely with the research teams. The interview transcripts were reviewed along with LeTUS's website and a sampling of the curriculum and publications produced by LeTUS. From these data, an initial write-up was produced (D'Amico 2003). In 2004, additional data were collected in the form of focus group interviews with teachers, graduate students, and researchers along with individual interviews with three of the four codirectors and an interview with a district leader from Chicago. In addition, a larger range of the project's papers and documentation was reviewed. From these data, a final case study was produced, structured to answer the core questions the metastudy was exploring (D'Amico 2005). To verify data interpretation, while writing both the initial write-up and the final case, members of the LeTUS community were contacted via phone or e-mail to check on specific facts or to review short passages of the text. When a full draft was completed, it was sent to those individuals who participated in the study for comment. In this way, any remaining issues with data interpretation were clarified before the final version of the case was completed.

2. "Work circle" is a term developed and defined by the LeTUS participants, and everyone who was interviewed agreed that it has come to be more associated with the Chicago/NWU site's design process. The label "design team" is not one that the interviewees employed but rather one I am using to distinguish the two practices.

3. This shift in the provision of professional development in Detroit was a significant one. The LeTUS participants from Detroit have written about it (e.g., Fishman et al. 2003), and many discussed it in interviews for the LeTUS case study (D'Amico 2005). These documents can be reviewed for a more detailed treatment of the transitions.

4

Examining a Novel Partnership for Educational Innovation: Promises and Complexities of Cross-Institutional Collaboration

Lisa Rosen

This chapter examines a novel, cross-institutional partnership to create, implement, and study the effectiveness of a Web-based Professional Development Support System (PDS2) for video case-based professional learning by literacy coaches and teachers. This effort was part of the work of a larger initiative called the Information Infrastructure Systems (IIS) project. Anthony S. Bryk and Louis Gomez, principal investigators for the IIS project, analogized the partnership around PDS2 to a "three-legged stool" comprised of different forms of expertise generally found in different kinds of institutions: a research leg, a commercial leg, and a professional/clinical leg. Based on this model, the work on PDS2 joined: 1) the IIS project team, an interdisciplinary research-and-development group housed at the University of Chicago's Center for Urban School Improvement; 2) Teachscape, a "technology-enabled professional development services company"; and 3) individuals closely associated with the Literacy Collaborative, a whole-school reform program focused on the improvement of literacy instruction through intensive professional development.[1] My discussion probes how this design for cross-institutional

partnership actually played out in practice and identifies the challenges
to and supports for its enactment.[2] Because the most novel—and also most
ambitious—dimension of this partnership was the inclusion of a commercial entity, my analysis focuses primarily on this aspect.

CRITICAL SUPPORTS FOR THE SUCCESS OF
CROSS-INSTITUTIONAL PARTNERSHIPS

Using this case to focus on the more general problem of creating cross-
institutional alliances in order to "scale up" educational interventions, I
argue that the success of such alliances depends on the development or
presence of four interrelated supports: 1) relational trust; 2) shared understandings (not only of the work the partners are undertaking together
but also of the partnership itself); 3) structures or mechanisms for regular,
ongoing communication, particularly individuals who can act as "boundary spanners" and convey information between organizations; and 4)
leadership to keep the partnership on track and ensure the effectiveness
of these mechanisms. My analysis demonstrates that these supports are
essential for the productivity of any interorganizational partnership but
particularly those involving alliances between academic and commercial
entities.

Relational Trust

Partnerships are fundamentally about relationships. In addition to any
explicit formal agreements, such relationships are also grounded in informal, tacit understandings of mutual expectations and obligations between individuals: taken-for-granted assumptions about how individuals
should behave. Relationships between partnering organizations and the
individuals who make up those organizations are also characterized by a
degree of mutual dependency that creates a sense of mutual vulnerability
within such relationships. This sense of mutual vulnerability is a particularly significant element in the development of what Bryk and Schneider
(2002) call "relational trust," an important social resource for coordinated
action.[3] According to Bryk and Schneider, relational trust accrues when,
within social exchanges, 1) understandings of mutual expectations and
obligations are synchronized, 2) expectations are fulfilled by actions, and
3) those with more power in a given situation take steps to reduce their
counterpart's vulnerability. When expectations are violated, trust is with-
drawn. Individuals' judgments as to whether expectations have been fulfilled are shaped by a combination of their prior history and experience,
personal and cultural beliefs, and discernments of the intentions they

believe to be motivating others' actions (discernments that are shaped by the previous two factors). When not based on judgments formed through previous interactions, people have been found to rely on reputation, stereotypes, and/or cultural similarities or differences to form judgments about others' behavior and intentions. Bryk and Schneider argue that, in educational contexts, discernments of intentions tend to organize around four key considerations: respect, personal regard or caring, competence, and integrity. My analysis demonstrates that while relational trust is fundamental to any institutional partnership, it is particularly important for alliances between academic and commercial entities.

Shared Understandings

Shared understandings are another essential element in the coordination of work between organizations, appearing as a particularly prominent theme in the literature on interdisciplinary collaboration. For example, Gallison (1999), borrowing a concept from cultural anthropology, defines "trading zones" for interdisciplinary collaboration as domains of contact between diverse groups for the purposes of exchange or trade. Gorman (2004, 2005) distinguishes two kinds of trading zones. In what he calls a "boundary object" (Star and Griesemer 1989) trading zone, different groups participating in a domain of contact view the object at its center in different ways. These divergent understandings may not be articulated and are thus "frequent sources of misunderstanding" in such partnerships (Gorman 2004, 29). However, in what Gorman calls a "shared mental models" trading zone, there emerges a more common understanding that allows participants from different domains to contribute to the development of new knowledge. Following Gorman, my own analysis demonstrates that cross-institutional partnerships, if they are to involve codevelopment of new knowledge and deep cooperation rather than simply exchange, require a "trading zone" based on shared mental models.

Ongoing Communication and Leadership

Wohlstetter, Smith, and Malloy (2005) argue in their review of research on "strategic alliances" between diverse organizations that the success of such alliances depends on the establishment of mechanisms (e.g., formal and informal roles, processes, structures, and norms) for ongoing communication and sharing of information to enable the coordination of activity between organizations (cf. Kanter 1994). A particularly important role in the present case was that of "boundary spanner": individuals within the partnering organizations who understood the vernacular or worldview of the other partner(s) and could serve as translators between them (Wenger 1998). Various individuals at different points in the project's development performed this role. However, this translation most frequently occurred between the IIS group and one or the other of the two partnering organizations; there was no individual whose responsibility it was to ensure communication across all three legs of the partnership. Rather, as we shall see, Bryk performed this role on an ad hoc basis, particularly when misunderstandings arose as a consequence of the absence of such communication between all three partners. The example of Bryk's informal role also speaks to the importance of leadership. Wohlstetter et al.'s review confirms that effective leadership of strategic alliances (as in any organization) is essential to their productivity, particularly for 1) the initial championing and architecting of the partnership in its early stages, 2) ensuring the effectiveness of alliance activity in relationship to the partnership's goals once it is under way, and 3) getting the partnership "back on track" if it falters or strays from these objectives.

THREE STAGES IN THE DEVELOPMENT OF THIS WORK

The IIS group envisioned PDS2 as a Web-based tool that would allow a user such as a school-based literacy coach to 1) search for specific, digitally indexed video content and associated assets (such as analyses of the teaching and learning in the videos, suggestions for professional development, and so on); 2) create a library of personalized resources arranged according to the specific needs of her individual context; and 3) network and collaborate with other educators around this content via e-mail, on-line learning groups, and other in-system communication tools. Actually creating the system would require expertise in three large domains: 1) *content development* (obtaining, editing, and preparing for inclusion in the system video footage of everyday literacy practice in actual classrooms—as opposed to "staged" lessons featuring only "best practices," as is more typically the case with professional development videos in education—as well as building a variety of resources around these lessons, such as student work, commentary, and discussion prompts to support literacy coaches' and teachers' use of these materials), 2) *technical development* (software engineering to create a Web-based technical platform including a searchable multimedia database as well as tools for customizing its resources and promoting online networking and collaboration around them), and 3) the design of *social practices* (e.g., professional development) to support use of the system in a way that advances high-quality teaching and learning.

The work on PDS2 proceeded in three distinct phases (the alpha, beta, and gamma stages) corresponding to the way in which the IIS group conceived of all its efforts to develop tools and social practices for use in schools: from their early incarnation as (frequently "buggy" and unstable) prototypes being developed and tested among a small community of users under relatively optimal conditions, to their refinement and continued testing by larger numbers of users outside the community of their development, and to their ultimate release for widespread use as stable (possibly commercial) products. Each stage posed unique issues and challenges and placed different demands on IIS group members and their collaborators as well as on the partnership itself. In what follows, I analyze the issues and challenges the partnership faced at each stage of the work on PDS2 in relation to the analytical themes discussed in the previous section.[4]

The Alpha Stage (2003–2004): Conceptualizing and Initiating the Work

The primary partnership activities in the alpha stage were conceptualizing the partnership, developing a prototype, and securing funding.[5]

Conceptualizing the Partnership: Aspirations and Ambiguities

Bryk and Gomez envisioned the partnership with Teachscape constituting a new kind of vehicle for "scaling up" technological solutions to problems of educational practice: a way to marry the clinical and academic insights of researchers and practitioners on the one hand with the capacity existing in the commercial sector to create robust, "scalable" technical products on the other. They also viewed the commercialization of products emerging from such partnerships as potential sources of revenue to fund further research and development. For his part, Teachscape chief executive officer Mark Atkinson hoped that his company would not simply develop the technical platform functionality required for PDS2 but also might make some of the system's content available for commercial use as well as learn from the research surrounding it. In short, Atkinson, Bryk, and Gomez shared the ambitious hope that the partnership would attain a level of deep, long-term collaboration that would result in getting more useful, evidence-based tools (not just PDS2 but possibly other tools as well) in the hands of educators and also generate revenue.

However, as we shall see, this conception of the partnership was not fully shared among all three of the partnering entities. Specifically, members of the Literacy Collaborative leg of the partnership were not privy to the early conversations between Bryk, Gomez, and Atkinson in which the latter formulated the deeper aspirations discussed previously and were thus more inclined at the outset to view Teachscape as simply a technology vendor. This was a consequence not only of a lack of communication and prior relationship with the company but also of a fundamental duality built into the partnership's contractual structure: in spite of the deeper aspirations discussed previously, Teachscape was actually a subcontractor hired by the project to develop and maintain a piece of software. Thus, the IIS project was simultaneously Teachscape's client and also its partner.

This dual way of conceptualizing interorganizational relationships is not uncommon in the business sector. However, there is no established model in academia for conceptualizing relationships with commercial actors other than the traditional "vendor" conception. Consequently, participants lacked a shared mental model to guide their work together. Moreover, as later discussion shows, the dual nature of the relationship created a degree of social ambiguity that may have made it more difficult to develop shared understandings of the partnership because of the tensions or contradictions between the "vendor" and "partner" aspects of the relationship and the unfamiliarity of the "partner" model. For example, while "partnership" (much like marriage) connotes a degree of mutual give-and-take as well as shared investment in a joint undertaking, "vendor" implies a somewhat more impersonal, contractual exchange of fees for services. These different aspects call forth different ways of "framing" social interaction (Goffman 1986) and therefore not only different expectations for behavior but also different ways of interpreting that behavior. The difficulty negotiating and reconciling these different aspects was aggravated by the fact that the vendor aspect was both more explicit and formal (e.g., codified in a written contract) and also more common than the partnership aspect, which involved a novel way of thinking about the relationship between commercial and academic entities. Consequently, expectations were clearer for the vendor than the partner aspects.

Developing a Prototype

Bryk and Gomez had recruited to the IIS group two individuals, Nichole Pinkard and Scot Wheeler, who not only shared their IIS colleagues' vision for the tool but also had the understanding of the software development process required to translate this abstract vision into concrete technical requirements. Having such boundary-spanning individuals within the IIS group at this stage was an essential support for specifying the features and functions they hoped the tool would perform and communicating these to their Teachscape colleagues. Pinkard subsequently recruited Denise Nacu to perform the role of "rapid prototyper" for the project: someone who would be able to create a "mock-up" of the tool in order to render in visual form what it might look like and be able to do from a user's perspective. These renderings provided a concrete focus for further conversations between the IIS group and Teachscape. Through a series of regularly scheduled meetings and with the help of Nacu's visual renderings, the IIS group and Teachscape developed a shared mental model of the tool and its actual features and functions. As mechanisms for ongoing communication, the previously mentioned boundary-spanning roles and these regularly scheduled meetings not only contributed to the development of a shared understanding of the system but also built trust because they allowed the partners to demonstrate the qualities that Bryk and Schneider argue are essential for the development of such trust, particularly competence and integrity.

Securing Funding

A major challenge at the alpha stage was securing sufficient funding for the project. To that end, the IIS group attained a "teacher quality" grant from the Institution of Education Sciences (IES) to conduct a randomized clinical trial studying the value added by PDS2 to the effectiveness of the Literacy Collaborative's training program for literacy coordinators. The grant provided resources primarily to fund 1) the software engineering work to develop a prototype version of PDS2 and 2) beta-level research on its use: a study of the impact of the Literacy Collaborative program—with and without the addition of PDS2—on teacher practice and student learning. However, a significant consequence of the IES grant was the imposition of deadlines that intensified the work of both technical development and content development. This intensification of work, in turn, had consequences for the partnership.

Specifically, after the initial period of idea formation and prototype development, the work of technical development and of content and social practice development tended to proceed on parallel tracks. Thus, the Literacy Collaborative leg of the partnership (which was exclusively involved in content and social practice development) had little interaction with the Teachscape leg, relying on LeAnne Sawyers (the IIS team member leading this work) to serve as an intermediary. Consequently, while trust and shared understandings developed at this stage in a dyadic fashion among subsets of the partners (e.g., understandings of the *tool* between the IIS and Teachscape and of the *content and social practices* for its use between the IIS and its Literacy Collaborative partners), no similarly shared understandings or trusting relationships developed across all three. As we shall see, this absence of ongoing communication, shared mental models, and trust would surface as an obstacle to project efforts in later stages, in which more concerted collaboration across all three entities was required.

The Beta Stage (2003–2006): Developing an "Implementation Curriculum"

By the fall of 2005, Teachscape had developed and launched a fully functional prototype of the tool, and the content development team had completed an initial set of video cases.[6] With this work behind them, a subset of the latter team (Sawyers and Patricia Scharer of the Literacy Collaborative at Ohio State University) turned their attention to constructing and documenting a series of three distinct implementation trials: pilot efforts to support engagement with the system by users with differing degrees of expertise and training in order to learn what kind of scaffolding or professional development would be required to support its effective use. Intensive work on the first two trials further strengthened bonds of relational trust between Sawyers and Scharer (and thus between the IIS and Literacy Collaborative legs of the partnership). As a result of what they had learned from these first two trials, the two approached the third trial (in Chicago's Area 15, a "subdistrict" within the Chicago public schools) with very specific, shared conceptions of how the implementation should proceed, viewing this as an ideal opportunity to test their emerging understanding of what an "implementation curriculum" for the tool would optimally entail.[7] However, because of the intensification of work discussed previously and the lack of mechanisms for ongoing communication, they did not share the lessons they had learned from the first two trials with Teachscape.

A Troubled Attempt to Deepen the Partnership

Teachscape, for its part, was also particularly interested in and enthusiastic about the idea of mounting an implementation trial in Area 15, for two reasons. First, the trial would involve an entire region of a large urban district and thus came closer to the type of context in which the company would typically work. Second, Teachscape hoped to make the tool a part of its existing platform at some point in the future and viewed this implementation trial as a key opportunity to learn what kinds of supports would be required for people to use it effectively. At the same time, Teachscape was also under increasing financial strain at this time, so Atkinson wanted to move quickly on this work for the sake of its potential business benefits. For these reasons, the project decided to use the implementation trial in Area 15 as an opportunity to deepen the partnership by codeveloping an implementation curriculum for the area. However, this effort did not get very far before difficulties arose.

The Loss of an Important Boundary Spanner and the
Lack of a Shared Mental Model for Implementation

Throughout the work of prototype development and in the early stages of the implementation work, a Teachscape staff member, Mike Scorski, had acted in the role of project manager for the work on PDS2, attending the implementation trials and serving as a liaison to Teachscape and a boundary spanner between the company and the other partners. However, Scorski left the company early in the beta stage of this work. Consequently, Teachscape lacked a liaison to communicate back to the company the lessons that the content team was learning from the trials, which, as discussed previously, the IIS team had also not taken the initiative to communicate. Thus, as discussed previously, the content team approached the work with a firm perspective shaped by these lessons that Teachscape did not necessarily share or understand. Moreover, as result of the decision to collaborate in Area 15, Teachscape brought new people into the project that, in the words of an IIS team member, "didn't share the same kind of background that the rest of us had . . . nor the same kind of deep understanding of either where we had come from or even the system itself." These conditions resulted in disagreements over how the implementation should proceed.

Aggravating this situation was the fact that the content development team perceived that Teachscape wanted to move more quickly toward developing a scalable implementation model (i.e., toward taking the work to the gamma stage) than they themselves were ready to move. As a member of that team explained,

> I kind of thought Area 15 could be a really great opportunity to do an implementation right. . . . And knowing full well that that might not be absolutely scalable but let's see, if it's done the way we think it should be done, does it work? And then, there was suddenly a lot of interest in the implementation and using that Area 15 work as a way to develop a scalable, efficient, implementation model that could be immediately replicated and used from there.

This perception may or may not have been correct. However, it was certainly the case that Teachscape approached this work with a somewhat different lens as a consequence of the kinds of demands a commercial entity faces that universities do not. For example, while Sawyers's team was interested in Area 15 primarily as an opportunity "to do an implementation right," Teachscape had to think not only about "doing it right" but also about doing it right on a large scale and being able to replicate that over and over again. Speaking generally of the differences in how universities and commercial entities approach research-and-development work, Atkinson remarked,

> The thing that is frustrating around these collaborations for [companies] like Teachscape . . . is that huge, huge sums of money . . . go to running experiments at remarkably small scales. . . . An idea is not the same when you run the experiment at a small scale than when you run it at a big scale. It forces the design to change. . . . It's sort of like "[let's] spend ten billion dollars figuring out how to change 10 teachers and . . . let's get that right [first]," and then the presumption that 3 million teachers will do it [similarly] afterwards. Run the experiment. Spend a little less time on building and more on running the experiment at scale, so that you are learning about what the issues about scale are.

Given limited time and the absence of mechanisms for ongoing communication, project members had not fully articulated their respective goals for the work prior to undertaking it, nor had they discussed what it would really mean to scale up the tool, a prospect about which the content development team, as we shall see, felt considerable uncertainty.

Lack of Consensus on Partners' Roles

Moreover, the project also did not fully consider how this new undertaking might differ from their prior work and the implications of this for each organization's role. As a member of the content development team observed,

> The roles were not clearly either worked out in advance or even given time to get it clear before we had to jump into the stuff. So it turned into sort of a confrontation of expertise instead of a colleagueship of expertise. . . . The coordination had been simpler when [the roles were] clearly defined: "Here is the content development. Here is the tool development. And here, we are [designing social practices] and kind of keeping those three things parallel."

A lack of time for substantive discussion about how to organize the work and the lack of established mechanisms to facilitate such discussion aggravated this confusion and allowed the perception that Teachscape wanted to move faster than the other partners to go unchecked and unaddressed.

In retrospect, one of the content team members acknowledged that she and her colleagues also likely had an overly narrow perception of Teachscape and that this probably contributed to the difficulties. For example, they perceived the company as simply a software development firm when in fact the majority of its business was actually devoted to providing professional development services, much of which involved video. As one member of the team remarked to me at the time of this misunderstanding, "We are the staff developers, they are the technical people," implying that the content team should therefore lead the professional development work. This misperception was partly a consequence of the ambiguities arising from Teachscape's dual role as both a vendor and a partner in this work. Indeed, in spite of the more ambitious goals that Bryk, Gomez, and Atkinson had for the partnership, the language of the grant actually defined Teachscape's role rather narrowly, limiting it to the domain of technology development (i.e., vendor). Moreover, as Atkinson noted, "In the grant, we are a subcontractor for technology development. We are not a collaborator." He had "thought that . . . that contractual relationship" would provide an initial basis for ultimately deepening the partnership. However, in the absence of sufficient opportunity to develop a fuller understanding of Teachscape's business, this narrow "technology vendor" conception tended to govern how the other project members (with the exception of Gomez and Bryk) perceived the company.

Academic Norms and a Suspicion of Commercial Entities

At the same time, given norms within academia (and especially education) that promote suspicion toward the motives of commercial actors (e.g., the assumption that they are more concerned with profits than student learning), the individuals involved may also have brought to this work negative preconceptions that shaped their interactions with Teachscape. For example, such preconceptions may have decreased their motivation to develop a deeper understanding of what the company was actually about and created a disinclination to trust their intentions. Moreover, Bryk and Schneider (2002) argue that when expectations for behavior within relationships are violated, individuals tend to fall back on stereotypes to explain others' behavior and interpret their intentions, a tendency that works against the development of relational trust. In the present case, Teachscape may have inadvertently violated a tacit expectation (implicit in the "technology vendor/subcontractor" frame) that the company should defer to the other partners' expertise in professional development. This violation, coupled with a lack of prior history or shared culture, may have caused members of the content team to fall back on stereotypes about the motives of commercial actors. This example suggests that the development of relational trust is both particularly difficult and particularly necessary in the context of partnerships between academic and commercial entities.

might actually want to accomplish together in terms of scaling PDS2 for more widespread use.

A Modest Plan for Scaling Up

Bryk ultimately succeeded in bringing the group together for a series of conversations in which they began to plan some new collaborative work that would involve commercializing the content of PDS2 in a modest effort to scale up the coaching academies. And, while by the time of this writing, the group had not yet addressed the outstanding issues around royalties and control of the system's assets that would have to be resolved prior to such commercialization, they had at least made a commitment to broach the subject at a future meeting. Bryk explained how, through this series of conversations, the group was able to devise a plan for scaling up use of the system that addressed many of the challenges and concerns discussed in the previous section:

> The way this was framed before was that we would be sort of giving our materials to Teachscape to market and there would be some royalty coming back and it would be like they would take control of it. In the context of the conversation, it shifted around to, well what if we change the [problem] and what if this was a professional development program of Ohio State, Lesley, and the Center for Urban School Improvement at the University of Chicago, and Teachscape was basically a service provider? And . . . Mark was very clear that . . . if they got into any of the human side of this activity they would want to look to hire people trained by the Literacy Collaborative . . . and have them [the Literacy Collaborative] develop a training quality control procedure.

Clearly, this shift was a consequence not only of Bryk's leadership in persuading all of the parties to return to the table but also of Atkinson's sensitivity to the content team's trepidations around the prospect of commercialization and their desire to maintain a strong hand in matters of quality control and his consequent efforts to reduce their sense of vulnerability in relation to these issues. The latter efforts also demonstrated Atkinson's (and therefore Teachscape's) respect for the expertise of his Literacy Collaborative colleagues and also the company's integrity in terms of the shared goal of promoting high-quality teaching. His actions in this regard consequently built trust. At the same time, in an effort to compensate for having neglected to share with Teachscape lessons learned from the three implementation trials, the IIS group also held a meeting specifically devoted to this purpose, at which they shared with Teachscape a number of conference papers and other research reports. This meeting not only served the latter goal of sharing findings from their research but also helped build trust between the partners and a more common understanding of the issues surrounding scaffolding literacy coaches' use of PDS2 assets, particularly at scale. In short, by the time of this writing, the partnership not only had rebounded from the difficulties discussed earlier but also had, in Scharer's words, begun to "touch its toe" into the waters of scaling up.

CONCLUSION

My analysis validates previous findings regarding the importance of trust, shared understandings, ongoing communication, and leadership to the productivity of collaborative work more generally and cross-institutional partnerships specifically. At the same time, it also extends current understanding by illuminating the special importance of these factors for partnerships between academic and commercial entities in particular. Next, I elaborate some of the additional lessons this study holds for others wishing to undertake similar partnerships.

The Need to Develop New Institutional Arrangements

One lesson concerns the project's challenges reaching the intellectual property and revenue agreements necessary for scaling up the use of PDS2. Given the multiple institutional interests involved, these difficulties suggest the need to either develop new institutional arrangements between existing organizations or develop new kinds of organizations that can support taking research-based innovations to scale via commercial channels. This includes mechanisms for engaging the question of potential commercialization from the outset of the partnership rather than deferring such discussion to a later stage of the work.[10] As Atkinson remarked,

> I would sort out a lot of the longer-term objectives earlier on. And be very clear that research is not the end in itself, but for us that there actually is a business objective beyond supporting a research activity: . . . Once we have a tool and a social context of use and a set of outcomes that we believe in, how would we bring that to scale [and] where would everyone's interests lie?

The Need to Develop Shared Mental Models for Commercialization

Atkinson's reference in the previous quotation to the need for much earlier discussion of "the business model" for taking the innovation to scale implicates a more fundamental challenge suggested previously:

the presence of a powerful norm within academia (and especially education) that promotes suspicion of efforts to commercialize the products of
research. Companies clearly require a commercial incentive to invest or
otherwise become involved in research endeavors. Thus, creating and
sustaining partnerships between academic and commercial entities to
bring research-based educational innovations to scale will require directly
confronting what Atkinson referred to as "a mind-set problem in the
academy about commercial solutions," which makes "commercialization . . . a bad word." This will necessitate developing not only the new
institutional arrangements discussed previously but also shared mental
models for commercialization that recognize the need to accommodate
the interests and priorities of both researchers and commercial actors in
partnerships of this nature.

This chapter has focused—perhaps disproportionately—on the difficulties and challenges the collaborating entities faced in their work on PDS2
so that others might learn from this project's experience. However, lest
there be any question about the overall positive character of this work, I
wish to stress that every individual I interviewed stated that, in spite of
the difficulties, they would not hesitate do it all over again. At the same
time, as their remarks throughout the chapter illustrate, they also clearly
learned lessons from this effort that would cause them to do it differently
in the future.

NOTES

I wish to thank LeAnne Sawyers, Cynthia Coburn, and Mary Kay Stein for their
contributions to my analysis of this case.

1. For more information on each of these projects, see http://www.iisrd.org
(IIS), http://www.teachscape.com (Teachscape), and http://literacycollabora-
tive.org (Literacy Collaborative).
2. The study used an ethnographic approach because this is the most appropriate method for understanding social processes as they unfold. I relied primarily
on observation of work activities (especially project meetings) and repeated, in-
depth, semistructured interviews at key junctures with approximately seventeen
individuals representing each of the three legs of the partnership, including project leaders. Over the course of four years between 2003 and 2007, I spent more
than seventy-five hours observing such meetings. In addition, I observed and
participated in countless hours of informal conversation with project members,
especially members of the IIS group, as I was myself a member of this group
as its "in-house ethnographer." All such observations were typed up as field
notes. Interviews generally lasted from forty-five minutes to two hours and were
audiotaped and transcribed. Both interviews and observations were guided by

the research questions organizing the larger "Meta Project" study. Likewise, I manually coded all interviews and observational data using codes derived from these questions and also tracked change over time in the issues with which these questions were concerned. Analysis of these data involved identifying patterns in how individuals behaved and in how they talked about their work and interpreting these patterns in relation to various internal and external contexts as well as in relation to current theory on institutional partnerships, collaboration, and so on.

3. While the theory of relational trust was developed to understand the accrual of trust between individuals *within* organizations, my analysis assumes that its insights apply to interactions *across* organizations as well. The literature on institutional partnerships also identifies the presence of trust between partnering organizations as key (Austin 2000; Robertson 1998; Waddock 1989; Waide 1999; Wohlstetter et al. 2005) but does not address the social dynamics involved in the accrual or decline of trust as does Bryk and Schneider's theory.

4. Although I use this three-stage formulation to organize my discussion, the stages should be thought of as heuristics for understanding key aspects of the work and the partnership around it rather than as entirely discrete or strictly chronological categories. Indeed, while it would have been ideal to proceed through the three stages in sequence, practical considerations meant that the work sometimes "straddled" two stages at once, as the project, for example, simultaneously grappled with alpha-level issues of design while also implementing a beta-level study of the tool's use.

5. This stage also involved initial content development and pilot testing. However, because this activity did not involve Teachscape, I do not discuss it in this chapter. For a discussion of this aspect of the work, see Sawyers et al. (2007).

6. A video case consists of a segment of classroom footage, accompanied by an ensemble of additional assets, including samples of student work, assessment data, commentary by the teacher, commentary by PDS2 authors with expertise in literacy practice, frequently asked questions, and suggestions for professional development.

7. For a detailed discussion of the implementation process, see Sawyers et al. (2007).

8. Ironically, this is the very challenge that Atkinson had warned of during discussions of the Area 15 implementation trial.

9. For a discussion on this point, see Sawyers et al. (2007).

10. As this is one of the few cases of "technology transfer" in education, educators could perhaps learn from other fields—most notably biotechnology—that have successfully established such new institutional relationships and mechanisms (see Powell 1996).

II

ROLE OF TOOLS
IN BRIDGING
RESEARCH AND PRACTICE

Tools are artifacts (e.g., curriculum materials, observation protocols, and rubrics) that embody research knowledge in ways that are directly usable in practice. Because they are positioned—in theory—to influence large numbers of teachers and classrooms (Ball and Cohen 1996), tools are important carriers of research knowledge in large-scale efforts to improve practice. Unlike the cases in part 1, where the researchers played a key role in bringing research to practice (and thus limiting the number of teachers who could be reached), the cases in this part feature tools as the key mechanism for bridging research and practice.

There are different ways to conceptualize the manner in which tools embody research to influence practice. Within the linear model (see chapter 1), tools are often viewed as a way to disseminate research knowledge to practitioners. In this view, research knowledge is produced by external researchers, captured and packaged into tools, and then transported across contexts to teachers in many schools. The goal is to embody effective, research-proven practices in minute-by-minute plans and highly specified training guides in order to ensure that teachers will replicate the research-proven practice as faithfully as possible.

The linear model's reliance on dissemination as the avenue by which research makes its way into practice privileges a "breadth" notion of scale (how many teachers have been reached?), a notion that downplays the challenges teachers face when asked to implement new practices in ways that hold true to the deeper principles underlying the research (Coburn 2003). Implementing new practices, we now know, requires learning on the part of teachers and others in order to take root and flourish in effective ways (Cohen and Barnes 1993).

All the tools discussed in this part take learning into account but do so in different ways. Some embody specific research-based practices that teachers are taught how to enact. Others are designed to shift the way that practitioners think about their day-to-day work. Some—conceptual tools—focus on changing practitioners' thinking as a way to prompt changes in their practice; others—practical tools—focus on changing the routines of practice as a way to shift practitioners' thinking (Grossman, Smagorinsky, and Valencia 1999). Regardless of their approach to learning, however, all the tools discussed in this part bridge research and practice by scaffolding the learning of practitioners so that they will be able to create and maintain a set of practices that is aligned with research-based knowledge.

In chapter 5, Amanda Datnow and Vicki Park examine how Success for All (SFA) has used a highly specified and comprehensive set of tools to improve students' reading performance across hundreds of elementary schools across three decades. Rooted in a series of research-and-development projects that date to the mid-1970s, SFA—at least in its earliest manifestations—represents the ideal type envisioned by proponents of the linear model. Rather than rely on the mechanism of dissemination alone, however, teachers received extensive professional development to learn how to implement programs that embodied these research findings. In recent years, SFA has shifted toward what they call "goal-focused implementation." Here, research knowledge is still embedded into a tool, but practitioners are encouraged to use their judgment to adapt the approach to meet the specific local context in response to local data. Chapter 5 investigates these two different logics and their implications for the implementation process and student achievement.

In chapter 6, Gina Ikemoto and Meredith Honig use the case of the Institute for Learning (IFL) to illustrate how tools can be used to guide the thinking and actions of district and building-level leaders who are engaged in systemic efforts to improve teaching and learning at all levels of their organizations. Rather than prescribing detailed practices for faithful execution by practitioners, IFL leaders have drawn on decades of cognitive science research to design tools that help practitioners to identify and label research-based concepts (e.g., Accountable Talk® and Clear Expectations), develop understandings of these concepts through active learning in professional development sessions, and apply these concepts in their daily work. Central to the IFL's theory of action is that tools scaffold learning by enabling thinking and actions that the practitioner is not yet capable of performing alone. This chapter investigates the impact of this approach to tool use on district change efforts.

Finally, in chapter 7, Juliet Baxter uses the Quantitative Understanding: Amplifying Student Achievement and Reasoning (QUASAR) case to illustrate how research-based tools can help middle school teachers develop shared visions of exemplary mathematics instruction and student performance and learn to assess and improve their own practice and their students' performance with respect to those visions. This case traces the development of QUASAR tools from their beginnings as frameworks for guiding research, to their adaption by practitioners in the local settings in which the researchers worked, and to their publication in teacher education materials that are used widely across the country and internationally.

5

⌒⌀

Success for All: Using Tools to Transport Research-Based Practices to the Classroom

Amanda Datnow and Vicki Park

The purpose of this chapter is to examine how Success for All (SFA), a comprehensive school reform model that has been implemented in schools for almost two decades, uses tools to bridge research and practice in an effort to improve student achievement. Success for All is a school-wide approach to reading instruction that spread rapidly in this country throughout the 1990s and is used in approximately 1,000 schools today (2010). Historically, SFA sought to bring research knowledge to practice by building it into an instructional program and then providing extensive professional development to assist teachers in implementing the program with fidelity. In many ways, it represents the ideal type envisioned by proponents of the linear model of research–practice linkages. However, as we will explain, in recent years, SFA has changed its approach somewhat, relying more on practitioner knowledge. Research knowledge is still embedded into tools and carried into schools, but practitioners are expected to use their judgment to adapt the approach to meet the specific local context in response to local data. Furthermore, SFA has developed mechanisms to incorporate the wisdom of practice into its ongoing refinement of the SFA program. This chapter investigates the shift in logic of the research-into-practice relationship and its implications for the implementation process and student achievement.

For this analysis, we draw on data from a qualitative case study of the role of research and practitioner knowledge in SFA that involved interviews, observations, and document analysis at the Success for All Foundation (SFAF) and two SFA schools in California.[1] We begin this chapter by providing an overview of the SFA program and its conceptualization of the relationship between research and practice. We explain the development of specified tools for teaching and learning as a key feature of the program. We show how SFA trainers assist educators in the use of these tools and in understanding the research behind them. We then explain that while locating evidence for school improvement primarily in formal research, the project has broadened its notion of what constitutes valid knowledge by incorporating practitioners' knowledge of implementation in order to meet local needs.

OVERVIEW OF SFA

SFA is a whole-school reform model that concentrates on early literacy intervention. The SFA reading curriculum is comprised of an Early Learning program for prekindergarten and kindergarten students; Reading Roots, a beginning reading program; and Reading Wings, its upper-elementary counterpart. Originally developed by Robert Slavin, Nancy Madden, and a team at Johns Hopkins University, the program is currently based at SFAF in Baltimore.

Relying on an aggressive approach to improving teaching and learning, SFA is highly specified and comprehensive with respect to implementation guidelines and materials for students and teachers. The program's instructional method for increasing student achievement centers on three main strategies: research-based instructional techniques for teaching reading, cooperative learning, and the use of data and ongoing assessment. Concrete tools are provided for each of the three strategies, including detailed minute-by-minute lesson plans, training guides for teachers and principals, materials for students, instructions for how to structure joint learning among students, and software to assist in the gathering and use of data.

Major components of SFA include a ninety-minute reading period every day; the regrouping of students into smaller, homogeneous groups for reading instruction; quarterly assessments; and one-to-one tutoring. Teachers are expected to follow SFA lesson plans closely, which involve an active pacing of activities during the ninety-minute reading period (Madden, Livingston, and Cummings 1998). Almost all materials for students are provided, including reading booklets for the primary grades, materials to accompany various textbook series and novels for the upper grades, as well as activity sheets and assessments for all grade levels. There is an assumption in the program, by virtue of its specification, that research-based knowledge for school improvement can be created by external groups, packaged, and transported across contexts. SFA's founders and developers conceptualize tools (e.g., training guides and lesson plans) as carrying research-based knowledge and making it available in as many contexts as possible.

The SFA model also takes a specified approach to the adoption process. SFAF requires that the majority of a school's teaching staff vote for program adoption before they provide them with materials and technical assistance. The program also asks that schools employ a full-time SFA facilitator, organize a Solutions Team to help support families, and organize biweekly meetings among Roots and Wings teachers. The principal of an SFA school is responsible for ensuring staff motivation and commitment to the program as well as adequate resources to support it. The role of the SFA facilitator is to ensure the quality of the day-to-day implementation of the program by supporting teachers, monitoring the progress of all students, and managing assessments and regrouping efficiently (Madden et al. 1998).

Over the past fifteen years, the number of schools implementing SFA has changed substantially, beginning with a handful of schools and peaking in the mid-1990s when serving over 2000 schools, many of which were newly adopting the program. SFAF is now working in approximately 1,000 schools, many of them long-term implementation sites, and assisting in related projects in five other countries. Most SFA schools receive Title I funds and serve large numbers of low-income and minority students. Although the majority of SFA schools at the elementary level, SFAF also works with a smaller number of preschools and middle schools.

Over the years, SFA has garnered an impressive record of gains in student achievement. Since its inception, SFA has been the subject of more than fifty quantitative research studies and several in-depth qualitative studies. Several reports have summarized the results of such studies. Most notable is the meta-analysis of research on comprehensive school reform models by Borman, Hewes, Overman, and Brown (2003). Their meta-analysis includes 232 studies on twenty-nine models. The studies were chosen according to rigorous inclusion criteria. After analysis, they grouped the models into four categories depending on the quality of evidence (i.e., research evidence from control group studies or third-party control group studies), the quantity of their evidence (i.e., the number of studies and their generalizability), and the statistical significance of their results. They found only three models that they considered *proven models* based on the previously mentioned criteria. SFA was one of these three models. Another recent summary of research conducted by the American Institutes for Research's Comprehensive School Reform Quality Center evaluated the quality and effectiveness of twenty-two widely adopted comprehensive elementary school reform models. It found that only SFA and one other model (Direct Instruction) received a "moderately strong" rating in "Category 1: Evidence of Positive Effects on Student Achievement" (Comprehensive School Reform Quality Center 2006). A more recent large randomized study of thirty-eight SFA schools also found positive effects favoring SFA over regular classroom instruction (Borman et al. 2005).

A CONCEPTUAL FRAMEWORK FOR UNDERSTANDING THE ROLE OF TOOLS

In order to understand SFA's use of tools, it is important to conceptualize the relationship between research knowledge and practitioner knowledge for school improvement and the role tools might play in this process. Hatch and White (2002) concisely articulate two central issues about knowledge for school improvement that relate to this issue. First, there is the problem of how to capture knowledge so that schools can implement it. Second, there is a critical question of how the local knowledge of educators and the knowledge developed by researchers or others outside schools relate to each other.[2] Cochran-Smith and Lytle (1999) suggest at least three ways that research knowledge and practical knowledge might come together to support teacher learning and school improvement. First, they describe *knowledge for practice* as that in which university-based researchers generate what is commonly referred to as formal knowledge and theory for teachers to use in order to improve their practice. In this model, research and theory are translated into advice, training for teachers, or tools that carry research knowledge into schools. This view sees teachers as consumers of knowledge and assumes that knowledge for teaching can be tested through rigorous methods and codified. Second, *knowledge in practice* is the knowledge that resides in the practice of expert teachers. The assumption is that teaching is a spontaneous activity that is constructed in response to the particulars of each classroom context. In this case, one would expect to see not tools that derived from the work of researchers or those outside the school context but rather tools developed by expert teachers themselves, even in the form of shared learning that might take place among teachers.

Cochran-Smith and Lytle's (1999) third conception of the knowledge for school improvement, *knowledge of practice*, eschews the divide between formal and practical knowledge found in the other two perspectives. The authors argue that the formal knowledge–practical knowledge distinction is problematic because it reifies power and status differentials between university-generated knowledge and teacher-generated knowledge, ultimately separating teachers from researchers. Instead, the knowledge-of-practice perspective argues that teachers learn best when they interrogate their own practice through action research and work within inquiry-based communities of practice. In this conception of knowledge for school improvement, tools would likely be generated by teachers rather than by researchers outside schools.

In the sections that follow, we argue that SFA initially began its use of tools using the assumptions associated with a knowledge-for-practice conception. This conception shaped how the project thought about tool development and provided support for teachers to use these tools. However, as the project has matured, it has shifted its strategy, embracing a strategy of tool development and use that is closer to the knowledge-in-practice conception.

THE ROLE OF RESEARCH IN
BUILDING AND VALIDATING SFA TOOLS

First implemented in 1987, the SFA model was an outgrowth of a series of research-and-development projects that date to the mid-1970s. From the initial stages of the project, cofounders Robert Slavin and Nancy Madden framed their overriding purpose as improving educational opportunities for children from disadvantaged backgrounds by creating replicable school change. A major aim of the SFA developers was to design tools that embodied existing research knowledge on teaching and learning that could be transported across various contexts. That is, SFA was premised on the knowledge-for-practice model. Underlying the creation of such tools was the belief that if teachers used practices that were supported by research findings, their teaching would be more effective and that one way to get teachers to use these practices was to embed them in tools. The developers still firmly believe that "educational outcomes will never change on a serious scale until the core technology of teaching, down to daily lessons and teacher behaviors and up to school and district organization, comes to embody well-validated principles of practice" (Slavin, Madden, and Datnow 2005, 262).

As noted previously, SFAF provides concrete and accessible tools for teaching and learning because they believe that teachers need tools that are easy to use. Detailed teachers' manuals, videotapes modeling strategies for students and teachers, computer programs (e.g., Alphie's Lagoon, which is an after-school computer-based intervention program), and data analysis software are important foundations for the program. They are the vehicles by which research knowledge is carried into classrooms and schools.

In some circles, SFA has been critiqued for being too "scripted" because SFA is seen as a "teacher-proof" curriculum. However, program developers stand behind their decisions to provide detailed program materials, arguing that specified tools are the key to changing teacher practice. Speaking about the detailed instructional delivery guidelines for program implementation, Robert Slavin remarked, "We're trying to get a proper balance [between implementation fidelity and adaptation], but I think if you're truly serious about change, about having teachers use research-based practices every day, you've got to be pretty explicit and pretty well thought out to have that take place." For instance, cooperative learning has always been a centerpiece of the program, but specified routines and student procedures have been developed in order to enable teachers to practice more explicit modeling. This arose from the belief that although teachers generally understood cooperative learning standards, translating it into concrete practice was another matter. Tools in the form of specific instructions for how to structure cooperative learning for students are thus now a key feature of the program.

SFA also uses research to validate its tools. Building on the existing research base, program components of SFA have been subject to research-based trials, and great care appears to have been taken in ensuring that each component is supported by data. The development of SFA was informed by comprehensive reviews of existing research on cooperative learning, effective early reading practices, parent involvement, and professional development. Once the components of the program were investigated through reviews of research, they were then tested in school settings using quasi-experimental, matched control group designs before becoming part of SFA. Slavin et al. (2005) explained,

> Since it was first conceived, Success for All has been designed as a means of creating conditions in which teachers would use the results of rigorous research everyday. Each of the major components of the program was designed to operationalize practices known from research to increase the achievement of students at risk. At the outset, and again as the program developed, SFA researchers have carried out reviews of research in many areas relevant to practice to inform us about effective strategies. (263)

Thus, there is a great deal of "formal" research knowledge on the effects of SFA and evidence that this research knowledge informs the program and its continual development (Slavin et al. 2005).

SFAF continues to focus its efforts on building and refining the SFA model through systematic research of the program components. Slavin shared that the model was frequently updated, noting that each year manuals, tools, and instructional practices are being refined and new program components are regularly added. With new program components, the SFAF developers use a piloting process within SFA schools based on quasi-experimental methods. Slavin believes it was the responsibility of SFAF to provide schools with "well done, matched control [studies] . . . and now randomized experiments to evaluate the program." Often the pilot studies are part of formal research projects being conducted by SFAF staff. One of the schools we visited, School B, was involved in two research studies related to SFA. This school was piloting a new video teaching tool for phonics and a computer-assisted tutoring program. This research on the effectiveness of a particular SFA tool is distinct of course from research that is embedded in the tool itself, which embodied research knowledge in its initial development. The process is iterative, as research on the effectiveness of the new tool is incorporated to further refine it.

TRANSFERRING AND BUILDING KNOWLEDGE: THE ROLE OF TOOLS AND TRAINING

In conjunction with developing user-friendly, research-based tools, the SFA program relies on extensive, ongoing training in how to properly use the tools. Trainer–school relationships around the use of program tools act as the central linkage in which program goals are realized. SFAF views regionally based trainers as the main supporters of successful program implementation and have structured their trainer–school relationships around a coaching model (SFAF 2005). Thus, understanding how SFAF is structured with respect to the training and support of schools is important to making sense of the process of how the trainers support educators' use of the tools and take knowledge about tool use back to the organization for further tool refinement.

It is helpful to have a brief background on the trainers themselves. In the early development of the program, the researchers themselves also performed training roles. However, as the program grew, the SFA team quickly began to see the value of recruiting trainers who had extensive background working as practitioners. Not only did most of them have experience implementing the program, but practitioners also had firsthand knowledge of dealing with the realities of different school communities. Overall, the implementation staff tends to have a wealth of clinical experience working in schools and/or related fields. That is, they had what

Cochran-Smith and Lytle would call knowledge of practice. Regional area managers have knowledge of local contexts because they have experience working as teachers, facilitators, or support providers. New trainers are minimally required to have a bachelor's degree, professional certification in their designated field, and five years of experience in education. Individuals with experience in using the SFA program are preferred. Senior trainers also have two to four years of SFAF training experience.

SFAF provides initial and ongoing professional development to build trainer expertise in the program's tools. This is critical to ensuring quality implementation, as trainers must be very knowledgeable about the tools in order to assist school educators in using and adapting them. One established trainer mentioned that in a given year, she participates in a one-week Experienced Trainer Institute, multiple team (regional) meetings, and national training institute sessions. New trainers participate in a three-week "train-the-trainers" program organized by the New Trainer Institute, which is also coupled with cotraining sessions with more experienced trainers. SFAF holds annual conferences for trainers to share strategies for working with schools and discuss successful and unsuccessful program adaptations they have observed. During these conferences, trainers also engage in discussion about current research that is related to SFA, such as new research on strategies for teaching English-language learners. Trainers then use this research when they are meeting with school educators to help them understand why particular program components are necessary. Thus, trainers are simultaneously building their expertise about the research base of the program components and the implementation process.

The SFA trainers assist educators in using program tools with a coaching model. According to the SFAF (2005), professional development is composed of three main components: intensive initial training, ongoing coaching, and goal-focused planning for all program members. Professional development for teachers and teacher leaders includes initial training in reading strategies, instructional delivery methods, and monitoring of student progress using assessments. SFAF also provides training for principals and district leaders and offers a Leadership Academy to give leaders an opportunity to share and reflect on practices as well as to set and monitor their progress within and across districts.

Face-to-face interactions between schools and trainers provide the main mechanism by which schools address questions about adapting the program tools to fit their local context. With the emphasis on continuous improvement, SFAF asks schools to commit a significant portion of their human and financial resources to professional development activities. Madden described the endeavor as "interaction heavy" because, typically, SFAF staff spend approximately twenty-six days at the school site in the first year of implementation. Each school receives telephone meetings two to three weeks after trainings to answer questions regarding implementation. There are two on-site support visits over the year to observe students' strategy use in classrooms, to meet with teachers and administrators, to review data on student progress, and to set new goals. In addition, there are six follow-up telephone meetings to provide teachers with further training and support for their implementation of the program. The meetings are held on a quarterly basis to answer teachers' questions and help with troubleshooting, goal setting, and assessment issues. In general, SFAF has unlimited, informal telephone support for all staff members. Through these vehicles, trainers and other SFAF staff both help educators use SFA tools most effectively and help educators understand the research knowledge that underlies the program tools.

THE EVOLVING ROLE OF RESEARCH AND PRACTITIONER KNOWLEDGE IN SFA TOOLS

Over time, SFAF has broadened the types of knowledge it draws on the use and ongoing development of tools. This is reflected in its change regarding fidelity to implementation. SFAF has decided to reevaluate the implementation quality by using a goal-focused approach because it found that schools and trainers were overly focused on visible details of the implementation rather than the theory underlying their use. Superficial engagement with the program seemed to result in compliance to mandates and fidelity to implementation but did not necessarily translate into enhanced student outcomes in all cases. The new theory is that the effective use of tools is driven by understanding the purpose and conceptual development of the tool, hence bridging knowledge for and knowledge of practice. Madden shared the following:

> [When we started SFA] we spent much more time on the activities and just getting teachers fluent with the activities so that they would be utilizing the concepts and lately we've sort of presented it more conceptually first, and then gotten down to how to, and I think that's where we get a much richer implementation by the teachers if we can get them to do both of those things.

Thus, SFAF increasingly emphasizes an understanding of the theory behind the tools, as it has found that it was important for teachers to understand the concepts behind the tool in order to utilize the tools more effectively or adapt them to fit the needs of students. The professional development approach of SFAF discussed earlier relates to this program goal.

Similarly, while SFAF had a strong focus on fidelity to the model, it now allows some adaptations to the model if those adaptations are aimed toward improving student outcomes and meeting the individual school's goals. Slavin described the shift:

> So we've gone through this big change toward what we call a goal-focused implementation process, in which we try to have a different kind of conversation with schools, get our trainers to stop focusing on those minutiae, and rather focus on student performance and making more explicit use of internal school data, and picking issues that are of a particular concern to them, and then monitoring data more closely on those particular issues, and deciding. . . . It was very much in response to concerns that schools had expressed and ideas that they come forward with about ways to do this more effectively.

The shift in stance toward fidelity to implementation allows the schools greater freedom in making adaptations that were geared toward student outcomes. Although program fidelity is still expected on a number of key dimensions (e.g., the reading curriculum, cross-grade grouping, and full-time facilitator), SFAF's measurement of the quality of implementation differs, as it now provides space for innovative practices arising from the needs of specific schools. The theory appears to be that program fidelity should serve program effectiveness rather than fidelity for its own sake. The implication here is that some of the knowledge for school improvement lies within the tools and support provided by SFA in its research-based program but that some also lies in the experience of educators.

As part of the shift toward goal-focused implementation, frequent dialogue between school educators, trainers, other SFAF staff, and the SFA directors informs the ongoing development of tools. This is obviously a change from the early development of the program when far fewer people, in a far less diverse set of roles (e.g., mainly researchers), were informing development. Expressing the viewpoint of other practitioners we interviewed, a teacher commented,

> [SFAF researcher and trainers] want to know how the questioning is going. . . . So they are listening to us, and they want to know. . . . So you feel like they are going into classrooms, talking to teachers to find out what is working and what is not. So I really feel like the research is coming from us.

Confirming this perception, Madden indicated that some of the "best changes" to the program are a result of the feedback from schools. She described the process:

> A sort of situation arises where a school has some feedback to give us, you know, they want to let us know that they've figured something out . . . or

they're having a special problem, and then maybe I'll go out and take a look at it and spend some time to really get out and understand it, or [another staff member] will go and work on what is the issue, how can we learn from it, or how can we help with it, and then we take that back to the development organization and say what can we do realistically to use this information.

This shift from a focus on pure fidelity to one focused on schools' needs appears to have substantially changed the relationship between the SFAF staff and the educators in the schools they work with. In the past, some teachers used to complain about SFA's rigidity (Datnow and Castellano 2000). However, SFA trainers who were previously referred to by some teachers as, "SFA police," are now seen as valuable sources of instructional support. Whereas in the past trainers would meet only with administrators or with whole staffs to share the results of their "implementation checks," they now meet one-on-one with teachers to help them improve their practice. An SFA facilitator explained how the relationship between trainers and teachers had become one characterized by support:

> When we first started . . . they would come in and watch the teachers, "Are you following the schedule? Are you doing Adventures in Writing on Day 3?" . . . And they've lightened up on it. Now they come in and they are looking and listening to the kids and seeing, "Okay, what's the conversation the kids are having? Are they using the strategies?" . . . Not so much, "Here's a schedule." And I think it has been beneficial for the teachers and for them. It lets teachers have some flexibility. . . . But I think they are more focused on what the student outcomes are and supporting teachers so that those kids have those outcomes.

One teacher reiterated this view: "They trust our judgment that we are doing the program, that we are following the components, and if we add something, if we lengthen it, if we shorten something, if I do it on the wrong day, it's not taking away from the overall comprehension of the program." An SFAF area manager confirmed, "If you can do [an SFA component another] way and still get the same outcome, then all the more power to you. But it really takes an understanding and an acceptance of what the rationale is behind the activity." One might argue that in this way, SFAF is attempting to link knowledge for practice and knowledge of practice, helping teachers understand how to successfully adapt research-based tools based on their own experiences.

SFAF helps teachers understand the rationale behind activities through explicitly modeling desired behaviors. This is an extension of the learning theories they also apply to students. Slavin shared, "Part of our theory of action has to do with trying to get away from the script but still have teachers understand what they are doing by showing things directly to kids that then model that strategy for the teachers." For example, to build teacher capacity, cooperative learning is not only utilized in student learning but also applied in teacher development. Madden indicated that "having teachers work together on these instructional concepts makes it easier for them to grow and refine their skills." As teachers become more skilled adapters and users of SFA, they can ideally better meet their students' needs.

Overall, the emphasis on goal-focused implementation points to the ways in which SFA has broadened its notion of what counts as valid knowledge in the development of the program. While still maintaining a heavy reliance on traditional research (knowledge for practice), knowledge of context and understanding how to adapt tools have gained more prominence since the program's inception (knowledge of practice). The continual development of SFA appears to rely more now on the knowledge of educators implementing the program. This practitioner knowledge described by SFAF staff and school practitioners as being gathered informally is not research per se but more nearly informal, internal feedback gathered by trainers and the developers themselves. Thus, researchers work alongside practitioners, frequently consulting with them about their craft and adapting the model accordingly.

CONCLUSION

SFA is a case of how reform developers shift the way they use tools to carry research-based practices to schools. Undoubtedly, there is considerable "formal" research knowledge informing the initial development of the program and its continual development. At various points in time, both social science research (i.e., on program components such as cooperative learning) and evaluation research (i.e., on the outcomes associated with SFA implementation) have been conducted. Furthermore, the development of accessible pedagogical and learning tools tested by research continues to be a cornerstone of the SFA model. The knowledge of SFA trainers, many of whom were former SFA teachers, is also integral to the continual development of the model and its implementation strategies. The trainers serve to bridge the gap between research at SFAF and the work of practitioners in schools.

However, while there is a reliance on rigorous, quantitative research methods in informing model development, there is now also very strong commitment to learn from teacher practice and the implementation of SFA by local educators. There are efforts to gather educators' insights and incorporate them into the model. In other words, there is an acknowledgment on the part of SFAF that the tools do not carry *all* the knowledge that is needed for improvement. Rather, there is also a role for disciplined adaptation, which brings practitioner judgment much more into the equation.

The continual development of SFA demonstrates how developers, trainers, researchers, and practitioners work together to improve teaching and learning by drawing on both research evidence and local knowledge of implementation. Moreover, with the organization's shift to goal-focused rather than pure fidelity-focused implementation, educators seem to feel that there is more flexibility in the model and thus greater ability to reach improved student achievement. However, the actual effect of the goal-focused implementation strategy (in comparison to the earlier approach) has not been tested. It would be difficult to parse out the effects of the new strategy given that it has taken place alongside many other developments in the ways SFAF works with schools.

Our hope is that the findings of our study will spur further research on research–practice linkages with respect to other examples of educational reform. It is important to unpack how various educational reformers design and use tools to link research and practice, particularly given the current emphasis on scientifically based educational research. Second, we believe that there is a need for theory building with respect to research–practice linkages in the development of tools for educational reform. Additional research is needed for understanding the complex ways in which research and practice intersect and the contributions of tools to that process. While there are many studies on the effects of reform models and other educational interventions, seldom do researchers take a close look at the tools that are embedded in such models, how and why they were developed, and with what outcomes for practice. The chapters in this volume provide one step in the direction of further understanding the role of tools in educational improvement, but much more work needs to be done.

Finally, as an education community, we need to continue to search for ways for educational research to influence practice, and we must approach this problem broadly rather than narrowly as current policy frameworks might suggest. Current federal policies are promoting a narrow definition of evidence-based practices, emphasizing the supremacy of "scientifically based research" with preference for random assignment or at least experimental or quasi-experimental designs (Berliner 2002; Erickson and Gutierrez 2002; Smylie and Corcoran 2006). As Smylie and Corcoran (2006) conclude,

> It has created an impetus for "product-oriented," "what works" interpretation of evidence based practices. It puts a premium on validation and transportation of discrete programs and practices and emphasizes fidelity of

implementation over more dynamic process of change and mutual adaptation in context. (2–3)

Slavin has been a vocal advocate for educational practices guided by scientifically based research and has written extensively about appropriate methodology for evaluating programs and criteria for establishing effective practices (Slavin 2002, 2003). At the same time, as the experience of SFA reveals, even in cases where tool development is driven by research, the use of such tools is informed by educators who bring their own knowledge and experience to bear in their decision making in the classroom. Teachers, therefore, are an integral part of the research–practice linkage, and their role in implementing programs needs to be recognized as such.

NOTES

This research was supported by grants from the Spencer Foundation and the MacArthur Foundation to the Learning Research and Development Center of the University of Pittsburgh. The opinions reported herein are the authors' own and do not represent the positions of the funders. We are greatly indebted to Robert Slavin, Nancy Madden, the staff at SFAF, and the educators in two SFA schools for kindly participating in our research. We also wish to thank Cynthia Coburn and Mary Kay Stein for their helpful comments on earlier drafts.

1. For this investigation, we chose study methods because it enabled us to examine SFA in real-life contexts and allowed us to present the perspectives of those actually implementing or working with the program (Yin 2003). Because we were interested in gathering data from multiple perspectives, our study focused on SFAF and two SFA schools. In keeping with the tenets of case study research, the sites and participants were chosen purposefully to address our research questions. From SFAF, we interviewed Robert Slavin and Nancy Madden, cofounders of SFA and researchers at Johns Hopkins University. We also interviewed several other SFAF staff, including an SFA trainer, the director of training for SFAF, two area managers, an implementation officer, and an individual in charge of policy. We also interviewed two individuals who had worked at Johns Hopkins University when SFA was being developed there. Each of these interviews lasted one hour or more. Data collection took place during the 2005–2006 school year.

We also gathered qualitative data during site visits to two SFA schools. The schools were recommended to us by an SFA area manager as experienced SFA sites. We sought sites in the state of California for logistical reasons. School A had been implementing SFA since 2000, and School B, which recently became a charter school, had been implementing SFA since 1999. Both of the schools are Title I schools, serving large numbers of low-income students. The majority of the students in both schools are Hispanic. Both are large schools serving more than

1,000 students each. The schools are located in different school districts, one in a very large urban district and one in a midsize district.

Our data collection at each school involved interviews, focus groups, and classroom observations. At both schools, we conducted interviews with the school principal. At School A, we also interviewed the SFA facilitator. Because School B is so large, it has individuals at each grade level, rather than just one facilitator, helping to facilitate SFA. Thus, we interviewed the assistant principal who oversees SFA and several lead teachers who served as SFA facilitators at School B. At School A, we conducted a focus group with four regular classroom teachers from different grade levels. At School B, we also interviewed five teachers from various grade levels. All interviews were tape-recorded and transcribed. In both schools, we observed classroom instruction in approximately ten classrooms during the SFA ninety-minute reading period. We took field notes during classroom observations. We also observed an SFA Experienced Site Conference in January 2006.

To analyze our data, we coded the interview transcripts based on the areas of inquiry guiding this study. First, we coded the data for examples of conceptions of the relationship between research and practice. In doing so, we searched the data for SFA staff and educators' conceptions of research. We noted instances where practitioner knowledge seemed to become increasingly important in the ongoing development of SFA. Second, we coded data that gave information on how program components and materials were developed and used, hence revealing the role of tools in the program. Coding was done with the aid of qualitative data analysis software called HyperResearch, which allowed us to sort the data based on code names and then generate reports. We also coded documents using the same coding scheme. For the purposes of confidentiality, pseudonyms are used for the names of all schools, persons, and places. However, we are unable to keep the identities of Robert Slavin and Nancy Madden confidential given that they are the leaders and founders of SFAF.

2. Hatch and White (2002, citing Lehming and Kane 1981) define knowledge in the following way: "Knowledge consists of information and understandings derived from research, practice, or both; it is empirically or socially validated; and it can reside in ideas, theories, explanations, advice, programs, materials, or technologies" (120).

6

✑

Tools to Deepen Practitioners' Engagement with Research: The Case of the Institute for Learning

Gina Schuyler Ikemoto and Meredith I. Honig

Federal and state policies over the past fifteen years have called increasingly on district central office and school leaders to use "research" or "research-based" programs and practices to foster districtwide improvements in student learning. Some school systems are responding to these new demands by seeking assistance from intermediary organizations that develop materials and processes designed to help practitioners engage with research-based ideas. Studies of intermediary organizations suggest that they can hold promise in this regard (Burch 2002; Gallucci, Boatright, Lysne, and Swinnerton 2006; Honig 2004). But are intermediary organizations actually realizing this promise? If so, what do intermediary organizations do when they help practitioners use research? What kinds of materials and processes seem particularly useful for helping practitioners engage research-based ideas and apply them to their practice? Answers to these questions would help practitioners decide whether and how to partner with various intermediary organizations as a means of using research to improve education.

We address these questions with data from an in-depth case study of the Institute for Learning (IFL), located in the Learning Research and Development Center at the University of Pittsburgh. Since 1995, the IFL has assisted more than twenty-five urban districts in using research—mainly research on how people learn—to ground efforts to strengthen student learning districtwide. As a cornerstone of its work, the IFL compiles and develops tools to help district practitioners engage with research. We draw on data from two mixed-methods studies of IFL's collaboration with eight urban districts to investigate the IFL's efforts to link research and practice and the role of tools in these efforts.[1]

We use ideas from sociocultural learning theory to conceptualize tools as materials and processes that can both constrain and enable thinking and action in ways that support understanding and application of new ideas. We argue that the IFL tools tended to serve at least one of three functions: naming and defining concepts, structuring learning activities during professional development sessions to support practitioners' understanding of concepts, and prompting activities practitioners could implement in their day-to-day practice to help them apply concepts to authentic activities. Practitioners' use of IFL tools shaped their understanding of research concepts and their engagement with particular ideas. The tools appeared to be more effective when the IFL supported practitioners' tool use by providing opportunities for social engagement, modeling, embedding knowledge from both research and practice into tools, linking tools to practitioners' local situation, and adapting tools over time. We conclude with implications for efforts to engage practitioners in using research.

SOCIOCULTURAL LEARNING PERSPECTIVES ON THE FUNCTION OF TOOLS IN LINKING RESEARCH AND PRACTICE

We turned to sociocultural learning theory to ground our analysis because it helps elaborate how particular types of materials, called tools, coupled with certain assistance relationships, can engage practitioners in new work practices. This theory's treatment of tools stems in part from Vygotsky's foundational work in this area suggesting that psychological tools support human learning much like physical tools (such as a hammer or shovel) support physical activities (Vygotsky 1978). Contemporary theorists have elaborated that psychological tools are "reifications" or the manifestation of an idea (Wenger 1998)—in this case, the specific form that research-based information may take. Tools enable or deepen individuals' engagement in work practices by "specify[ing] the parameters of acceptable conduct," communicating messages about what the individuals should and should not do (Brown and Duguid 1991, 33). Tools also constrain thought and action by directing people's attention away from particular ways of thinking and doing. For example, curriculum materials communicate messages to teachers regarding how they should teach particular knowledge and skills to students, and, in the process, they limit teachers' engagement in other work practices. Tools also scaffold thinking by prompting action, which provides people with an experience on which they can reflect (Wertsch 1998).

From this perspective, not all materials qualify as tools. To be a tool, a set of materials must have some semistable aspects—that is, it must constrain and enable thinking and action in particular ways across settings and over time. This is not to say that tools cannot be adapted and evolve. Rather, at any given time, tools carry particular ideas in which tool designers and providers aim to engage others. Tools are also distinct from other materials in that they do not simply broadcast a set of information. Rather, tools often "trigger" negotiations among individuals about which actions to take to meet particular goals (Brown and Duguid 1991). Any social setting may feature tools. However, whether materials actually function as a tool depends in part on whether they help users deepen their engagement with particular ideas.

By definition, all psychological tools aim to prompt thinking and action (Wenger 1998). However, not all tools emphasize thinking and action in the same ways. *Conceptual tools*, for example, foreground thinking. Such tools typically take the form of "principles, frameworks, and ideas" (Grossman, Smagorinsky, and Valencia 1999, 13). They can include theories that are broadly applicable across a range of settings. For example, Grossman and colleagues describe how the idea of curriculum alignment operated as a conceptual tool by focusing teachers' attention on the goals of their lessons and guiding a thought process in which they considered whether and how planned instructional activities related to what they wanted students to know and be able to do.

Practical tools also aim to prompt new thinking and action but foreground action. Such tools generally take the form of "practices, strategies, and resources" that have "local and immediate utility" (Grossman et al. 1999, 13–14). For example, a lesson plan developed by a curriculum developer may aim to communicate particular concepts by suggesting specific strategies that teachers might use in their classrooms. While the broad concept of "curriculum alignment" aims to prompt action by shifting thinking, the lesson plan prompts action to shift thinking.

Sociocultural learning theory suggests that access to a tool alone does not ensure that practitioners will use the tool to particular ends. Additional forms of assistance may also be essential to practitioners' engagement with tools over time (Tharp and Gallimore 1988). Accordingly, intermediary organizations may help practitioners use research by assisting them in engaging with research-based tools. For example, intermediary organizations can assist practitioners by making research ideas embedded in tools more explicit and helping practitioners understand how to maintain the integrity of those ideas when using the tool. Sociocultural learning theory suggests that such assistance may include the provision and facilitation of social opportunities through which practitioners grapple with new ideas embedded in tools and the relevance of those ideas to their own practice. Through dialogue, participants have opportunities to challenge each others' beliefs and interpretations of problems and events and engage in conversations that can lead to shared understandings and deeper engagement in activities that would otherwise not be possible by individuals operating alone (Brown and Duguid 1991).

Intermediary organizations may also assist with tool use by modeling how to use the tool or new work practices that the tool prompts. Such models help practitioners visualize how research-based ideas can be carried out in practice prior to attempting to execute application of the ideas themselves. Models can be particularly useful when modelers employ metacognitive strategies that bring their "thinking to the surface" and make it "visible" (Collins, Brown, and Holum 2003, 3) so that observers understand not just what to do but why.

FINDINGS

We found that the IFL created or collected several different types of tools to support practitioners' engagement in research-based ideas. Practitioners' accounts and observations suggested that these tools contributed to practitioners' understanding and use of research-based ideas. However, the tools were most effective when they were accompanied by assistance from IFL. We elaborate each of these claims in the sections that follow.

Tool Development

We found that IFL staff either developed tools themselves or used tools created by others as a core part of their strategy for helping district practitioners use research—especially research about how people learn—to inform their own practice. Tools tended to serve three functions related to helping district practitioners integrate new research ideas into their practice: 1) naming and defining concepts from research, 2) structuring learning activities during professional development sessions to support practitioners, understanding of those concepts, and 3) structuring authentic activities that practitioners could engage in as a means of applying concepts to their day-to-day practices.

Tools That Named and Defined Concepts

The IFL created a series of conceptual tools that named and defined particular ideas. In doing so, these tools provided conceptual scaffolding that helped practitioners access and understand research-based concepts. As suggested by sociocultural learning theory, these tools aimed to prompt action by presenting specific ideas and a language for defining and elaborating those ideas as a main lever of change. For example, the Principles of Learning (POLs) are nine statements about the characteristics of environments that promote rigorous teaching and learning. (See figure 6.1.) They established a common language that practitioners could use to make sense of particular concepts. They also aimed to provide a framework or lens that structured practitioners' attention and thinking as they observed teaching and learning environments. In doing so, the POLs enabled a new conceptualization of high-quality classroom instruction.

The District Design Principles (DDPs) constituted another IFL tool that named and defined concepts. The DDPs were statements that emphasized features of district environments that supported use of POLs, such as two-way accountability and a culture that emphasized continuous learning at all levels of the system. By naming these features of the district environment and defining them, the IFL provided district leaders with a research-based framework for conceptualizing the district's role in supporting rigorous teaching and learning and for assessing whether their district's policies and structures were set up to support use of POLs.

Tools That Structured Learning Activities during Professional Development Sessions

IFL staff also developed tools that aimed to support practitioners' understanding and use of research-based ideas by structuring their engagement in particular learning activities during professional development. Given their emphasis on engagement in action as a main vehicle for change, these tools are examples of "practical tools." For example, IFL staff created an interactive CD-ROM to support practitioners' understanding of the idea of clear expectations. We observed this CD structuring a learning activity by prompting practitioners to view videos of classroom practice and negotiating with colleagues whether the idea of clear expectations was evident in these videos. After entering their decision, the CD provided them with feedback on their assessment.

Organizing for effort—Everything within the school is organized to support the belief that sustained and directed effort can yield high achievement for all students. High standards are set, and all students are given as much time and expert instruction as they need to exceed or meet expectations.

Clear expectations—Clear standards of achievement and gauges of students' progress toward those standards offer real incentives for students to work hard and succeed. Descriptive criteria and models that meet the standards are displayed in the schools, and the students refer to these displays to help them analyze and discuss their work.

Fair and credible evaluations—Tests, exams, and classroom assessments must be aligned with the standards of achievement for these assessments to be fair. Further, grading must be done against absolute standards rather than on a curve so that students can clearly see the results of their learning efforts.

Recognition of accomplishment—Clear recognition of authentic student accomplishments is a hallmark of an effort-based school. Progress points are articulated so that, regardless of entering performance level, every student can meet the criteria for accomplishments often enough to be recognized frequently.

Academic rigor in a thinking community—In every subject, at every grade level, instruction and learning must include commitment to a knowledge core, demand for high thinking, and active use of knowledge.

Accountable Talk®—Accountable Talk® means using evidence that is appropriate to the discipline and that follows established norms of good reasoning. Teachers should create the norms and skills of Accountable Talk® in their classrooms.

Socializing intelligence—Intelligence comprises problem-solving and reasoning capabilities with habits of mind that lead one to use those capabilities regularly. Equally, it is a set of benefits about one's right and obligation to make sense of the world and one's capacity to figure things out over time. By calling on students to use the skills of intelligent thinking—and by holding them responsible for doing so—educators can teach "intelligence."

Self-management of learning—Students manage their own learning by evaluating feedback they get from others, by bringing their own knowledge to bear on new learning, by anticipating learning difficulties and apportioning their time accordingly, and by judging their progress toward a learning goal. Learning environments should be designed to model and encourage the regular use of self-management strategies.

Learning as apprenticeship—Learning environments can be organized so that complex thinking is modeled and analyzed in apprenticeship arrangements. Mentoring and coaching will enable students to undertake extended projects and develop presentations of finished work both in and beyond the classroom.

Figure 6.1. Principles of Learning

IFL staff also regularly developed what they referred to as "task sheets." These task sheets served as practical tools by structuring activities that assisted practitioners in engaging in research-based ideas. For example, in one professional development session, IFL staff asked participants to discuss a paper by Spillane and colleagues on the idea of distributed leadership in groups. Had the IFL just asked the group to read the article, the article might have served as an example of a tool that carried information without necessarily prompting action. However, the IFL staff also provided an accompanying task sheet with guiding questions for the groups to consider that served to prompt action. For example, one task sheet included the following question:

> Spillane et al. write, "Leaders do not work directly on the world; their actions in and on the world are mediated by a continuum of artifacts" (p. 32). Think of an artifact used in your present leadership context and discuss how it mediates your work.

In this way, the task sheet transformed the article into a tool to help practitioners engage the concepts in the article by participating in activities that promised to enhance their understanding of those concepts and how they related to their own practice.

Tools That Structured Authentic Activities
to Apply Concepts to Day-to-Day Practices

A third type of practical tool prompted practitioners to engage in "authentic activities"—coherent, meaningful, and purposeful work that individuals carry out as part of their regular day-to-day responsibilities—as a primary means for engaging practitioners in research-based ideas. The IFL's signature tool, the LearningWalk® routine, exemplifies this type of tool because it prompts practitioners to examine research-based ideas (such as the POLs) in the process of conducting an authentic activity (such as observing classrooms). The IFL defines a LearningWalk® routine as "an organized walk through a school's halls and classrooms using the Principles of Learning to focus on the instructional core" (Institute for Learning 2003, 4). They involve multiple "walkers" that spend five to ten minutes in each of several classrooms looking at student work and classroom artifacts and talking with students and teachers. During LearningWalk® routines that we observed, participants focused their attention on particular attributes of teaching and learning represented in the POLs—such as evidence of clear expectations—and then gathered in the hall to discuss what they observed and implications for steps the school could take to improve teaching and learning.

Evidence That Tools Deepened Practitioners'
Engagement with and Use of Research

To what extent did IFL tools impact practitioners' understanding of research-based concepts and their day-to-day practice? Drawing on practitioners' accounts plus observations of their participation in IFL activities over time, we argue that engagement with IFL tools deepened practitioners' understanding and use of research-based ideas, particularly for district leaders and principals who were the primary targets of the IFL's work.[2]

In interviews and observations, school and district administrators across our case study districts repeatedly credited the IFL with "deepening" or "shifting" their understanding of research-based ideas about learning. In the words of one administrator, his or her work with the IFL "changed my thinking. It's totally changed my thinking about how kids learn." Many central office administrators emphasized that the IFL's tools helped them deepen their understanding of the following research-based ideas: effort-based intelligence, two-way accountability, focusing the organization on instruction and learning, everyone as a continuous learner, and making instruction public.

Respondents consistently reported that two IFL tools—POLs and LearningWalk® routines—were particularly useful. For example, district and school leaders reported that the POLs helped them deepen their understanding of high-quality teaching by providing them with shared ideas and a common language they could use to make sense of practice together. Interview data suggest that practitioners at all levels in all the case study districts used language consistent with the POLs at least somewhat routinely, especially such terms as "accountable talk®," "clear expectations," and "academic rigor." Respondents indicated that these terms provided them with a framework that influenced their classroom observations and the guidance they provided to principals and teachers about how to strengthen their practice. Some respondents attributed changes in their daily practice directly to the POLs. In one principal's words, "It's been very useful, at least when I go into a classroom I know what to look for . . . it's given me a language to use when I'm giving feedback to teachers." Respondents also reported that the LearningWalk® tool was a particularly useful tool because it triggered negotiations among their colleagues in ways that supported their understandings about the research on high-quality teaching and how it related to their own practice.

Despite these generally positive views, a few principals in each of the case study districts expressed frustration with their perceived inability to implement some of the IFL ideas themselves and to involve their teachers deeply in engaging those ideas. For example, in one district, several participating principals took issue with the expectation that they should be responsible for training teachers on IFL ideas, noting that they had little time or training to do so.

Central office administrators and principals across our case study districts also credited the IFL and its tools with helping them change their policies and practices in ways they believed would strengthen teaching and learning. For example, the majority of central office administrators whom we interviewed reported that their work with the IFL helped them develop skills related to the research-based concept of instructional leadership that influenced how they supervised and supported principals. This support included the kinds of questions they posed to principals, what they looked for when visiting schools, and the types of assistance they offered principals.

Impacts on conceptual understandings did not necessarily precede impacts on practice. Some central office administrators and principals noted that the IFL tools helped them change practices, which then helped them deepen their conceptual understanding. These reports were consistent with sociocultural theories' emphasis on learning as participation in practice. For example, one district respondent explained how his district required principals to get into the habit of observing classrooms. These observations provided fodder for discussions in meetings, and this furthered understanding about research-based ideas and how they related to the instructional practice that was observed during the school visits.

Assistance with Tool Use

The previous section provides evidence that district practitioners most closely involved with the IFL credited the IFL with deepening their thinking about and engagement in research-based ideas. Many of these practitioners credited IFL tools with these outcomes. However, our observations suggest that the tools alone did not contribute to these outcomes. Rather, the tools, combined with forms of assistance, promoted these outcomes in practitioners' thinking and practice. We anticipated some of these forms of assistance in our conceptual framework, including opportunities for social engagement and modeling. However, we also found that the IFL enabled tool use by providing additional forms of assistance not anticipated by our conceptual framework, including embedding both research-based and practitioner-based knowledge in the tools, linking tools to practitioners' local situation, and adapting tools over time.

Providing Social Opportunities to Make Sense of Research-Based Ideas Embedded in Tools

As part of their work with district practitioners, IFL staff engaged them in countless formal and informal dialogue-rich social processes that helped practitioners make sense of what particular research-based ideas meant and implications of those ideas for their practice. The formal opportunities typically occurred during monthly daylong professional development sessions that the IFL held for stakeholder groups within the district, such as district leaders, principals, and/or coaches. Unlike some conferences or professional meetings characterized by formal presentations or the transmission of information to attendees, the IFL's daylong professional development sessions typically featured multiple and lengthy opportunities for groups of practitioners to discuss and engage with tools. The IFL structured these opportunities by focusing the content of the conversations and by encouraging practitioners to respectfully challenge each other's ideas.

Characteristic of these dialogues were opportunities for district practitioners to socially construct the relevance of particular ideas or forms of work practice to their own ongoing practice within parameters set by the tool. As one district leader explained, these opportunities to grapple with the meaning of new ideas in light of their own practice had a much greater impact on his or her practice than exposure to the same ideas absent opportunities for social construction:

> In my work in graduate school, I had some experience with WalkThroughs, which is the early iteration of LearningWalks. And I'd had my requisite courses in psychology of learning and all that stuff, but I hadn't really had the opportunity to practice it. So I've learned enormously from the work [with the IFL].

Some tools, like the LearningWalk® routine, included in its design prompts for practitioners to engage in rich conversations about classroom observations even if IFL fellows or others were not present to trigger and facilitate such dialogue. However, as the previous quote suggests, the IFL staff further enhanced practitioners' engagement with that tool by providing opportunities during professional development sessions for practitioners to discuss the LearningWalk® tool and how it should be used in practice.

The IFL also facilitated opportunities for practitioners to engage with their counterparts in other districts around particular tools. For example, several practitioners reported that IFL staff put them in communication with practitioners in other districts who had more experience with LearningWalk® routines. These opportunities were particularly useful in helping them understand how particular research-based ideas could be actualized in practice, especially when practice in their own districts fell short of the forms of participation prompted by the tools. One principal explained the value of such opportunities: "It wasn't until we went to

New York City and I got to talk to the people [principal and teachers] there that I really understood how this all fits together."

Modeling

IFL fellows also modeled how to engage with IFL tools in ways that seemed to foster practitioners' engagement with research-based ideas. This finding was not surprising given that sociocultural learning theory suggests that modeling can help practitioners visualize how research-based ideas can be carried out in practice. IFL fellows provided these visual models by stepping into the role of a central office administrator or school principal and demonstrating how the local leaders might look for evidence of a particular POL while on a LearningWalk® routine or how to structure walks in particular schools. One district leader noted that by watching the IFL fellow conducting LearningWalk® routines, he or she was able to develop a more vivid picture of what the LearningWalk® routines were supposed to involve than he or she was able to develop using the tool alone.

Interviewees across our case study districts reported that this modeling helped them determine how they could apply tools and research-based ideas in their day-to-day work. One principal explained how modeling helped him or her develop a deeper understanding of the POLs than he or she would have with only the CD tools:

> People who just had that overview coverage and been given the CD on it [the POLs], they're not there. . . . It wasn't until I started going to [IFL trainings] . . . that I really saw how it [the POLs] impacted and made change. . . . I could actually see examples of good teaching. I could see examples of good questioning. I could see examples of high academic rigor. I learned most of those examples when I did those intensive trainings.

Modeling seemed a particularly powerful form of assistance in part because it generally involved opportunities for IFL fellows to "make thinking explicit." For example, while on LearningWalk® routines, fellows typically provided a running narrative of how they were positioning themselves in classrooms, what they were directing their attention toward, and how they were thinking about what they were seeing to help make visible the mental work involved in such classroom observations. When asked to identify what she considered the most important features of her work with district practitioners, one fellow highlighted, "The idea of making thinking visible . . . the meta-level of stepping back and reflecting on what supported your learning, and what the implications of that are for what you're going to do when you try to support someone else's learning." IFL fellows regularly labeled strategies they were using during their professional development sessions.

Embedding Knowledge from Both Research and Practice into Tools

Beyond the conditions anticipated in our conceptual framework, the IFL also fostered tool use by crafting tools with knowledge from both research and practice. Interviewees across our case study districts who had opportunities to contribute to tool development reported that this experience both helped them personally understand the ideas and resulted in tools that were more likely to resonate well with their colleagues. For example, when the IFL created the POLs, staff members began by compiling an initial draft of the characteristics of effective learning environments based on their reading of learning research. The IFL then convened representatives from four districts and learning researchers in a series of meetings over almost three years to debate the meaning of the research and the initial draft of the POLs. During this process, district staff used research to surface examples from teaching practice in their own districts that supported or contradicted the research and, with the researchers, moved back and forth between the information from research and practice to come to a clearer understanding of what the research might mean for district practice. These debates resulted in a consensus regarding what the research considered the characteristics of teaching and learning that enabled all students to learn at high levels and what language to use to communicate those principles in ways that resonated with practitioners. As such, the final set of POL statements incorporated knowledge from both research and practice.

IFL's willingness to incorporate practitioner knowledge improved the efficacy of the tools and the degree to which they resonated with practitioners. For example, one central office leader reported,

> I think some of the things [this district] has done with [an IFL tool] has shown up in their [the IFL's] work. I know our literacy coaches will point out that certain things the IFL now says [about how to use the tool] are based upon their experiences within the district.

Multiple interviewees from this district said that the IFL's willingness to adapt the tool in response to literacy coaches' input yielded a tool that was more practical and useful both for their own and for other districts.

Linking Tools to Practitioners' Local Situations

IFL fellows actively assisted district practitioners in linking their use of the tools to their own local district situations. Across role groups, respondents reported that the fellows' "responsiveness" and efforts to "tailor" their work to the specific interests and needs of their districts helped them and others in their districts continually draw on research-based ideas. IFL fellows relied primarily on two strategies in this regard. First, IFL fellows created new tools in response to a particular problem of practice within a given district. In the words of one IFL staff member, "We see a district, and there's a particular kind of need that that district has. . . . And so then we decide, 'How are we going to meet that need?'" For example, the IFL launched a strand of work called "disciplinary literacy" in response to district leaders' concerns that their large comprehensive high schools were not supporting high-quality teaching. As part of this work, the IFL developed tools that specified the nature of high-quality teaching within each of the content areas and tools aimed at developing the capacity of high school teachers to embed this type of teaching in their day-to-day practice.

Second, IFL fellows adapted existing tools to fit aspects of a given district's situation. For example, in one district the IFL adapted the LearningWalk® protocols to prompt practitioners to investigate not only whether they saw evidence of rigorous teaching and learning but also to look for evidence of teachers realizing their state mathematics standards in their classrooms. In another district, the IFL adapted its tool related to Accountable Talk® to support district practitioners' understanding of how Accountable Talk® fit with their district's reading curriculum.

Practitioners reported that the IFL's willingness to create new tools and adapt existing tools was particularly helpful. For example, one district leader argued that the IFL's assistance in applying tools to local situations was a key strategy for helping their district access and use research knowledge:

> [The IFL has been] helping us to translate that [research] into good practice and then really applying it to our own situation. So translating the research to practice across the country and then adapting it to our own situation, I think, was the perfect flow.

While IFL interviewees consistently reported that contextualizing tools was an important strategy, they also indicated that it could be labor intensive and that the IFL as an organization struggled with how to improve efficiency of this approach. Given that the IFL did not want fellows to "reinvent the wheel" in each partner district, it created what we would call "core" tools, such as a standardized Learning Walk® protocol, and then encouraged fellows to adapt the tool to fit the local context. Several IFL fellows said that it was particularly important for them to be involved in the adaptation process—rather than allowing practitioners to adapt the tools by themselves—so that they could assist practitioners in maintaining the integrity of the research-based ideas that the tool was designed to support.

Adapting Tools over Time

IFL enabled practitioners' use of tools by updating and improving the core tools over time. These updates occurred in response to emerging research or lessons learned from efforts to use the tools in districts. For example, the IFL created multiple iterations of its LearningWalk® tool in response to implementation problems that it encountered in the field. More specifically, some practitioners tended to use the LearningWalk® routines to evaluate teachers rather than to investigate and figure out how to support teachers' practice. The IFL staff reported that they believed that an evaluation thrust would threaten the open and trusting dialogue that was at the heart of the POLs that the LearningWalk® routines ultimately aimed to support. In response to this information from practice, the IFL developed a series of training sessions for practitioners to complete before conducting LearningWalk® routines to help practitioners understand the relationship between the LearningWalk® protocol, teacher support, and teacher evaluation. Over time, these trainings became a formal part of the LearningWalk® tool. Thus, the IFL adapted its core LearningWalk® tool over time, and fellows could then further adapt the tool to fit with specific situations in individual districts. This willingness to adapt tools over time was crucial because it increased district leaders' and principals' willingness to engage with the tools.

CONCLUSIONS AND IMPLICATIONS

Our findings suggest that the IFL's tools—in conjunction with intentional, structured assistance provided by the IFL—enabled practitioners to engage research-based ideas in ways that shaped their thinking and their actions. The types of assistance that seemed particularly powerful featured modeling and social opportunities for practitioners to make sense of research-based ideas embedded in tools. In addition, we found that the IFL's tools were particularly useful when the IFL included knowledge from both research and practice in their tools, linked tools to practitioners' local situations, and adapted tools over time.

These findings have several implications for efforts to engage practitioners in using research. First, the IFL case highlights that not all materials may be promising catalysts for practitioners' research use. Our work with IFL districts and beyond suggests that the term "tool" is often used indiscriminately to refer to a host of materials that do not necessarily reflect the features of tools that sociocultural learning theorists have found make materials fundamental instruments of learning. For example, some people refer to research summaries as a tool based on the argument that these documents make research ideas available to practitioners. However, these documents do not necessarily fit sociocultural learning theory's definition of "tool" if they do not prompt users to engage in new ways of thinking or acting. The IFL case suggests that research providers and users might do well to scrutinize so-called tools and other materials that promise to help them link research and practice for the features of tools outlined and elaborated here.

Second, the IFL case underscores that tools alone are not enough. Adaptable assistance seems essential to helping practitioners actually use tools to impact their own thinking and actions. Such assistance involves a number of challenging activities that might be beyond the capacity of most intermediary organizations to engage. IFL staff who work directly with school district practitioners in assistance relationships typically have deep expertise in teaching and educational leadership and a keen ability to read and make use of challenging research-based ideas. They are also located in a national university-based research center where they have access to research and researchers, including their founder and executive director, Lauren Resnick, an expert on learning. Furthermore, the IFL has made a significant investment in staff dedicated to tool development—staff whose job is to collect lessons learned from research and experience, to incorporate that information into tools, and to continually revisit and revise IFL tools based on experiences using them in districts over time (Honig and Ikemoto 2007).

When considering whether to partner with a particular intermediary organization for assistance with evidence use, district leaders might investigate the extent to which their prospective partners have the potential to provide the kinds of assistance that maximizes the degree to which practitioners can use research-based tools to change their practice. In our experience, such organizations are few and far between. Accordingly, public and private funders should consider how they can make strategic investments in building the capacity of intermediary organizations and others to develop tools—and to assist practitioners in using tools—as a means of deepening practitioners' engagement with research.

NOTES

Research for this chapter was funded by the Spencer Foundation and the John D. and Catherine T. MacArthur Foundation as part of the "Meta Study on the Relationship between Research and Practice." We thank Cynthia Coburn and

Mary Kay Stein, principal investigators of the metastudy, for their feedback on various drafts of this chapter and related papers. Thank you to Lauren Resnick for her careful reading of our work and all the staff of the Institute for Learning who welcomed us in (one of us for many years) to learn with them about their experiences.

1. For this chapter, we draw on data collected between 2001 and 2006. Data from 2001 to 2005 come from two mixed-methods studies of the IFL's relationships with eight urban districts conducted by the first author and colleagues at the RAND Corporation (Marsh, Kerr, Ikemoto, and Darilek 2004, 2006; Marsh et al. 2005). Between 2005 and 2006, both chapter authors conducted additional data collection activities in one of the original eight districts and in another district that had recently initiated a partnership with the IFL. This second wave of data collection focused specifically on IFL efforts to link research and practice. For this chapter, we drew on approximately 150 documents, interviews with eighteen IFL staff members and 153 district and school leaders across eight partner districts, focus groups with 118 teachers across three districts, and nearly 200 hours of observation notes. (For an elaboration of our methods, see Honig and Ikemoto 2007.)

We coded data in several phases using NUDIST (QSR6) software. First, we used low-inference categories to sort through basic dimensions of the IFL's district partnerships, including how the IFL intended to assist districts in accessing and using research-based ideas, how the IFL actually provided this assistance, outcomes associated with these efforts, and conditions that helped or hindered these efforts. Second, we recoded our data using higher-inference concepts related to how the IFL provided assistance to districts, including their development of tools and how they supported tool use. We also asked key IFL respondents and a RAND researcher who led their IFL research to review our draft report carefully and highlight consistencies and inconsistencies with their interpretations of events. We used respondent reviews as an additional check on construct validity and the overall reliability of our analyses.

2. For more extended accounts of the IFL impacts, see Honig and Ikemoto (2007), Ikemoto (2007), and Marsh et al. (2005).

7

QUASAR: The Evolution of Tools to Support Educational Improvement

Juliet A. Baxter

Tools, such as student assessments, curricula, and protocols for observing classrooms, have the potential to bridge research and practice by communicating theory and knowledge. Well-designed tools embody important generalities (research-derived patterns or theory) connected to illustrations of specific instances of teaching and learning. The design of these tools is not a trivial undertaking. This case presents two sets of tools that were developed for use in research but then successfully adapted to assist improvement efforts in practitioner settings. By looking closely at how individuals in two different educational contexts (i.e., researchers in a university setting and teachers and teacher educators in inner-city middle schools) generated, used, and modified tools over a five-year project, the Quantitative Understanding Amplifying Student Achievement and Reasoning (QUASAR) project, we surface one specific but perhaps replicable way in which tools that carry theory and useful knowledge might develop.

The tools developed by the QUASAR project offer an unusual example of applying research to practice. Typically, research findings identify a "best practice" or a particularly effective mathematics program that is then imported to schools and classrooms. Research results are intended primarily to certify that a particular program or practice "works." In QUASAR, however, research influenced practice in a very different way: instead of using research findings to certify "what works," QUASAR participants adapted and repositioned tools initially created for research purposes—data collection instruments, analysis protocols, and even the data themselves—to support changes in practice. In so doing, QUASAR researchers paid close attention to the contexts and needs of practitioners. While using the tools, practitioners suggested extensions that would help them refine their practice. This created a dynamic between the researchers and practitioners that nurtured the development of tools that communicated theory and promoted improvements in practice.

Community-of-practice theory (Lave and Wenger 1991; Wenger 1998), especially ideas related to the development of knowledge and practices within and across groups, provides a useful framework to examine how tools were developed and used in the QUASAR project. As will be seen, QUASAR included working groups of researchers and practitioners that formed communities of practice with sustained relationships, shared ways of working together, and communication that was both rapid and efficient (Wenger 1998). I argue that these three dimensions characterize the QUASAR organization and that the QUASAR groups worked together, as well as independently, in ways that developed tools that supported productive links between research and practice.

The chapter begins with a brief overview of the QUASAR project: its goals and organization. The second section presents two tools developed by the QUASAR project, noting how each changed over time as different groups worked with each tool. The tools progressed through three variations or generations. My analysis identifies patterns and critical factors in the development of each generation of tools. The chapter concludes with a discussion of how joint negotiations between researchers and practitioners can lead to the development of tools that in turn foster improvement in practice.[1]

OVERVIEW OF QUASAR PROJECT

The QUASAR project was funded in 1989 by the Ford Foundation to both improve and study mathematics education in high-poverty middle schools. QUASAR pursued a vision of middle school mathematics that differed from the standard fare at the time of learning computational procedures. QUASAR envisioned challenging mathematics, in which students pose questions, develop multiple solutions to problems, explain and justify their mathematical thinking, and make sense of mathematical concepts (Silver, Smith, and Nelson 1995; Silver and Stein 1996). From 1990 to 1995, the QUASAR project supported mathematics teachers at six urban middle schools across the nation and resource partners (typically mathematics educators from nearby universities) to develop more rigorous instructional programs and to improve their pedagogical skills. At the same time, QUASAR researchers studied the practitioners' efforts by collecting classroom data and performance-based measures of student learning.

To assess changes in students' understanding, QUASAR researchers analyzed data from the National Assessment of Educational Progress (NAEP) as well as instruments developed specifically for the project. These results consistently documented the positive impact of the QUASAR project on students' understanding of mathematics. For example, when the performance of QUASAR students on released NAEP items was compared to a demographically similar sample studied in NAEP (designated by NAEP as the "disadvantaged urban" sample), QUASAR students generally outperformed students in the NAEP sample, especially on constructed-response tasks that required students to generate an answer rather than select from a given set of choices (Silver and Stein 1996). The QUASAR students also compared favorably to the entire NAEP sample, especially considering that NAEP's national sample significantly outperformed NAEP's disadvantaged urban sample on virtually all NAEP tasks (Silver and Stein 1996).[2] In addition, project-designed measures of student performance documented the positive impact of the QUASAR project. For example, an open-response assessment of problem solving (the QUASAR Cognitive Assessment Instrument [QCAI]) showed clear trends in the growth of students' understanding, reasoning, and problem solving as well as a link between cognitively demanding mathematical tasks and gains in student learning (Stein and Lane 1996).[3]

Organization of QUASAR

QUASAR encompassed a university-based research effort, QUASAR central, located at the Learning Research and Development Center at the University of Pittsburgh and six geographically diverse practice sites; its organization was key to how tools were developed and evolved. Principal investigator and project director Ed Silver created and oversaw QUASAR central, which was organized into three branches: assessment, program development, and documentation. The assessment branch, directed by Suzanne Lane, developed and administered the QCAI (Lane 1993), a collection of open-ended mathematical tasks that assessed students' (a) understanding of mathematical concepts and their interrelationships and (b)

capacity to use high-level reasoning to solve complex mathematical problems (Silver and Stein 1996). The program development branch, directed
by Margaret S. Smith and Catherine Brown, supported the development
of site-specific curricula and professional development efforts at each site.
In addition to intense support, the program development branch also
prepared specific feedback for each site, drawing on data from the other
two branches, that is, assessment and documentation. The documentation
branch, directed by Mary Kay Stein, documented and analyzed the nature
of mathematics instruction at each site. Formal documentation visits took
place three times a year, each of which included videotaping and observation of three successive days of mathematics lessons as well as interviews
with teachers, students, principals, and resource partners.

Each of the six practice sites included a middle school in an urban,
high-poverty community and one or more resource partners. With the
goal of improving the mathematical opportunities afforded to traditionally underserved students, QUASAR central financially and substantively
supported these local partnerships between middle school teachers
and resource partners. Unlike many highly specified or centralized approaches to instructional reform, the QUASAR approach assumed that
local experts would be best positioned to identify strategies and curricula
that would work and be sensitive to local conditions.

In the QUASAR project, each research branch and each practice site
formed a community of practice, sharing goals and regularly working
side by side. QUASAR central managed the work across these various
communities. Rather than demanding compliance with a predetermined
style of operation, the project leaders sought to establish general principles within which each community would have the autonomy to build
its own programs and ways of working.

Nevertheless, cross-community coordination was essential: each community of practice was responsible for a task that would contribute to
the overarching goal of finding ways to provide opportunities for underserved students to learn challenging mathematics. The documentation branch sought to develop ways to examine what was happening
in the QUASAR classrooms. The assessment branch worked to design a
psychometrically rigorous instrument to assess students' mathematical
understanding. Each practice site developed curriculum and professional
development activities to support teachers in improving students' opportunities to learn math. Consequently, QUASAR's success depended on
the work of multiple, overlapping groups or a network of communities
of practice. The tasks undertaken by each community of practice were
highly interrelated, requiring clear and timely communication.

Learning within and across QUASAR's communities of practice occurred by the continual negotiation of meaning around the shared work

(Wenger 1998). Due to the sprawling network of communities that comprised the QUASAR project, learning across communities heavily depended on boundary objects, "artifacts, documents, terms, concepts, and other forms of reification around which communities of practice can organize their interconnections" (Wenger 1998, 105). Because boundary objects are meant to be used by multiple communities of practice and sit at the nexus of perspectives, they have the potential to coordinate perspectives and spur similar forms of learning across multiple communities (Star and Griesemer 1989). Boundary objects do not speak for themselves, however. The ways in which individuals interpret boundary objects that "cross into" their community of practice will depend on how their participants, together, negotiate the meaning of a boundary object for their work.

In the QUASAR project, the tools discussed herein (initiated first within the research communities and then traveling to the practice sites) came to play the role of boundary objects. As we shall see, each tool served as a "point of focus" for the negotiation of meaning within practice communities by fostering meaning-making that ultimately led QUASAR teachers to new ways of understanding student learning and seeing their practice.

THE DEVELOPMENT OF THREE
GENERATIONS OF QUASAR TOOLS

Each of the QUASAR tools evolved over time as the research communities and the six practice communities used them to negotiate new understandings of the joint enterprise in which they were engaged. Table 7.1 summarizes the features that distinguish each generation, progressing from tools for research purposes to tools that support changes in practice to tools for broad dissemination. This section tells the story of how the research instruments, frameworks, and data associated with the two research arms of QUASAR (assessment and documentation) were developed and made their way to practice. The story focuses on two tools initially developed by QUASAR, tracing their development and their evolution into succeeding generations of tools. The two tools initially developed in QUASAR were (a) the QCAI, an assessment of students' understanding, and (b) the Mathematical Tasks Framework (MTF), a conceptual framework used to analyze lessons from QUASAR classrooms. Both of these tools were designed to address research goals, yet, through the interaction among the research and school-based communities of practice in QUASAR, each led to new tools that supported teacher and student learning at the sites.

The QCAI and MTF tools provided a means of developing shared understandings across the research and practice communities of practice

Table 7.1. Features of Three Generations of QUASAR Tools

			Generation		
			First: Research	Second: Change practice	Third: Disseminate
QUASAR Tools	QCAI	Form	Performance assessment tasks and rubrics	Task packets of performance assessment tasks, student responses, and rubrics	Book of multiple, data-based examples of performance assessment tasks, student responses, and rubrics
		Purpose	Assess students' understanding of challenging mathematics	Curriculum materials for classroom instruction and professional development	Communicate research findings and provide tool to support different way of assessing mathematical understanding
	MTF	Form	Analytical framework	Teacher-specific data on classroom instruction and composite case	Book of data-based cases showing how factors affect cognitive demand of mathematical tasks
		Purpose	Analyze factors that affect cognitive demand of mathematical tasks	Professional development at sites: new lens to observe in classroom	Communicate research findings (e.g., factors) and provide tool (i.e., case study) to support different way of looking at classroom instruction

within the QUASAR project. These boundary objects were not static, however; each changed over the course of the QUASAR project as different communities of practice interpreted and adapted the tools for local contexts. As will become evident, the application of these tools to practice was not completely designed in advance—by either the researchers or the practitioners—but rather evolved over time as the various communities worked to bring challenging mathematics to underserved students. By looking at each generation of tools, we can examine how communities of practice use boundary objects in different ways to support and make sense of their work.

First Generation: Tools Intended as Research Instruments

The QCAI and the MTF began as research instruments: the first to assess students' understanding of challenging mathematics and the second to analyze classroom instruction intended to support students' learning of mathematics. The first generation of both the QCAI and the MTF were carefully designed and rigorously tested research instruments intended to support the QUASAR goals of building fundamental understandings for the field and monitoring performance at the sites. Each facilitated communication among the QUASAR communities in two ways. First, each embodied a vision of challenging mathematics. Second, each provided data that informed the work of the QUASAR researchers and the QUASAR practitioners. Thus, the first-generation tools connected the work of the different communities of practice by reifying a vision of challenging mathematics and providing meaningful data and analyses.

The first-generation version of the QCAI was developed by the assessment branch to measure students' understanding of challenging mathematics. At the time that QUASAR began, relatively few performance-based assessments that measured high-level knowledge, reasoning, and communication skills were available. Moreover, none had been designed for or tested on large numbers of students. Indeed, there was considerable skepticism that large-scale, performance-based assessments that were technically sound could be created. The assessment branch produced the QCAI, a collection of open-response tasks and associated scoring rubrics that required students to explain and justify their solution strategies. The rubrics included three components: mathematical knowledge, strategic knowledge of mathematics, and mathematical communication (Lane 1993).

While the QCAI had considerable face validity, Lane and her colleagues demonstrated its technical adequacy as well (Lane, Stone, Ankenmann, and Liu 1995). They articulated a conceptual framework to analyze QCAI tasks and scoring rubrics, ensuring that each reflected the construct domain of mathematics (Lane 1993). Other QUASAR researchers conducted an empirical study and found that the QCAI tasks elicited cognitively complex performances (Magone, Cai, Silver, and Wang 1994). In a later study, Lane et al. (1995) concluded that the assumptions that underlie item-response theory were met by QCAI tasks, supporting the validity of inferences or generalizations from the QCAI data. Through the development and testing of the QCAI, the QUASAR project made significant contributions to the psychometrics of performance assessment.

But beyond these contributions to research, the QCAI also contributed directly to the practitioner communities in QUASAR by providing data on how well their students were learning mathematics. At the end of the first year, the assessment branch prepared a projectwide summary showing gains in student performance from the fall to the spring. This report was intended to inform planning of curriculum and professional development for the following year at each site. Thus, the QCAI began as a research tool, developed by QUASAR central to assess progress at the sites and inform the sites of their progress in helping students engage in challenging mathematics.

Similar to the QCAI, the MTF was originally intended to support the research efforts of QUASAR. The documentation branch designed the MTF to analyze videotapes and narrative summaries of classroom instruction (Stein, Grover, and Henningsen 1996). The MTF (see figure 7.1) focuses on a segment of classroom activity—referred to as a task—that addresses a particular mathematical idea (Stein and Smith 1998). A task can be relatively brief or extend to an entire class period.[4] The MTF captures the progression of a task from printed form in instructional materials to setup by teachers to implementation by students. The power of the framework is that it highlights changes in the cognitive demands of tasks as they pass through the three phases. A printed task can present lower-level (e.g., memorization or procedures without connections to concepts) or higher-level (e.g., procedures with connections to concepts and doing mathematics) demands. When the teacher introduces the task to students (i.e., sets up the task), the nature of the task can change. Higher-level tasks can decline and become procedural. Again, as students begin to work on a problem (i.e., the implementation phase), the task can decline to a lower level of demand given the hints and explanations offered by the teacher. The framework includes factors associated with the maintenance of high-level cognitive demands (e.g., teacher presses for justifications, explanations, and meaning through questioning, comments, and feedback) as well as factors associated with the decline of high-level cognitive demands (e.g., teacher shifts the emphasis from meaning, concepts, or understanding to the correctness or completeness of the answer) (Stein and Smith 1998; Stein et al. 1996).

The first generation of both the QCAI and the MTF were carefully designed research tools, intended to collect and analyze data that would inform the QUASAR work. In addition, each functioned as a boundary object, carrying the researchers' vision of challenging mathematics instruction (the MTF) and competent student performance (QCAI) to the sites. The sites used each boundary object to envision ways to support their work with students: to better understand and change their practice. As the sites participated with the boundary objects, they reified ideas germane to their work in the schools. For example, the QCAI offered specific questions that assessed students' understanding of challenging mathematics. The accompanying scoring rubric revealed a nontraditional means of evaluating students' work, supporting a different practice for assessing students' thinking by looking at levels of understanding and communication as presented in the QCAI rubric. Similarly, the MTF offered a vision of challenging mathematics instruction that helped frame and interpret teachers' practice. Both the QCAI and the MTF functioned

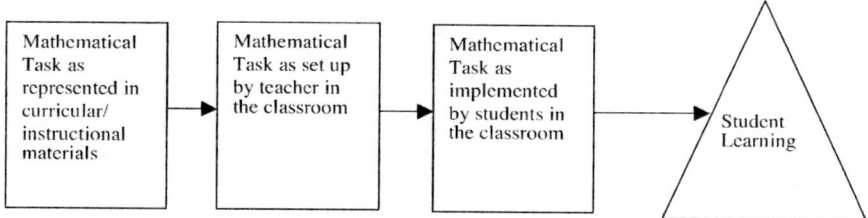

Figure 7.1. Mathematical Tasks Framework *Source:* Adapted from Stein et al. (1996).

as boundary objects by identifying elements of the vision and practice of a research branch and then traveling to the sites. Once at the sites, the QCAI and MTF stimulated questions and suggestions that would support the work in the schools. The conversations among the sites and QUASAR central led to the second generation of each tool.

Second Generation: Tools to Change Practice

The second-generation tools were designed and used in very different ways than the first-generation tools. QUASAR central developed the first-generation research tools, specifying detailed protocols as to their use at the sites and subsequent analysis. In contrast, the second-generation tools addressed needs at the sites as identified by the QUASAR practitioners. The second-generation tools used data from the QCAI and MTF to provide specific feedback to teachers and to substantively shape materials for classroom instruction and professional development. In addition, each site determined how the second-generation tools would best support their efforts to change practice. The second-generation tools illustrate how the refinement of shared goals, dynamic relationships between researchers and practitioners, and the incorporation of data can support changes in practice.

In the development of both the QCAI and the MTF second-generation tools, summaries prepared by QUASAR central stimulated questions and requests by the sites. The projectwide summary of student results on the QCAI prompted teachers and resource partners at the sites to ask for additional reports that summarized the QCAI data by school and by teacher. In addition, the practice sites asked for sample assessment tasks to share with students. The assessment branch responded to this request by preparing sample task packets. Each task packet included a QCAI item, a scoring rubric, and student responses that illustrated the different levels of the rubric (Parke, Lane, Silver, and Magone 2003).

The assessment branch sent teachers at all six sites these second-generation QCAI materials. With their resource partners, teachers decided how best to use these materials with their students. Many QUASAR teachers developed lessons using the QCAI scoring rubric to help students learn how to reason and communicate their mathematical thinking. In this way, the materials in the task packets actually became a source of classroom curriculum at the QUASAR sites. It is important to note that standards-based curricula were not yet available at this time, so most sites were cutting and pasting together activities to form their own curricula. The resource partners also saw the potential of these materials as a support for professional development.

In several sites, the resource partners used these second-generation materials to help teachers examine students' understanding, evaluate their curriculum, and teach more challenging mathematics. For example, at one site the resource partners had struggled to engage the teachers in substantive discussions of what it means to understand mathematics. During the QUASAR work in the early 1990s, many teachers still equated understanding with correct solutions. One teacher questioned the need to look beyond right answers: "The answer is the most important part; if they've got it right, there's no need to look at the explanation" (Parke and Lane 1997, 27). The Circle the Decimal Task, shown in figure 7.2, provided resource partners with the opportunity to challenge this assumption. Many students could select the right answer for this task, but they had difficulty explaining their thinking.

For example, the three students, whose work is shown in figure 7.3, had selected the correct answer yet offered very different explanations. After reviewing the students' responses to this item, the teachers noticed how explanations can provide insights into students' understanding. Student 1 clearly understood how the decimal quantities related to each other. The response of student 2 offered no insights into how the student understood decimal values. Student 3's response revealed an area of confusion: the more zeros, the smaller the number. This was the first substantive discussion the teachers at this school were able to have about students' conceptual understanding (Parke and Lane 1997). As another teacher noted, "[Analyzing students' responses] opens our eyes as to what was taught versus what was learned" (Parke et al. 2003, 13).

Circle the number that has the greatest value.
.08   .8   .080   .008000

Explain your answer.

Figure 7.2.   Circle the Decimal Task

Student 1. .8 is 8 tenths.
       .08 is 8 hundreths [sic]
       .080 is the same one.
       .008000 is 8 thousandths. This is how they look: [The student drew a
       picture illustrating the relationship between tenths, hundredths, and
       thousandths.]
Student 2. It has the greatest value.
Student 3. The 8 is the greatest because it has no zeros before the number or
after the number. The more zeros, the lesser it is.

Figure 7.3.   Student Responses to Circle the Decimal Task

This episode illustrates how the second-generation QCAI functioned as a boundary object: through participating with the task packets, teachers developed important ideas needed to change their practice. The boundary object, in this case the task packets, helped the teachers examine and better understand their practice.

The MTF served a similar function around both curriculum selection and implementation. The MTF identified typical patterns of decline (in the cognitive demands of tasks) that resonated with QUASAR teachers and resource partners (Henningsen and Stein 1997). For example, after hearing one of the QUASAR researchers at a conference identify the pattern of a high-level task (a "doing-mathematics" task) declining into "unsystematic and nonproductive exploration" on the part of students, one of the QUASAR teachers commented, "That is exactly what happened to my 'tape roll toss' task!" The MTF was perceived as a powerful tool for interpreting what happened in classrooms when challenging mathematical tasks did not elicit high levels of student learning as expected. One QUASAR teacher noted that the analysis of factors that led to the decline of challenging tasks (see figure 7.1) was especially revealing. She recalled her and her colleagues' responses when they first heard of the MTF:

> Well, I think we all kind of laughed because we'd all been there. I think at that point we could recognize it [the decline of tasks], but we'd never really–at least for me, I had never really thought about it as, "Oh yeah, that happens all the time." (teacher interview)

This was a critical juncture in the QUASAR work. The teachers, resource partners, and researchers in the QUASAR project all agreed that the MTF captured an important phenomenon that many had experienced or observed in the QUASAR classrooms. The MTF offered a way to label, talk about, and analyze this phenomenon. The QUASAR teachers asked for more detailed and personalized feedback—specifically how the tasks in their own classes progressed.

QUASAR central responded to the request for formative feedback by developing analyses of each teacher's instruction using the MTF. Thus, the second generation of MTF materials began with tailored reports for each site and teacher. The sites, in turn, used the MTF reports to support professional development in different ways. For example, the resource partners at one of the sites used the framework to focus peer observations on the cognitive demands of lessons (teacher interview). A second site reviewed curricula using the MTF. The teachers looked at the curricula they were using "to see what the characteristics were of the tasks that seemed to be producing learning" (teacher interview).

The response to the MTF was enthusiastic. To build on that excitement and the potential to look at instruction in a very different way, QUASAR central decided to write a composite case that illustrated important features of the MTF. QUASAR central believed that an abstract analysis would not have the same impact as a highly contextualized case. As Silver explained,

> Rather than providing people with an abstract presentation of data of the sort that I give in my talk and what you give in published articles and so on, we thought it would be interesting to try to create a more grounded version of this. And we didn't want to show videotape because that would particularize it to some teacher in some particular setting in some particular classroom. (teacher interview)

A team of QUASAR central researchers, one of whom was an experienced teacher, wrote the first composite case drawing on elements that had been observed across many teachers' lessons. This case can be viewed as a second-generation revision of the MTF tool. The composite case offered the QUASAR sites an example of two of the data-based patterns of the MTF in a narrative structure, one in which the teacher let the cognitive demands of the tasks decline during the implementation phase and one in which the teacher was successful in maintaining the level of cognitive demand. The case stimulated lively conversations that surfaced ideas and concerns central to the QUASAR work (teacher interview).

The second generation of the MTF supported the QUASAR work in two ways. First, the teachers asked for and received individual feedback as to how well they were selecting, introducing, and supporting cognitively demanding tasks in their classrooms. In addition, the composite case offered the teachers a vision of how cognitively demanding tasks can be used in classrooms. The case presented the complexities when teaching challenging mathematics rather than a set of steps to be followed.

The second-generation versions of the QCAI and MTF point to important factors in the development of tools in the QUASAR project. Practitioner use and response to the first-generation tools shaped the development of the second-generation tools. In both instances, practitioners first were exposed to the research instruments and then requested modifications that would support their work. This dynamic relationship between QUASAR central researchers and practitioners at the sites is a hallmark of the QUASAR work. The shared goal—increasing students' opportunities to engage in challenging mathematics—linked the work of the researchers and the practitioners. Thus, the researchers' work had the potential to support the practitioners' work, but the input of the practitioners was needed to bring about the modifications of the first-generation tools that would enable the QCAI and MTF to support the work of the practitioners. By participating with the boundary objects, QUASAR participants and researchers were able to come to new understandings of what it means to teach and learn mathematics for understanding.

In addition, the second-generation versions of both the QCAI and MTF were data based. Teachers received tailored summaries of their students' performance on the QCAI, and the MTF analysis provided direct feedback on their classroom instruction. Both summaries provided detailed feedback on the teachers' practice and the effect of their practice on their students' understanding. The second-generation tools also made use of actual data in a second, less personalized but equally meaningful way: to illustrate important ideas. The QCAI task packets included assessment items and actual student responses that illustrated the various levels of each rubric. By analyzing these student responses using the scoring rubrics, teachers, as well as their students, were helped to envision competent student performance in mathematics. Similarly, the composite case drew on data from the MTF analyses of hundreds of lessons to present an episode of classroom instruction that highlighted many issues teachers face when they work to teach challenging mathematics.

Third Generation: Tools to Disseminate Research and Change Practice

The third generation of the QUASAR tools extended the QUASAR work to a broader audience, that is, teachers and teacher educators who were not involved in the QUASAR project. Dissemination beyond QUASAR presented two challenges. First, the data-based examples that had engaged the QUASAR teachers in the second-generation tools might not be as compelling to non-QUASAR teachers. In addition, the support for the interpretation and use of the second-generation tools that QUASAR central had provided needed, somehow, to be replaced. As the sites worked with the second-generation QCAI materials, QUASAR researchers observed the ways in which the sites incorporated the QCAI task packets and the MTF composite case into their instruction and professional development activities. They noted which assessment tasks were most successful in provoking teacher and student learning as well as the variety of ways in which teachers and resource partners interpreted the assessment tasks and the sample student responses.

Ultimately, QUASAR researchers wrote two books: one presenting task packets on the items from the QCAI (Parke et al. 2003) and a second using cases to present the MTF (Stein, Smith, Henningsen, and Silver 2000). Each book offers a theoretical framework that is grounded in multiple, detailed, data-based examples. The QCAI book includes twelve to fifteen student responses for each task. Each sample task has been scored, and a justification for each score is provided. These materials are offered as a way to engage teachers in conversations about students' work and what we can learn about students' understanding from reviewing their work with a rubric. Similarly, the MTF book includes a chapter suggesting how to read and reflect on the cases. This third generation of MTF materials was a collection of cases intended for a broader audience, that is, teachers and teacher educators not directly involved in the QUASAR project. The cases were published in a book, *Implementing Standards-Based Mathematics Instruction: A Casebook for Professional Development* (Stein et al. 2000) with guiding questions to encourage teachers to reflect on and evaluate their own instruction. Mathematics educators, professional developers, and international educators have embraced this book of cases and a second edition was published in 2009 (Stein, Smith, Henningsen, and Silver 2009).[5] In 1997, funding from the National Science Foundation supported the Comet Project, which resulted in three additional case books based on the QUASAR work (Smith, Silver, & Stein, 2005a, 2005b, 2005c). Each casebook focuses on a different mathematical topic: rational numbers and proportionality, algebra, and geometry and measurement.

The intent of each casebook is to provoke inquiry into the nature of teaching that supports student learning. The casebooks are not intended to offer models of good teaching or "best practices" that yield predictable results. Rather, the QUASAR books offer data-based examples and theoretical frameworks as a starting point for conversations intended to help teachers examine their teaching and the ways in which it supports or inhibits student learning. The books are designed to foster participation in thousands of more distant communities, participation that leads to the negotiation of meaning around assessment and instruction. As a boundary object, the books reify the QUASAR vision of challenging mathematics supported by data-based examples of assessment and instruction that are consistent with that vision.

CONCLUSION

The QUASAR project developed tools in distinctive ways to link research and practice: the QUASAR tools supported researchers' study of student and teacher learning as well as practitioners' efforts to develop curricula and pedagogy that would provide opportunities for underserved students to engage in challenging mathematics. Consistent with earlier work on communities of practice (Lave and Wenger 1991; Wenger 1998), the present analysis of the three generations of QUASAR tools reveals the importance of sustained relationships, shared goals, and clear communication. In addition, the QUASAR work offers insights into the design and use of tools that can inform efforts to bridge research and practice.

Importance of Data in Development and Dissemination of Tools

QUASAR used data in novel ways: data provided the foundation for both the QCAI and the MTF. The former was designed to collect data on students' understanding of complex mathematics, while the latter used data to identify productive and less productive patterns in teachers' use of cognitively demanding tasks. The QUASAR tools communicated complex ideas. The tools provided nuanced examples of teaching and learning that could be captured in frameworks and then illustrated with data. The data were integral to the tools in that they provided support, so the tools could travel and be used in thoughtful ways. The QUASAR tools immersed practitioners in data-based experiences from which they could learn.

Importance of Focusing the Work

The tools served a cuing function, signaling what was important to the QUASAR work and the QUASAR participants. For example, the MTF clearly focuses teachers on one aspect of mathematics instruction: the selection and enactment of cognitively demanding mathematical activities. Many aspects of mathematics instruction vie for teachers' attention (e.g., use of manipulatives). The MTF focused QUASAR practitioners on challenging tasks, thereby restricting the problem space so that researchers and practitioners could develop shared understandings that informed the work.

Importance of Participation That Requires Judgment

The tools also created an increased demand for participation that required judgment. This was especially evident in the second- and third-generation tools. The task packets based on the QCAI, for example, engaged teachers and students in analyzing student responses to assessment items. In addition, QUASAR practitioners received the task packets without protocols for their use. Each site reviewed the task packets and determined how best to use them. Uses of the tools varied across the sites, but the intent behind the tools was to develop habits of mind rather than routines.

The QUASAR story reveals one way in which tools that carry theory and useful knowledge were developed. In the QUASAR project, knowledge spread from research universities to schools and, equally important, from schools to researchers. Initially, research influenced practice through the efforts of QUASAR central to develop research tools to study the impact of classroom instruction on students' understanding, but as the project unfolded, practitioners began to shape the work of the researchers in subtle and not so subtle ways. The second-generation tools especially reveal the fortuitous ways that knowledge was shared and interpreted as the practitioners requested and then determined how best to use QCAI task packets and MTF cases. As researchers and practitioners refined the QUASAR tools across three generations, the iterative character of their interactions revealed the critical role of boundary objects, such as the QUASAR tools, in the sharing of knowledge. By fostering a dynamic relationship among researchers and practitioners, the QUASAR project created opportunities for the resulting communities of practice to jointly use data to study students' understanding and teaching that supports that understanding.

NOTES

I wish to thank Ed Silver, Margaret Smith, and Cynthia Coburn for their careful reading and thoughtful comments on earlier versions of this chapter. I am especially indebted to Mary Kay Stein, who supported this work in so many ways.

1. The present case study was designed to examine how knowledge was developed and used in a research project. The study was conducted in two phases: an initial phase to determine the extent to which different types of knowledge (e.g., research and practitioner knowledge) played a role in the QUASAR project and a second phase during which data were collected, analyzed, and critiqued to develop an understanding of how knowledge was created and shared in QUASAR. Key participants were interviewed: the leadership for QUASAR as well as support staff (six individuals); local QUASAR participants, including teachers and teacher educators (five individuals); and academics who were part of organizations that influenced the QUASAR work (three individuals). All interviews were audiotaped and transcribed. Transcripts were hand coded to identify patterns in the development and use of knowledge in QUASAR. In addition, an annotated

bibliography was created for the extensive set of publications that resulted from the QUASAR project. Internal documents from the project were available as well. A draft of the case study was given to all key participants, who then provided feedback that resulted in a revision of the case study.

2. For the NAEP tasks that assessed problem solving or conceptual understanding and for tasks that measured less traditional areas of the middle school curriculum (e.g., statistics and probability), the QUASAR students matched or outperformed NAEP's national sample on many of the tasks (Silver and Stein 1996).

3. In addition, high school algebra is viewed as a gatekeeper course that determines access to higher mathematics and science courses. At most QUASAR sites, the number of students taking algebra in ninth grade increased. One site showed a striking increase in the number of QUASAR eighth-grade students who passed a qualifying exam for placement in ninth-grade algebra. At the end of the first year of QUASAR, only 8 percent of the students at this site qualified for algebra. In contrast, at the end of the fourth year of the project, more than 40 percent passed the qualifying exam (Silver and Stein 1996).

4. It is the transition from one mathematical idea to the next that signals the end of one task and the beginning of a second task, not a change in class grouping arrangements.

5. More than 10,000 copies have been sold to date.

III

DEVELOPING CONDITIONS TO FOSTER KNOWLEDGE DEVELOPMENT IN SCHOOLS

To date, debates about the relationship between research and practice have largely focused largely on the research side of the equation. Commentators have focused on improving the quality of educational research (Feuer, Towne, and Shavelson 2002b; Lagemann and Shulman 1999; Slavin 2004), on certifying research-based approaches (Cook 2002; Slavin 2002), and on building new bridges to carry research knowledge into schools (Hood 2002; McDonald, Keesler, Kauffman, and Schneider 2006). Comparatively little attention has been provided to the practice side of the equation. More specifically, there has been little attention in this debate to the conditions in schools that are conducive for engaging with new ideas and approaches and making substantive, lasting change.

Yet there is plenty of research that documents how conditions in schools work against opportunities for teachers to learn new approaches, sustain research-based interventions, and use research in their decision making in meaningful ways. Teachers' work is largely private (Little 1990; Lortie; 1975). While teachers often experiment on their own in their classrooms and learn valuable lessons along the way, they rarely seek out research or research-based ideas to inform their experimentation (Hargreaves 1984; Hargreaves and Stone-Johnson 2009; Hiebert, Gallimore, and Stigler 2002; Huberman 1985). In part, this is because teachers find it difficult to integrate new ideas and approaches into the complexities of real classrooms (Coburn 2001; Hargreaves and Stone-Johnson 2009; Kennedy 1997, 2005). But there is also evidence that in the absence of opportunities to engage with others, discuss new approaches, and critically evaluate research-based ideas and approaches, teachers tend to discount research and other kinds of evidence if it challenges their existing ways of doing things (e.g., Hargreaves and Stone-Johnson 2009). And there are limited mechanisms to verify, capture, and share what they learn with others (Hiebert et al. 2002). Absent favorable conditions for teachers to engage with new ideas and each other, it seems unlikely that teachers will be able to engage with research-based ideas or any others in ways that help them improve their instructional approaches in widespread ways.

The two chapters in this part profile initiatives that work on the practice side of the research–practice equation. Each initiative sought to create conditions in schools for knowledge development and continuous improvement and, in so doing, also created a fertile environment for teachers to engage with research and research-based ideas. In chapter 8, Rebecca Perry and Catherine Lewis chart the development of Lesson Study (LS) in a San Francisco Bay Area school district over the course of six years. They show how teacher leaders developed a stable set of practices for teachers to plan, implement, study, and critique public research lessons in mathematics. Perry and Lewis argue that carefully developed tools to guide lesson planning alongside the publicness of LS surfaced differences of opinions and raised questions that led teachers to reach out to each other and others to learn more. The links that teacher leaders established with local universities and a local foundation created pathways through which new ideas and research flowed into and fed teachers' deliberation about their instruction. The norm in LS to invite outside individuals who can serve as a resource to participate created a venue for researchers and teachers to problem solve together about the challenges that teachers faced in their classroom. As LS developed and became institutionalized in the school, the culture of work shifted from individual and private to collaborative and public. Student achievement in mathematics soared.

In chapter 9, Laura Stokes describes an infrastructure for knowledge generation at a much greater scale. While the LS example describes the development of a system for knowledge development in a local school and district, the National Writing Project (NWP) is a national project that links together more than 200 school–university partnerships across the country that work with thousands of teachers to improve writing instruction in their local communities. Stokes describes how the NWP has created structures for inquiry that link local NWP sites to each other regionally and even nationally. This improvement infrastructure, as she calls it, functions to develop knowledge of writing instruction to support local improvement efforts. At the center of this endeavor is a set of norms of critique whereby teacher leaders work with each other and researchers to share practice and question new ideas and approaches, using evidence from student work from multiple classrooms as the arbiter of effective practice. These inquiry processes are nested in a set of relationships between local sites, regional working groups, and the national network as a whole that enables resources, research, and ideas to flow in to local sites but also enables the knowledge developed in local NWP sites to flow out to the larger network. In this way, the NWP has created a set of structures to capture, verify, and share local knowledge developed by teacher leaders at the intersection of research and practice.

8

⚜️

Building Demand
for Research through
Lesson Study

Rebecca Perry and Catherine Lewis

Richard Elmore (1996) has noted that U.S. education suffers not so much from lack of *supply* of good educational ideas as from lack of *demand* for them on the part of practicing teachers. Lesson study (abbreviated hereafter as LS), a form of teacher professional learning that originated in Japan (Fernandez and Yoshida 2004; Lewis 2002a, 2002b; Lewis and Tsuchida 1997, 1998; Stigler and Hiebert 1999), may support the development of demand for research among practitioners. In the United States, LS has been initiated and spread mainly by practitioners. In just a few short years (1999–2003), LS emerged at more than 335 U.S. schools across thirty-two states (Lesson Study Research Group 2004), and interest among practitioners throughout the United States has continued to grow at a rapid pace.[1] This chapter describes the development of one particularly well-realized case of LS in a school district in the western United States, where practitioners' use of research increased as they shifted toward public, practice-based forms of learning.

As illustrated in figure 8.1, LS consists of cycles of inquiry in which teachers consider the teaching of a particular topic as well as their long-term goals for student learning and development, collaboratively plan a "research lesson" that is taught by one team member while other team members observe and collect data, and use the data to reflect on the lesson and teaching and learning more broadly. One feature that distinguishes LS from many other types of practice-based professional development is the research lesson: a jointly observed classroom lesson that provides an opportunity to collect data on student thinking; to discuss a shared, live example of instruction; and to encounter in actual practice colleagues' ideas about the nature of good instruction (Lewis, Perry, and Murata 2006).

In this chapter, we draw on six years of interview and observational data on LS in Bay Area School District (BASD), a medium-sized semi-urban district where a small group of practitioners initiated LS in 1999.[2] Three of the four practitioners central to LS development in BASD were part- or full-time mathematics coaches participating in the regional coaching network of the West Coast Foundation (WCF), which provided them with partial salary support and professional development beginning in 1998. Over the six-year period of our study (2000–2006), BASD practitioners developed a substantial LS effort in the district, producing a subculture in which professional learning shifted from individual, private work to collaborative, public work. These LS practitioners had sustained access to knowledge about LS (from sources including Mills College) and to research-based knowledge of mathematics instruction (from WCF and

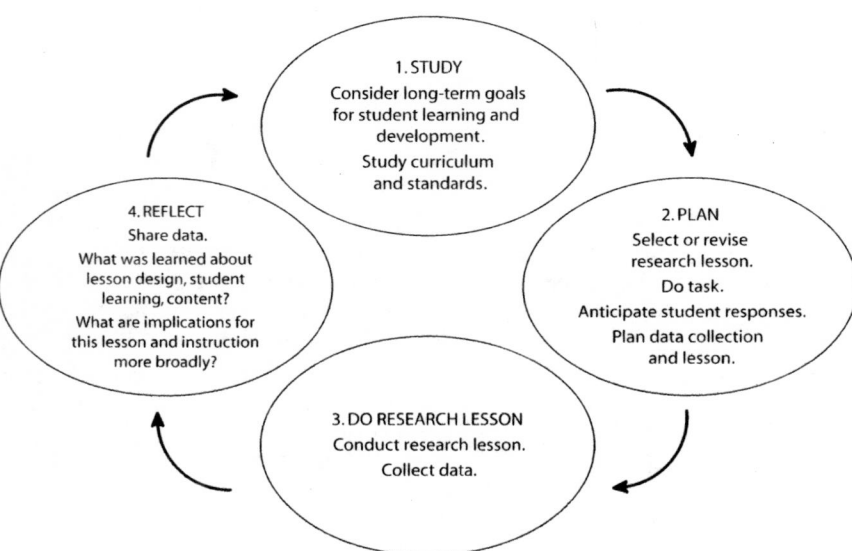

Figure 8.1. Lesson Study

other sources). Case data indicate that LS had consequences for the teaching culture, student achievement, and the relationship between research and practice. Thus, the case suggests the potential of LS to alter teachers' attitudes about research and build a demand for it and the use of it.

To illustrate these claims, we chart the development of LS in BASD across six years, arguing that three factors—the creation of public, practice-based learning opportunities; tool development and refinement; and increasing links to knowledge resources—enabled LS practice and teacher learning in the BASD to become increasingly research based over time. We end by describing the consequences of the LS effort for teachers and students and discuss implications of our findings for understanding the connection between research and practice.

THE EVOLUTION OF LESSON STUDY AND PRACTITIONER KNOWLEDGE BUILDING

LS began in BASD when two BASD practitioners sought a professional development model to support sustained, teacher-led improvement of classroom instruction. One of them (a half-time elementary teacher and half-time mathematics coach) recalls that she read about LS in *The Teaching Gap* (Stigler and Hiebert 1999) as part of her work with the WCF coaching network and immediately knew that it was the model they had been searching for: "I was sure we wanted to do lesson study. How to do it was much less clear." Independently, both these two BASD practitioners and WCF's program director of mathematics, Bob Williams, sought out further information about LS from various sources, including, coincidentally, the second author of this chapter, an LS researcher at nearby Mills College. The two BASD practitioners and two fellow mathematics coaches (hereafter, this group of four will be called "the leaders") invited district teachers to try LS. In the fall of 2000, twenty-six volunteer teachers responded to the LS invitation, and seven lesson study groups were formed, based on school location and grade level.

The LS process developed by the leaders involved two conscious adaptations to the Japanese models they had read about and seen: joint lesson observation was not required, and the idea that "lesson study is about the lesson, not about the teacher," was emphasized. The leaders thought these adaptations would help build initial comfort with LS among teachers who had not previously shared their practice with one another. Since the leaders knew the local teaching culture (from both teaching and coaching), they were well positioned to design these adaptations. Other initial LS guidelines were "pretty minimal," in the words of one leader, because of leaders' own limited knowledge of LS.

Participants received a small stipend ($500) and were asked to spend at least twenty hours over the year working in their teams to plan as many as three lessons. The seven groups varied substantially in their approaches, but six of seven groups conducted research lessons, and most teachers reported that the focus on the lesson rather than on the teacher promoted safe collaboration and supported their mathematics learning. Most teachers found that the benefits outweighed their initial discomfort with sharing their practice; in this way, the groundwork was laid during this first year for a continuing and expanding norm of public practice within the district's LS effort.

Over the course of the six years, the number of teachers participating in LS grew from twenty-six in the 2000–2001 school year to fifty-three during 2005–2006. In 2001, teachers at Foothills Elementary School voted to practice LS schoolwide, reallocating some of their faculty meeting time to LS meetings. Over 2000–2006, use of public, practice-based learning structures increased, and the publicness of practice (Lord, Burns, and Nikula 2003; Lord and Gorman 2004) extended beyond the pool of practitioners to involve researchers, university-based math educators, and foundation staff, thus creating new openings for practitioners to learn *in practice* from divergent perspectives. There was continued development and adaptation of LS tools. Both of these things, in turn, fostered the increased demand for and use of both external and internal knowledge resources. In the sections that follow, we provide evidence for each of these changes.

Increase in Public, Practice-Based Learning

Prior to beginning LS, opportunities for BASD teachers to learn from practice occurred mostly privately, with teachers working alone in their classrooms or occasionally with a mathematics coach. By 2006, opportunities for teachers to learn with colleagues by planning and analyzing live research lessons had become a routine part of district life for any interested teacher, for many new elementary teachers with BTSA[3] coaches, and for all teachers at Foothills Elementary, the schoolwide site. Large public research lessons (involving 75–200 participants) occurred at least yearly during 2000–2006; they typically included not only WCF mathematics program staff and Mills College researchers but also university-based mathematics specialists (from the United States and often Japan). By 2005, fourteen of twenty-two Foothills Elementary teachers had taught research lessons in front of their colleagues (and often in front of a much wider audience). Large public research lessons provided opportunities for exchange not only among practitioners from different locations and backgrounds but also between researchers and practitioners who were able to experience the classroom lesson (and sometimes the preceding planning sessions) together.

The practice-based learning structures were initiated, developed, and sustained by practitioners within BASD, supported in part by funds they obtained through their own grant writing as well as by funds from the WCF (for the coaches' salaries and some LS events) and the Mills College LS Group (mainly for collaboration with Japanese teachers). Mills College researchers provided some technical resources on LS and, at the request of the leaders, ongoing feedback on the BASD LS work based on observations and interviews. In general, however, BASD practitioners led their own LS work and also subsequently took leadership in work code-signed and funded by the WCF with the goal of improving mathematics instruction throughout the region (Perry and Lewis 2006). Ultimately, the increasing publicness of research lessons was important because it provided strong motivation for teachers to draw on research and expertise (in order to design a lesson of interest to colleagues) as well as an opportunity to use, refine, and spread research findings and ideas.

Refinement of LS Tools

Over 2000–2006, BASD practitioners used and refined existing LS tools derived from research on Japanese LS (such as a lesson plan template and protocols for lesson discussion and data collection) and also developed new tools. The tools fostered the growth and effectiveness of the public learning structures by supporting warranted discussion of student learning rather than a free-for-all critique of teaching. Tools also provided ways to communicate and spread ideas about instruction and about LS, providing scaffolding to help practitioners support culture change and construct new knowledge (Luria 1973; Wertsch 1991).

Tools helped support the development of shared standards about how to conduct LS and shared ideas about teaching, such as how to develop useful lesson plans. Initially, BASD leaders did not provide LS groups with a lesson plan template, and leaders found the lesson plans submitted by groups during year 1 disappointing since they did not summarize groups' learning in an easily shareable way. After seeing a research lesson by a Japanese teacher and reading his lesson plan during a public lesson, BASD leaders adopted his template as their own, providing spaces for teachers to record information including long-term goals for student learning and development, the rationale for lesson design, anticipated student responses, and data collection methods. Lesson plans developed during the early and later years of BASD LS work looked vastly different. The lesson plan of the year 1 group that included O'Neil, one of the founders of LS in the district, was just one page long, with a hypothesis, three lesson steps, a list of materials needed, and a note on the teacher's actions for each step of the lesson. In contrast, the lesson plan for her third-year group was a six-page document that laid out multiple lesson goals; analyzed what students already understood about problem solving, how their understanding needed to develop further, and how the lesson would contribute to this development; and suggested data points and evaluation questions for observers.

However, tools like the lesson plan template were not necessarily sufficient to spread knowledge. For example, the previously mentioned new lesson plan template initially evoked only perfunctory responses from team members. However, as teachers took part in research lessons, they began to elaborate their use of template categories like "anticipated student thinking," moving from superficial responses like "students will not follow directions" to detailed descriptions of what prior knowledge students would draw on. Although some of the tools (e.g., the lesson plan template and LS time line) were available in early LS resources, they were not necessarily seen as useful until LS had been tried and problems encountered. Finally, as teachers participated in these new public learning structures, they learned about new tools and new uses of tools from other sources, which they then borrowed. For example, teachers deepened their thinking about the category "anticipated student responses" after seeing live research lessons in which student thinking was discussed.

Increased Use of External and Internal Research-Based Knowledge

The publicness of research lessons and the development and elaboration of tools supported the development of a third change: from 2000 to 2006, BASD practitioners increasingly drew on both external and internal sources of research-based knowledge. First, the group drew on *external research-based knowledge* more over time. During the first year of their work, BASD LS groups drew minimally on research-based resources other than their own textbooks or resources that WCF provided to the coaches. After the first year of LS, when the leaders saw the varying quality of research lessons, they suggested two modifications designed to improve the quality of the LS process. They encouraged participants to start with existing curricula rather than planning a lesson from scratch and to involve a "knowledgeable other" by e-mail or in person. Over the subsequent years, the public lesson records, lesson plans, and transcripts of LS meetings all indicate increased use of external research-based knowledge, a category that here includes curricula and research articles and research-knowledgeable individuals, including WCF mathematics staff, content coaches from the district and region, Japanese mathematics educators, and university-based educators and researchers. For example, O'Neil reported how exchange of e-mails with WCF's Williams brought an alternate perspective to her LS group's planning of a lesson on fractions:

> He had us thinking about . . . fractions . . . in terms of proportional reasoning, which isn't the way that we had been thinking about it. . . . It impacted the lesson that we taught, because then we ended up doing a problem that had to do a lot with proportion. But also . . . it really impacted me . . . I was so stuck on thinking of fractions in a physical model representation. . . . Thinking of two-thirds not as the relationship between the two and the three but thinking of, "oh, there's this whole piece of it and two thirds of it is. . . ." So . . . it impacted my own understanding of fractions and content knowledge understanding.

In this instance, Williams provided unfamiliar research articles and curriculum and encouraged teachers to solve and compare student tasks and think about different representations of the same subject matter, thus helping teachers think in new ways about the mathematical relationship between fractions and proportional reasoning.

The involvement of knowledgeable outsiders also increased the range of ideas that practitioners encountered during public research lessons and debriefings. A Japanese practitioner invited to a BASD public research lesson collected data on the same student throughout the entire research lesson in order to see how the student's learning developed and to document the particular experiences that sparked or impeded student learning. After hearing the types of conclusions the teacher was able to draw out of his collected data, BASD leaders began to recommend widely this data collection approach. Similarly, during a postlesson discussion, a Japanese math educator asked his American colleagues why a student's incorrect solution had not been discussed by the teacher as a way to bring out similarities and differences among the students' methods. This question revealed an aspect of the Japanese teacher's philosophy of mathematics instruction that was surprising to some of the U.S. teachers and that is still talked about by the catchphrase "mistakes can be treasures."

Coding of the content of the lesson study meetings also suggests an increase, over time, in the use of research-based knowledge. First- and third-year group transcripts reveal that teachers' references to established sources (including curricula, standards, research literature, named experts/programs, and outside LS materials), while still not common occurrences during the meetings, increased from 2 to 9 percent of statements between years 1 and 3.[4]

Analysis of lesson plans also suggests increased use of external research-based knowledge. Later lesson plans more frequently combined practice-based knowledge with information from external research, suggesting that practitioners increasingly connected these two sources of information. For example, a lesson plan by a year 5 group studying subtraction included standards related to subtraction for neighboring grades, examples of student solution methods, and references to research the group drew on (including a National Council of Teachers of Mathematics research presentation; Carpenter et al., 1999, 2003; Ma, 1999). It also included statements about what the group did not know prior to their LS work and hinted at the way that LS supported their learning from each other and from practice: "as we explored a variety of subtraction strategies, we discovered that we, as teachers, were not always comfortable with the approaches that our students might present."

Second, BASD LS practitioners increased over time their use of research on their own practice, what might be called *internal research*, as they began to use systematic procedures for studying their own students. For example, teaching and observing a lesson enabled a group of BASD teachers to discover that providing a two-column table (as recommended by the textbook) for students to record data for a function problem actually undermined student understanding of the mathematics. This discovery sparked a series of further investigations by members of the LS team; for example, they conducted investigations to see whether the detrimental effect of the worksheet held for another function problem. This internal research has subsequently been used by them (and, on video, by many others) to illustrate how subtle features of lesson design can impact student learning (Mills College LS Group 2005). Over time, the increased focus of BASD practitioners on student thinking and student work greatly expanded the possibilities for internal research. Comparison of both lesson plans and teachers' discussions from year 1 and year 3 showed an increase over time in the frequency and specificity of references to student thinking. The year 3 group discussions showed more than twice the proportion of references to student thinking or student work than found in year 1 group discussions (18 percent in year 1 and 43 percent in year 3). During the same period, global and fixed-ability evaluations declined from 8 percent to less than 1 percent of statements during the postlesson discussion. Together, these data on knowledge sources and student thinking suggest that teachers were beginning to shift away from an evaluative mind-set and toward a knowledge-building mind-set, drawing more heavily on both external and internal knowledge sources.

CONSEQUENCES OF BASD LESSON STUDY

In interviews conducted after completion of LS cycles between 2001 and 2005, teachers reported a number of changes to their instruction and their collaboration as a result of their LS participation. Teachers reported changes in how they conducted research during their own instruction, including increased use of tasks that elicit student thinking and support student exploration, more experimentation with mathematical tasks before giving them to students in order to understand task demands and anticipate student thinking, more discussion and comparison of student solutions in the classroom (including incorrect solutions), more use of student data to inform instruction, and less tendency to "give" students mathematical answers. Teachers reported changes in collaboration including asking more questions of colleagues, more use of print resources to inform discussions with colleagues, increased discussion of student thinking, and increased interest in observing other teachers and discussing observations.

Given voluntary and shifting teacher participation in LS, study of the impact on students in BASD is difficult, except at the schoolwide LS site, where all students are taught by LS participants. Table 8.1 provides district California STAR test score data in mathematics and English-language arts for students in grades 2 through 4 from 2002 to 2005. Analysis focused on net changes in scores for all students who remained at Foothills Elementary compared with students who remained at other district schools. Over 2002–2005, the three-year net increase in mathematics achievement for students who remained at Foothills School was more than triple that for students who remained elsewhere in the district as a whole (an increase of ninety-one scale score points compared to twenty-six points), a statistically significant difference ($F = .309$, df $= 845$, $p < .001$). While a causal connection between the achievement increases and LS cannot be inferred, other obvious explanations, such as impact of other programs or of changes in student populations served by the school and district, were ruled out.[5] Schoolwide LS appears to be a primary difference between the professional development at this school and other district schools during the years studied. We found weaker and later results for language arts, which is consistent with the school's later use of LS in language arts.

Implications for the Relationship between Research and Practice

From 2000 to 2006, teachers in BASD built opportunities for public, practice-based knowledge development; refined, developed, and spread tools to support LS; and increased teacher-initiated use of both internal and external research. As they did so, student achievement at the schoolwide LS site improved at a significantly higher rate than that in the district as a whole, and teachers reported changes in both their instruction and collaboration with colleagues. We suggest that the development of a system to build and share practitioner knowledge was central to these changes.

Table 8.1. Mean Gain Scores on California STAR Test for Foothills Elementary versus Other District Schools

Grade at Beginning Period	One-Year Net Change						Two-Year Net Change				Three-Year Net Change	
	2002–2003		2003–2004		2004–2005		2002–2004		2003–2005		2002–2005	
	School	District	School	District	School	District	School	District	School	District	School	District
Mathematics												
2	16.47	22.93	25.05	8.12	23.85	13.59	5.55	16.34	6.6	4.04	90.59	25.84
N	59	920	62	926	62	842	53	850	58	851	51	796
SD	52.59	50.38	46.14	52.31	38.22	53.7	48.24	49.84	51.42	56.74	59.4	62.86
3	14.74	7.01	-13.92	-5.63	-23.66	-3.64	88.53	6.64	66.79	4.04		
N	65	908	65	934	62	950	59	837	62	862		
SD	42.88	44.17	38.65	42.46	46.71	46.58	62.89	53.19	58.36	61.73		
4	72.36	10.67	76.5	-0.41	84.35	9.74						
N	55	912	62	921	69	942						
SD	53.6	10.67	61.39	48	56.49	54.43						
Language Arts												
2	11.33	8.02	4.23	-2.79	-4.18	2.61	22.04	19.1	31.38	23.2	37.33	24.03
N	55	881	62	924	62	837	50	814	58	850	48	766
SD	34.53	36.14	38.98	36.04	37.54	35.36	31.6	33.01	39.32	34.11	25.93	37.36
3	19.18	17.33	16.48	13	27.48	26.34	33.34	17.48	28.61	17.76		
N	65	888	65	933	62	950	59	817	62	861		
SD	28.41	32.13	34.29	31.93	33.8	32.03	32.15	34.78	32.97	36.39		
4	-1.98	-0.08	13.73	0.72	14.64	5.45						
N	52	870	62	919	69	943						
SD	25.79	24.97	27.69	26.97	29.73	31.4						

[a]The state standardized achievement transitioned from the STAR-9 to the CAT-6 between 2001 and 2002. To maintain consistency in testing instruments across school years, we did not include data from the 2001 school year, although the data are available.

There are several implications of these findings for efforts to strengthen the relationship between research and practice.

First, this analysis suggests that public, practice-based professional learning can build practitioner demand for research-based knowledge. As noted at the outset, U.S. education may suffer from a lack of "demand" for research on the part of practicing educators (Elmore 1996). Over the years that they were involved in LS, BASD teachers increased their use of external research-based resources, including print materials and "knowledgeable others," creating a system in which teachers (and the Foothills principal) actively pulled in research-based resources to address the questions and instructional challenges surfaced by LS. Practitioners sought knowledge relevant to problems and goals they themselves had chosen to investigate.

We argue that the increasingly public nature of practice sparked the increased demand for research-based knowledge on the part of teachers. Leaders were initially surprised by the variable quality of the lesson plans produced by LS groups, so they modified the LS process to emphasize study of the best available curricula and consultation with knowledgeable others. Teachers planning research lessons knew that their thinking, as represented in both the written lesson plan and the enacted research lesson, would later be scrutinized by colleagues (and often by outsiders). As teachers planned research lessons with colleagues, they often bumped up against gaps in knowledge and competing assumptions about mathematics and teaching. Consulting books and knowledgeable others was one way they dealt with these gaps and conflicts (Mills College LS Group 2005). Within these newly developed public learning structures, research-based ideas became more important as tools to help make sense of confusion or conflicting perspectives, to anticipate student thinking or interpret student work, and to provide a compelling rationale for lesson design. Likewise, public knowledge-building structures probably rendered research more accessible to practitioners because puzzling points—like the difference between an "equation," a "formula," and a "rule"—could be discussed with colleagues, connected to specific instructional moves, and made sense of in light of particular student work or classroom events (Mills College LS Group 2005).

Analysis of LS group discussions from years 1 and 3 suggests that the influx of research-based knowledge may have changed the local teaching culture, as evidenced by a substantial increase in the proportion of time that group members spent discussing student thinking and work. In addition, significantly greater gains in achievement for students in the schoolwide LS school than in other district schools may be attributable to LS's role in supporting teachers' knowledge development and spread.

Second, this analysis suggests that practice-based learning structures provide a fertile site for research–practice exchange. As researchers and practitioners came together around practice-based learning, both parties benefited. Research about LS and about mathematics teaching and learning (introduced from Mills College and from WCF) shaped the BASD LS effort in many ways, such as supporting incorporation of ideas about mathematics teaching and learning from Japan and from local university-based researchers. At the same time, the BASD LS effort reshaped both the research agenda of the Mills College team and the professional development strategies of the WCF. For example, the current work of the Mills College team to introduce research-based materials to LS teams stems directly from our observation of BASD LS groups—of how useful they found research resources and how time-consuming it was to locate high-quality resources pertinent to their particular mathematical topics.

Joint participation in LS also seemed to reshape the power relationship between practitioners and those identified primarily with research and its application. BASD leaders appreciated from the very start of their work the central role of teachers' knowledge in LS; indeed, their 2000 presentation to a district mathematics symposium described LS as "a model of professional development in which teachers assume responsibility for researching and improving the practice of teaching." This is remarkably different from standard practice in the United States where researchers have responsibility for asking questions and seeking the answers. Over time, WCF mathematics staff and county and district office professional development specialists were called on not only to convey research-based ideas about good practice to LS groups but also to put their own thinking and practice out for scrutiny and discussion in LS groups and in large public research lessons; their research-based ideas needed to be evaluated in practice, not simply taken as correct.

In addition, research-based knowledge came to include not only the ideas suggested by specialists but also the data gathered by practitioners to judge the impact of the lesson on students. Research lessons created a new currency—observational data on students—for evaluation of research-based knowledge. In one LS cycle we observed, a teacher reported learning that the textbook's presentation of material is not necessarily the most effective for student learning; she expressed pleasure in her new-found role as researcher:

> So that's a good lesson for us, I think always to really question just because it's already done for you [in the textbook], is it really the most effective? . . . I'm thinking how would the lesson have been changed if we had started off with . . . ten and then seventeen and then . . . just these random numbers. . . . There would have been no vertical pattern. It's kind of fun to think about all

the different things you can kind of tweak [in the lesson] and then look and watch and see . . . what [students] do. Gee, I guess that's called lesson study. (Mills College LS Group 2005)

Her words suggest not only an increased demand for research information but also, for her, a new way of engaging with research.

As both full-time classroom teachers and specialists separated from full-time classroom practice used research to develop lesson plans, put their own teaching out for public scrutiny during research lessons, and analyzed whether research-based ideas were successfully translated into practice, the research–practice divide began to efface. Bringing research and practice into closer relationship sometimes required direct action by the BASD leaders—for example, when they persistently requested that a district literacy specialist develop a question to investigate rather than tell group members what was good practice or when they disinvited specialists who could not restrain themselves from dominating LS work—but other times the research lesson provided a naturally level playing field for the worlds of research and practice to offer knowledge about instructional improvement.

Third, our case suggests that successful development of LS depends on knowledge resources both within and outside the district. In BASD, the development of LS depended on a confluence of resources, including teacher leadership within the district; a regional foundation that made a substantial, long-term investment in regional mathematics instruction; and (initially) university-based LS expertise and feedback on the emerging LS work. As teachers took part in LS, they drew on information about the LS process and mathematics teaching and learning from multiple sources and put it to use in classrooms, in their discussions with other group members or non-LS colleagues, in public lessons, and in the information they passed on to others outside the district. Thus, practitioners' connections with individuals both outside and inside the district helped make available to district LS practitioners new ideas, approaches, and resources about mathematics instruction and facilitated dialogue about and translation of research ideas into practice.

Finally, this study highlights the importance of sharing expertise from research and from practice and the value of strong, mutually energizing human relationships that develop through the sharing process. For example, LS in the district owes a great deal to WCF, which functioned outside the standard research–practice (district-to-school) "pipeline" to provide intellectual, financial, and networking resources that helped BASD practitioners achieve their initial LS successes. Initial assistance with LS tools and feedback on the emerging LS work from the Mills College team also enabled district practitioners to adjust their LS approach.

While much of the information we initially provided is now available in print and video materials, the confluence of teacher leadership, practitioners' willingness to experiment, access to research-based knowledge and high-quality modeled practice, support for coaches, and formative feedback on the emerging work are still likely to be crucial resources for any site that wishes to emulate the professional knowledge development system that emerged in BASD.

NOTES

This chapter is based on work supported by the MacArthur-Spencer Meta-Study (subtitled Toward Producing Usable Knowledge for the Improvement of Educational Practice) and by the National Science Foundation under grants 9996360 and 0207259. Any opinions, findings, and conclusions or recommendations expressed in this material are those of the authors and do not necessarily reflect the views of any of the supporting foundations. The authors wish to thank Mary Kay Stein, Cynthia Coburn, and the rest of the metastudy team for the productive theoretical framework provided for the work and for their extensive formative feedback.

1. More current measures of the extent to which LS has continued to spread across this country currently do not exist.

2. Most data for this chapter are drawn from six years of research supported by National Science Foundation (NSF) grants. The NSF-funded research focused on LS implementation and impact in six sites nationally, including BASD. Data from BASD included interviews (one-half to one and a half hours in duration) of seventy-six teachers, district administrators, and LS leaders that focused on LS implementation and theory of action from the perspective of those engaged in the work; observation and documentation of workshops and of the meetings of about twenty LS groups; and ongoing e-mail communication. Additional interviews and new transcript analyses were conducted specifically for the metastudy. New data collected for the metastudy include eight interviews with individuals in BASD and WCF focusing on the relationship between research and practice in BASD. We also developed new coding systems for the LS meeting transcripts and artifacts collected that focused on the sources of knowledge used by teachers. We selected for intensive analysis two lesson study groups from a single BASD elementary school, Foothills Elementary, where teachers voted in 2001 to practice lesson study schoolwide. These two lesson study groups, one from the first year and one from the third year of the lesson study effort, were chosen to include the same lesson study leader as a team member. (Transcript analyses focus on the first three years of the district effort; at the time of manuscript preparation, qualitative data for the next three years were not transcribed for analysis.) Other teachers in the groups differed because of changes in teaching assignments and group design over the years. From the full complement of meetings held by each group (averaging about eight meetings each), we selected two meetings for coding: a planning meeting that took place before the group had finalized the lesson and the debrief-

ing discussion that took place after the lesson. Full written transcripts of these meetings were created and coded sentence by sentence for evaluative stance (e.g., global evaluation of the lesson and characterization of students in a way that connoted fixed ability), knowledge-building stance (e.g., questioning and making a proposal), and source of knowledge (e.g., established sources, student thinking or work, and teachers' own professional experience). We expected a shift away from global and fixed-ability evaluation (e.g., "that was a good lesson" and "he's a low student") and toward use of multiple knowledge sources (including knowledge from research, colleagues, and student thinking and work).

3. BTSA is the Beginning Teacher Support and Assessment program, a state-funded induction program cosponsored by the California Department of Education and the Commission on Teacher Credentialing.

4. While these figures are still quite low—much of the teachers' discussions remained focused on practice and the classroom implications of their discussions—we include them to focus the reader's attention on what we see as an emerging trend. The total number of coded sentences from the year 3 transcripts (2,913 lines) was larger than in the year 1 transcripts (1,853 lines), yet a higher percentage of sentences included references to established sources.

5. To rule out competing hypotheses about causes of the increased achievement, we identified other reform efforts that Foothills participated in during 2001–2005 and identified all other elementary schools that also participated in these reform efforts. Gains in achievement for students who remained at each of these schools for longer than one year were compared with gains for all students who remained in the district. Only one school other than Foothills showed any statistically significant achievement gains relative to the district as a whole, and that school did not show sustained gains over three years. We also investigated characteristics of the schools and staff that might influence student achievement and found no statistically significant differences that could plausibly explain why Foothills would show greater gains than other sites, as documented.

9

⌒⌒⌒

The National Writing Project: Anatomy of an Improvement Infrastructure

Laura Stokes

What if everybody really worked together making knowledge that was going to benefit us all? How would you organize that thing? I think that is part of what the writing project tries to do.

—National Writing Project national leader

The National Writing Project (NWP) is a nationwide network of professional development organizations—the 200 local "sites" of the NWP[1]—that aims to improve the teaching of writing at all grades levels, kindergarten through college. NWP sites are housed on university campuses and codirected by university faculty and K–12 teachers; these sites conduct a variety of professional development partnerships and teacher in-service programs in area schools. All local NWP sites support the development of an ever-growing community of leading teachers, called teacher consultants, who develop, coordinate, and lead these in-service programs. The NWP is notable because it has created a system of practices that enable teachers in sites across the country to generate, interrogate, test, and share knowledge about the teaching of writing. These knowledge-generating processes are not just local. Rather, the NWP has put structures in place that allow knowledge developed at one site to be shared with others and for resources that support knowledge generation to flow up and down the network from local to regional to national levels. These structures enable the building of cumulative leadership and knowledge capacity for the improvement of teaching. Thus, I argue, the NWP has created a unique asset for the nation's education system, one that is best described as an *improvement infrastructure* for generating and sharing teacher knowledge at scale.

In this chapter, I draw on data from a case study of the NWP[2] to illuminate the functions and contributions of this infrastructure. I begin with an overview of the NWP's approach to knowledge generation followed by a discussion of the concept of improvement infrastructure. I then illustrate both of these conceptions through the lens of a sixteen-site, three-year initiative within the NWP called Improving Students' Academic Writing (ISAW). I conclude with a discussion of defining features of the NWP that create and sustain its function as an improvement infrastructure.

KNOWLEDGE GENERATION IN THE NWP

The NWP structures its programs so that teachers draw from carefully designed experiences and resources to build knowledge about problems of teaching. In a speech at the NWP annual meeting in 2005, former Executive Director Richard Sterling said that the correct role for the NWP to play is to "work the problems" of teaching and to share successful practices widely with teachers who face those same problems. He used as an analogy the famous plea from space, "Houston, we've got a problem," and he suggested that the NWP can play the same role as the NASA engineers who "worked the problem" on the ground—using the same materials the astronauts had at hand—and then showed the astronauts how to save their own lives in space. One teacher participant shared her perspective about this role: "It seems like the writing project always finds where there is a struggle with teaching and takes it on, head-on. When there is a question about how something is done, or do we have that knowledge, then we look for it and we try to figure it out."

The NWP does not work from a linear conception of research to application in practice. Rather, the NWP believes that there are three necessary contributors to the knowledge that writing teachers must develop so that they can continually improve their teaching: 1) participation in the core discipline, that is, "doing writing"; 2) inquiries into classroom practice in multiple contexts; and 3) traditional theory-based academic research. NWP programs and activities vary widely in their structure and their content because they serve different audiences in different contexts, but they have in common that they focus on problems of teaching and involve teachers in writing, in examining classroom practice, and in learning from research. Teachers draw from these sources to generate knowledge that they and their colleagues can use.[3]

Development of problem-centered knowledge occurs at all levels of the NWP. Individual teacher consultants focus on teaching problems that they find most vexing in their own practice and important to their students. In so doing, they amass resources and develop classroom practices that will be germane to their colleagues who face similar challenges. At the site level, directors design programs strategically so that the site's community of teacher consultants can become more knowledgeable about the struggles that teachers in their service area face—for example, the teaching of English-language learners or of adolescent nonreaders or the integration of technology, redefinition of genre, and expansion of audience needed for teaching in the digital age. Regionally or nationally, multiple NWP sites can be organized, as in the ISAW program discussed here, to inquire into problem areas for the purpose of disseminating knowledge within and beyond the NWP network.

THE NWP AS AN "IMPROVEMENT INFRASTRUCTURE"

In its scale, longevity, and human capital capacities, the NWP stands out as a unique investment in the strengthening of teaching. There are 200 sites in the NWP,[4] located in all fifty states, Puerto Rico, the U.S. Virgin Islands, and the District of Columbia. On an annual basis, the NWP offers roughly 7,000 programs serving more than 92,000 individual teachers; nearly half these teachers participate in multiple programs, reflecting a "turnstile" capacity of about 135,000 participants annually. Between 6,500 and 7,000 teacher consultants are active in designing and delivering these programs annually. The concepts of "improvement infrastructure" and, within that, "improvement community" serve as a useful framework for understanding the function of the NWP and its contributions to education. In conceptualizing the NWP this way, I am borrowing from Douglas Engelbart's perspective on organizations.[5]

Infrastructure can be defined as the foundational structures and technologies that enable necessary work to get done. Highways allow trucks to carry supplies and people to get to work; phone lines and other communication systems facilitate transfer of information. Applied to organizations, infrastructure refers to the technologies and processes that enable an organization to do its work. Engelbart (1992) posits that organizations should aspire to creating three basic levels of infrastructure. Level A is the *core capability infrastructure,* or what is needed to enable people to do the core work of the organization. Level B is the infrastructure that enables the *improvement of core work* done at level A. Level C is an infrastructure that enables the *ongoing improvement of the improvement processes* at level B. Applying Engelbart's framework to education, the core activity is the teaching of students. The core capability infrastructure within the school organization (level A) is what enables core work to happen, such as the presence of teachers, books, and other learning materials; technologies for learning; and structures of time and space. The level B infrastructure is the system that surrounds classrooms—for example, schools and districts—that enables improvement in the teaching of students—for example, the presence of shared standards, high-quality curriculum and resources, good assessments of learning, and leadership that creates good conditions for teaching and for learning. The level C improvement infrastructures are what enable these level B infrastructures to improve their ability to improve teaching, or what Engelbart called "getting better at getting better" (Gonzalez 1998, preface). These include curriculum developers who produce new and better materials, creators of analytic tools that enhance the quality of school leadership, professional development networks and other institutions that develop new approaches to enhancing teacher quality, and so on.

Engelbart notes that the improvement-of-improvement level (level C) typically receives the least long-term strategic investment but that it is the most important: "The most important activity we can do is to develop the improvement infrastructure . . . and to encourage and fund cross-functional 'improvement communities' whose members work on common challenges to explicitly improve improvement . . . then that community itself thus becomes a knowledge accelerator (Gonzalez 1998, preface)." Within education, activity at level C—often deemed "reform" activity because it aims to strengthen districts' and schools' ability to support better teaching and learning—is typically conceived and funded as series of episodic projects rather than as investments in ongoing improvement. The challenges of real change, however, require sustained investment, a reality that practitioners are often more sensitive to than funders (L. Stokes 1997).

The NWP network, unlike typical professional development programs, operates as a long-term, sustained infrastructure for improvement. As suggested in figure 9.1, the NWP seeks to enable every site to develop itself as a local improvement infrastructure and community that serves local teachers and schools and to sustain a nationwide improvement infrastructure that is a knowledge accelerator for improving the teaching of writing.

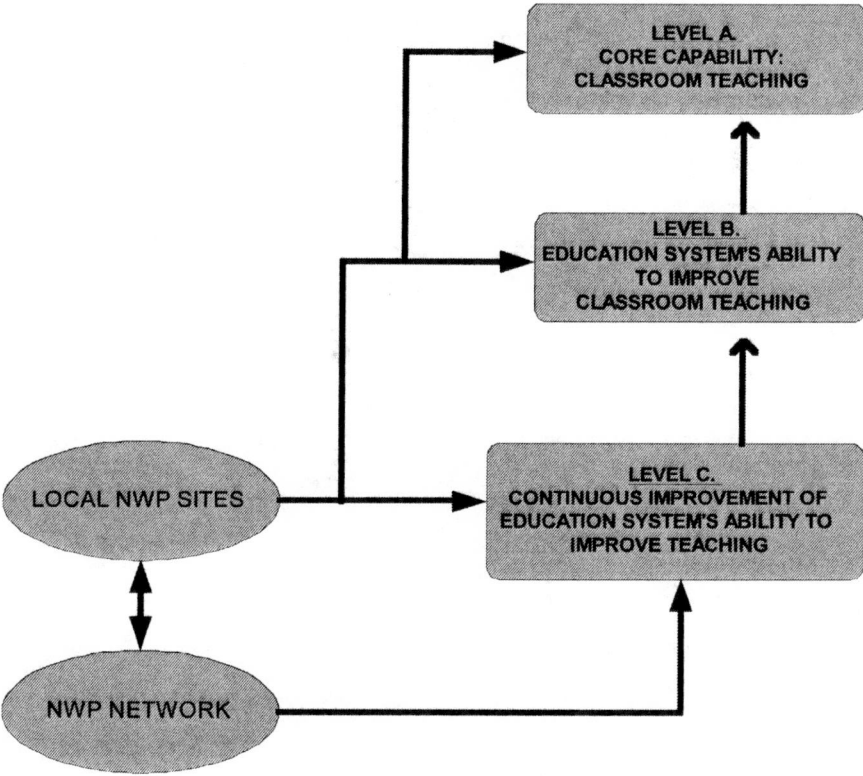

Figure 9.1. The National Writing Project as a National Improvement Infrastructure

The NWP makes direct contributions to schools at level A. NWP teachers develop, employ, and disseminate classroom practices that support students' learning and development of writing.[6] Local NWP sites make contributions to local schools and districts at level B. They provide direct professional development services in which teachers gain access to tested and refined practitioner knowledge and professional literature about classroom practices for teaching writing, designing the writing curriculum, and assessing student writing. At level C, the NWP's major contribution is its model. The network as a whole, the special-focus networks within it (such as ISAW, discussed here), and each site are structured to develop their own capacity to help districts and schools improve their writing programs. The NWP does this by building teacher knowledge about important problems of teaching, continually expanding and renewing its cadre of teacher consultants, and developing in-service programs designed to disseminate knowledge to districts and schools. These dimensions of the NWP—its model, its linked local sites, its knowledge resources, its people, and its programs—are the key components of the improvement infrastructure. A profile of one of the NWP's special focus networks—the ISAW project—illustrates the ways in which NWP acts as an improvement infrastructure for generating knowledge for teaching.

NWP IN ACTION: THE CALIFORNIA
WRITING PROJECT'S ISAW PROJECT

The California Writing Project (CWP) comprises sixteen sites, all housed on University of California or California State University campuses. In addition to grants from the NWP, the CWP receives varying amounts of state funding through the University of California, and sites garner additional funds through their home universities and fees for service to local schools and districts. As part of a state-sponsored evaluation of the CWP in early 1998, an advisory board member posed a question to the CWP directors: were they privileging personal writing in their programs and focusing too little on improvement of academic writing? The CWP's response to this question ultimately led to ISAW, a focused, multisite project aimed at developing and disseminating practical teaching knowledge about a difficult and urgent problem—helping high school students develop writing skills needed for success in college. The design of ISAW and teachers' experiences in it reflect NWP principles and knowledge-building processes at work.

CWP directors began by auditing the content of their core teacher institutes to assess the extent to which they were supporting future teacher consultants in addressing academic writing. According to the CWP director at the time, they found that they were doing an "abysmal" job of it. Site leaders agreed to begin involving teachers in more rigorous writing for professional audiences so that they, as teachers, would gain insight "in their bones," as one person put it, by personally experiencing rhetorical demands that are analogous to the demands that academic writing places on their students. Individual sites also launched new programs, for example, organizing yearlong teacher research groups focused on questions related to academic writing. A few sites had produced academic writing resources in the past—for example, professional development institutes, high school writing assessment programs, high school curriculum development, and libraries of resources for teachers. The CWP leaders held statewide meetings so that site directors could share what they had accumulated until, as the former CWP director said, "We had pulled out everything that we could from our network."

At this point, CWP leaders recognized that they were still not doing enough for teachers in this important problem area. They noticed that many districts were responding to the state's new high school exit examination,[7] which required a writing sample, by purchasing what the NWP teachers regarded as "canned formulas." Academic writing is quite susceptible to formulas (e.g., "the five-paragraph essay" and the "power paragraph") that do not reflect authentic discipline. In addition, NWP teachers themselves felt that they had not been well taught as writers in academia and that they needed more knowledge about this aspect of their discipline. One CWP leader recalled hearing "an impassioned plea at one of our meetings, that if teachers couldn't come to *this* project for what they were going to need, where could they go?"

Following this effort to amass existing knowledge, CWP launched the three-year project ISAW. They brought together teams of high school teachers (grades 9–12) from sixteen CWP sites, nearly eighty teachers altogether. There was a strong equity focus, with emphasis on involving teachers in schools with low college-going rates in order to give underserved students more opportunities to develop academic literacy. A number of Writing Program faculty from the University of California at Los Angeles, Davis, and Berkeley served as collaborators or consultants, participating in various ways throughout the program. Embedded within the ISAW project (and serving as its source of funds) was a state-commissioned evaluation study focusing on the extent to which high school students' academic writing improved from fall to spring. The evaluation framework demanded a common set of writing prompts, and the group settled on the University of California's "Subject A" examination, a quite challenging timed reading-and-writing task that students must pass in order to qualify for freshman English. It turned out that focusing on this well-defined but complex representation of academic literacy was advantageous for the knowledge development purpose of the project. The Subject A examination embodied well the analytic reading and writing skills that students need to succeed in college. It has strong credibility with teachers and is designed in a format that high school teachers can adapt into instructional units for their students. Further, it served as a rich starting point for dialogue and collaboration among high school teachers and university writing faculty.

The statewide group met three times per year for two to three days each time. In between those meetings, teachers were responsible individually and sometimes in small local study groups for experimenting in their own classrooms—trying new assignments, new teaching approaches, and new resources. In the whole-group meetings, teachers participated in a variety of activities designed to help them build knowledge about the teaching of academic writing. To better understand the nature of the literacy tasks demanded of students, teachers themselves wrote timed university essay tests and discussed with one another the analytic skills and composing processes needed for the tasks. Teachers also participated in discussions led by collaborating University of California writing program faculty, who presented their own research and practice associated with the nature of literacy in the academy and with students' development of literacy and with the application of theories about language, culture, text, and genre to the teaching of academic writing. Further, teachers engaged professional literature directly, reading and discussing books and articles that addressed university and state standards associated with writing competency, that offered examples of university students' writing as models of academic literacy, that presented theory- and practice-based approaches to the design of developmental curriculum for high school students, and that examined research on especially problematic areas that cropped up, such as the politics of genre, adolescent reading development, and language development of students learning English. Additionally, through formal demonstrations, teachers shared with one another practices that they were developing in their classrooms in between the whole-group meetings—new approaches to teaching revision, analysis of nonfiction text, and so on. These demonstrations were treated not as "how-tos" but rather as cases of practice made public so that the group could examine them. Embedded in these demonstrations were opportunities to analyze student work samples to link the practice with the student work it produced. Finally, in consultation with the University of California writing faculty, the teachers jointly assessed student papers, scoring them holistically against the University of California standards.

Through these learning processes, teachers identified a major gap in the available knowledge. Among all the resources amassed for the project (college and university faculty, high school teachers, and a full professional library), they could not find an explanation about how academic literacy develops across the full span of the high school years. The ISAW coordinator noted, "The dilemma with this whole issue is that most all of the research and theoretical stuff is about college kids. There is so little written about high school kids. So the teachers knew that they had to go back and solve the problem." To build this knowledge for themselves, the ISAW project leaders led teachers in painstaking analyses of matched pairs of student essays (fall to spring) from the full range of several hundred students in grades 9 to 12 and all language backgrounds. Teachers focused on naming precisely what degree of improvement was exhibited through the year for each of the multiple thinking, reading, and writing skills important to academic literacy and success. These analyses of features of the student writing were ultimately distilled into what became dubbed an "improvement rubric." The aim of the rubric was to identify all the developmental improvements that students made and to couch them in positive (nondeficit) language that both teachers and students could understand and would find helpful in furthering the development of literacy skills. ISAW participants wanted the rubric to reflect their grounded knowledge of how these skills evolved, and they wanted the rubric's language to be of practical instructional use for themselves and their students. In effect, they were building a new grounded theory of academic writing development, grades 9 to 12.

Between whole-group meetings, teachers tested the evolving rubric in their classrooms. They interrogated the rubric against their own criteria of explanatory value and usefulness for teaching: Do the terms used to describe student writing reflect a developmental perspective (not a deficit-based performance perspective)? Is the rubric applicable to the full range of teachers and students? Does it explain the developmental level of every paper from every student in grades 9 to 12? Is it usable and accessible for both teachers and students? Does it map well onto a sequential transition-to-college academic literacy curriculum? In this lengthily iterative process taking place over two years, teachers individually used drafts of the rubric in their own classrooms to assess student papers, to design lessons, to talk with their students, and to document students' progress over time. At the projectwide meetings, the teachers worked together to elaborate and refine the rubric based on sharing their efforts to use it in their own classrooms and on their ongoing joint analyses of student papers.

This collective effort ultimately produced an instrument that captured the range of writing characteristics students exhibit and developmental pathways they take as they develop academic literacy before college. Importantly, the rubric was made for use in classrooms as a guide for students as well as teachers. One participant, for example, noted that her students could use the rubric to self-assess their work and see what they needed to learn to "move over" toward higher scores: "When the students get their papers back . . . they would know what it would take to keep moving over because the rubric is elaborate. . . . They can look at it and say, oops, I forgot to counter my argument, oops, I didn't cite any text."

ISAW participants spanned the full high school grade span and taught students with a variety of language, ethnic, and community backgrounds. As the project unfolded, teachers split off into small groups to focus on specific problems within the broad area of academic writing in high school. Teachers of ninth grade, for example, worked on how to begin sequencing writing tasks that would eventually lead their students to the transition-to-college standards. Some teachers formed a study group focusing on improving the teaching of reading, especially of nonnarrative prose, an area integral to academic writing development. Others focused on scaffolding instruction for English-language learners. In this way, teachers were able to contextualize in practice the general ideas they formed and also develop context-specific practices to increase the robustness of collective understanding. Over the three years, participants created, refined, and shared among one another a wide range of specific practices, building up considerable knowledge usable for teaching. Much of this knowledge could then be captured in shareable formats and disseminated beyond the ISAW participants. Teachers reported sharing what they gained from ISAW in their own high school departments, in in-service programs (workshops, institutes, and study groups) sponsored by their local NWP sites, in articles in journals for teachers, in Web-based teaching modules, and in conferences of both the California and the National Council of Teachers of English. When California's Department of Education sponsored statewide professional development institutes, one ISAW participant and a colleague from her NWP site led a secondary-level program, designing it as an institute on academic reading and writing based entirely on the ISAW project. Distributing teacher-formed knowledge in ways such as these is expected in the NWP and central to its mission.

FEATURES OF THE NWP
AS AN IMPROVEMENT INFRASTRUCTURE

The ISAW project illustrates several features of the NWP that have enabled it to grow and ultimately sustain itself as a national improvement infrastructure for the teaching of writing.

Generative Structures for Teachers' Development of Knowledge for Teaching

The ISAW project unfolded in a way that is typical of processes of knowledge generation, testing, refinement, and distribution that occur and recur in roughly cyclical ways at every level of the NWP network. Activities are structured generatively as occasions for learning that, in the words of one NWP leader, are "all unified by a single activity that I would call critical inquiry." Critical inquiry involves teachers in asking how the ideas they are encountering through their core experiences of writing, of examining practice, and of reading research fit together and what the implications are for their teaching. The NWP leader explains how this works:

> So let's say that they [the teachers] are reading Debra Brandt's article, "Sponsors of Literacy" [Brandt 1998]. They [the teachers] don't just read it and

write it down, or say "literacy is sponsored." They look at the other two parts of their experience. They look at their [classroom] practice, and they look at their own experience of writing, and they bring that to bear on that professional reading: 'In what ways is this true? How is it true for me? How is it true for everybody? *Is* it true for everybody, is it true for some people and not for others?'

Thus, teachers in NWP programs are not expected to act as recipients of knowledge that is transmitted to them; rather, they are asked to form knowledge relevant to their teaching through thoughtful study and reflection within these generative learning experiences. Teachers engage in this knowledge making both individually and through dialogue within a professional community that is studying together so that the knowledge they generate, while it is contextualized by individuals in different teaching situations, is ultimately shared.

As illustrated in figure 9.2, all NWP activities begin with the identification of a problem of teaching. Pursuing these problems involves focused study, that is, amassing knowledge resources (university faculty, other teachers, and research articles and books), participating in generative experiences (writing, discussions of research, and examination of student work and classroom practice), and seeking insight through critical inquiry into all of them. Pursuing the problem further involves forming tentative knowledge for teaching and testing new ideas through iterative cycles of classroom experimentation, demonstrating for others and getting their feedback, and analysis of student learning. Testing and validating knowledge involves holding up new ideas to teacher-centered criteria of explanatory power and utility for teaching; it also involves ongoing integration of others' research and teaching. Some aspects of the refined knowledge can be captured and articulated in any of a number of the forms and forums by which the NWP makes practitioner knowledge transportable—including demonstrations of teaching, professional articles, teacher workshops, intensive seminars or institutes, curriculum units, books, and so on. These forums are used to distribute knowledge both within the NWP's own network infrastructure and beyond the NWP through its in-service programs in schools and districts. As is true in any knowledge-development process, new questions of practice arise that can launch new inquiries.

These inquiry processes occur continually and at all levels of the NWP. Local sites support the knowledge development of individual teacher consultants over many years as an ongoing investment in building leadership capacity for the site. Site leaders draw on the specialized knowledge areas of teacher consultants to design professional development programs for schools in their region. The NWP national office sponsors special-focus networks that individual teachers anywhere in the nation can belong to,

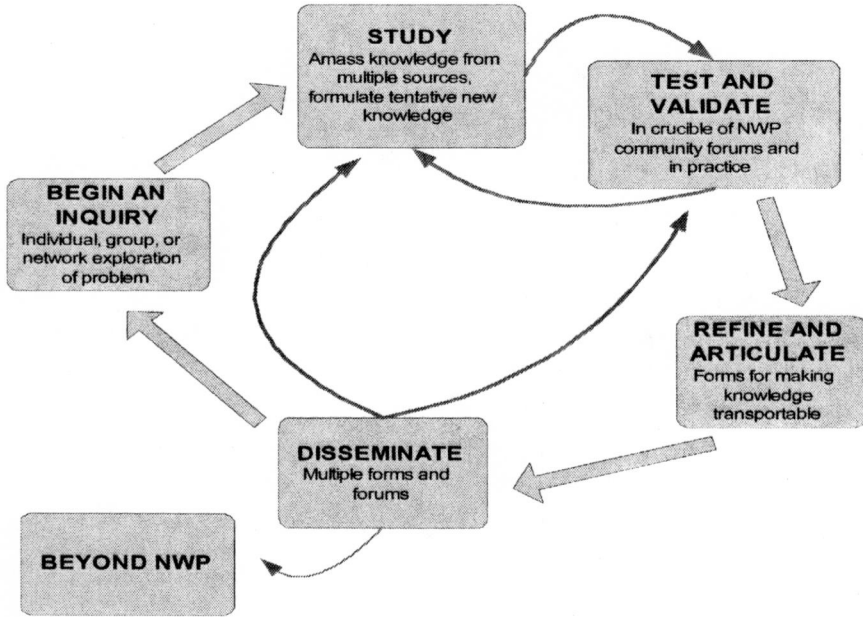

Figure 9.2. Producing and Distributing Refined Practitioner Knowledge in the National Writing Project

such as the English Language Learners Network and the Teacher Inquiry Community. These networks sponsor regional and national institutes, circulate articles and other resources to teachers, and invite teachers to share their knowledge through writing and presenting. Like the ISAW but reaching nationally, the NWP's New Teacher Initiative, Reading Initiative, and Technology Initiative are examples of structures that involve multiple sites in developing and distributing knowledge for teaching. The NWP website is a repository of massive quantities of research- and practice-based resources for teaching, available to any site directors, teachers, or others. These elements of the NWP infrastructure function to generate knowledge for the improvement of teaching.

The Role of University Faculty, Research, and Culture

NWP sites are housed on university campuses, are organized as ongoing partnerships between universities and schools, and are codirected by university faculty members. Further, two of the core values of the NWP culture are egalitarianism and respect for teachers' knowledge, and these values extend from kindergarten to university.[8] These aspects of the NWP model are significant to the quality of the knowledge resources available to NWP teachers. In any given year, some 500 to 600 university faculty members in English, rhetoric, linguistics, or education departments are directly involved in the work of NWP sites.[9] Whether they have ladder appointments or occupy lectureships, these faculty members are conducting research as well as administering and teaching in teacher education and writing programs. College and university faculty are key producers as well as "brokers" of the books and articles that NWP teachers read. The NWP's conception of learning as inquiry, especially when realized in a university–school partnership, helps foster a discourse culture that is more intellectual than that of schools.

At the same time, NWP programs tend not to reward uncritical consumption of ideas but rather to encourage teachers to interrogate research ideas in dialogue with one another in the same way that they test and critically interrogate knowledge from practice. Thus, teachers are not likely to accept on face value the results of a research study. Rather, NWP teachers make demands associated with utility and value in the world in which they teach. In the NWP, it is the leading teachers of NWP sites who are pursuing these cycles of knowledge generation, individually and collectively, with encouragement, direction, sponsorship, and collaboration from site leaders interested in the teaching problems at hand. And it is these leading teachers—as members of an ongoing professional learning community—who ultimately validate the quality of the knowledge for teaching by applying their own standards as practitioners.

A Codifiable Model for Building Teacher Knowledge

Ultimately, what the NWP provides to teachers and the field of writing as a whole is not a codified model of "how to teach writing" but rather a codified model for building teacher knowledge. From the perspective of the NWP, knowledge about teaching cannot be perfected and distributed as a fixed commodity. Treating knowledge as fully codified, in their view, not only misrepresents the true complexities of teaching but also serves to shut down the kind of inquiry and professional dialogue that fuels knowledge generation. At the same time, the NWP knows that a great deal has become known about the teaching of writing in the past several decades and that high-quality knowledge resources—especially those that are developed and refined through continuous study of classroom practice—can and must be distributed widely to teachers so that they can become more knowledgeable. Because of this approach, there are some who credit the NWP with leading the formation of a shared knowledge base about the teaching of writing—shared language and shared practices—that is rare in the profession.[10]

CONCLUSIONS

Knowledge that is both well tested and usable for teaching is an important educational asset that the NWP contributes to the nation's education system. Part of the NWP's unique ability to generate such knowledge lies in its deepest design principle, which says that knowledge making for the classroom must be in the hands (i.e., minds) of teachers, the users of the knowledge. The NWP's approach to knowledge formation breaks down traditional boundaries between research and practice by treating both as important contributors to knowledge that is usable for teaching. Further, the NWP does not see research and practice as the only major contributors to such knowledge; the NWP also sees knowledge gained from the experience of writing itself—from the reflective practice of the discipline and its craft—as a third source. Thus, in the NWP, the equation is not research + translation = knowledge for practice. Rather, the equation is (discipline experience + practice + research) + inquiry in professional community = knowledge for practice *and* for sharing among teachers.

Further, in the NWP, working relationships among K–12 teachers and college/university faculty are not special or temporary; rather, they are embedded as the regular mode of social interaction in the ongoing governance and knowledge-making enterprise of local NWP sites and the national network. The NWP professional community spans the K–12 university spectrum. While it is true that community members working in different academic contexts have greater or lesser access to knowledge resources from research or practice, the important principle is that all members come to the knowledge-making table with something to share, something to learn, and a desire to inquire into problems together.

Its distinctive design principles and generative structures are not the only reasons for the NWP's ability to generate knowledge for the nation, however. The NWP has operated continually for three decades and at a scale that may be unique in professional development programs. The NWP represents a different kind of improvement effort. It functions as an investment—one that sustains an improvement infrastructure that builds capacity, cumulatively over time, to generate educational "capital" (knowledge and professional leadership)—that teachers and schools can draw upon. Its most significant contribution is its combination of design, scale, lasting infrastructure, and accumulated assets that allow it to function and to keep growing as a knowledge generator for the improvement of teaching.

NOTES

I owe a great debt to my colleagues at Inverness Research: Mark St. John, especially, and also Barbara Heenan, Judy Hirabayashi, Kathleen Dickey, Allison

Murray, and Laurie Senauke. The National Writing Project management team, especially Judy Buchanan, made this study possible and cooperated as steadfastly, thoughtfully, and kindly as anyone possibly could. Each person I interviewed was willing to tell me their stories, dig up documents, and think hard about the questions I asked them. Cynthia Coburn of the metastudy team gave me invaluable guidance on several drafts.

1. As of February 15, 2008, there were 200 NWP sites. In 2003–2004, the year from which data from this report were drawn, there were 185 NWP sites. All data on numbers of NWP programs and participants are drawn from data gathered by Inverness Research.

2. The study was carried out in two phases. The first phase documented the NWP's "theory of action" related to how the NWP supports the development and spread of practitioner knowledge and how research and practice interact in the NWP. I conducted individual interviews with the NWP executive director and seven other members of the national leadership staff. I supplemented these by collecting publicly available and internal information. I coded interview transcripts according to key concepts linked to the research questions and created analytic memos to document emerging themes. To check my understanding, I prepared a slide presentation that outlined the emerging concepts and involved all the interviewees in lengthy discussion and feedback.

The second phase developed a "case within the case" to portray the NWP theory in practice. In consultation with the NWP leadership, I selected a program called Improving Students' Academic Writing (ISAW), a three-year effort undertaken by sixteen sites of the California Writing Project (CWP) between 1999 and 2002. I interviewed the two CWP leaders who created and directed ISAW as well as three teacher participants from two CWP sites. Additionally, I reviewed meeting agendas, professional literature (books and articles) used by the participants, the "improvement rubric" that was a major product of the collective effort, Web-based teaching modules that were produced from the project, and a published article about how practitioner knowledge from the ISAW program was distributed through a state-sponsored professional development initiative (Kittle 2004).

For background information on the history, design, scope, scale, and effectiveness of the NWP, I drew from data amassed over ten years by Inverness Research, where I am a senior research associate, as well as my own experience studying a number of NWP programs and initiatives. I also reviewed participant reports of the quality, value, and impact of NWP programs (Dickey, Hirabayashi, St. John, and Stokes 2003, 2004; St. John 1999; L. Stokes 2003), two evaluation studies of the NWP (Academy for Educational Development 2002; Olson and Land 2003), two books (Gray 2000 [a memoir]; Lieberman and Wood 2003 [a research study]), and an article about the NWP's theory and practice of scaling their work (McDonald, Buchanan, and Sterling 2004). I also drew on my personal experience as director of the University of California, Davis, site of the NWP in 1981–1986 and 1988–1990. On completion of the first draft, all informants reviewed it and offered individual feedback via e-mail or telephone. Additionally, I met with the NWP management team to get feedback on the analysis.

3. The roots of the NWP model go back more than thirty years to the founding of the Bay Area Writing Project by James Gray, a former high school teacher

teaching in the University of California, Berkeley, Teacher Education Program. His beliefs about what sources of knowledge were important to a teacher's effort to improve teaching—and about how research and practice relate—became embedded in the NWP as design principles that undergird NWP programs today.

4. As of February 15, 2008.

5. Engelbart is a technology innovator, credited with inventing the computer mouse and pioneering online communication and e-mail. His work on "groupware" helped create the intranet and the Internet, planted the seeds of Web 2.0, and underscores his vision of the need for worldwide knowledge sharing and collective generation to address urgent and difficult problems. For information about the Bootstrap Institute, which Engelbart created to bring his ideas about improvement infrastructure to organizational leaders, see http://www.bootstrap.org. Mark St. John, president of Inverness Research, first began applying Engelbart's ideas to education to help funders rethink the nature of their investments in reform.

6. For information about research and evaluation studies that document improvements in writing in NWP classrooms, see http://www.nwp.org.

7. The California High School Exit Examination was written into law in 1999.

8. Lieberman and Wood (2003) emphasize and illustrate the points in this section. In our ongoing study of the NWP over more than a decade, we have observed these values and principles over and over. See, for example, the Inverness Research report on the NWP's New Teacher Initiative, available at http://www.inverness-research.org and www.nwp.org. Issues of status difference can cause problems in NWP sites where the university faculty do not grasp these core values of the NWP model.

9. Based on annual site data collected for all sites by Inverness Research.

10. Lee Shulman, president of the Carnegie Foundation for the Advancement of Teaching, made this assertion in a research panel of the American Educational Research Association in April 2005.

IV

RESEARCH AND DECISION MAKING IN SCHOOL DISTRICTS

School district central offices are a key leverage point for bringing research and practice together for school improvement. District leaders make crucial decisions that can influence the instructional approaches used in schools. They select the textbooks that teachers use, make decisions about which instructional approaches to promote, identify interventions for struggling students, and create learning opportunities that encourage teachers to teach and school leaders to lead in particular ways. And some districts evaluate, assess, and make changes in their improvement efforts over time. In so doing, district leaders can play an important role in the degree to which instructional improvement efforts in schools are rooted in research and evidence.

However, prior research on the relationship between research and practice at the district level has identified a number of challenges that districts face as they seek to integrate research into their ongoing policy and practice. These studies suggest that district leaders can lack access to appropriate research either because appropriate studies do not exist (Corcoran, Fuhrman, and Belcher 2001) or because they may not be easy for district leaders to find and access (Corcoran et al. 2001; David 1981; Roberts and Smith 1982; West and Rhoton 1994).

Beyond access, school district central offices have complex organizational structures that create challenges for bringing research and practice together. Decision making is stretched across levels of the system and divisions, creating challenges of coordination and communication and fostering differences in interpretation, values, and priorities (Coburn, Touré, and Yamashita 2009; Kennedy 1982; Spillane 1998). Decision making in districts also exists in highly politicized and highly changeable environments (Englert, Kean, and Scribner 1977; Hannaway 1993). District central offices have multiple constituencies to serve and multiple layers of governance—above as well as below—to whom they must be responsive. Multiple interest groups inside and outside the district with different stakes and, at times, different values pressure district administrators to make particular decisions.

Finally, districts often lack the capacity to integrate research into their ongoing problem-solving processes. Few districts have systems in place to foster engagement with research and research-based ideas in a systematic way (Corcoran et al. 2001). Evidence use requires research literacy and skills at data analysis and interpretation (Corcoran et al. 2001; Mac Iver and Farley 2003). However, many districts appear to lack these capacities, frustrating their attempts to use evidence in decision making (Burch and Thiem 2004; Corcoran et al. 2001; David 1981; Honig 2003, 2004; Mac Iver and Farley 2003; Reichardt 2000).

Increasingly, school districts have turned to partnerships with external organizations to support their efforts to incorporate research and evidence into their practice (Datnow and Honig, 2008). The two chapters in this part profile attempts by external organizations to partner with school districts to increase the use of research to inform district practice and policymaking. In many respects, these chapters echo the challenges raised by earlier studies. However, by digging into and really trying to understand the dynamics of research use and the role of external providers in supporting this work, these chapters uncover strategic levers for supporting school districts in integrating research into their ongoing work.

In chapter 10, Cynthia Coburn reports on a longitudinal study of an initiative called Partnership for District Reform (PDR). PDR brought together an external research organization and a midsized urban school district to develop evidence-based practice at the district level. Coburn shows that work with the external organization brought research and research-based approaches into the district in unprecedented ways. But greater access to research did not always translate into substantive use of this research in decision making. Coburn argues that PDR was most successful in bringing research and practice together in the service of instructional improvement when it created conditions for district leaders and researchers to engage in discussions about research and research-based approaches outside the confines of a particular decision. In the absence of this kind of engagement, district personnel tended to use research in superficial or symbolic ways. Coburn also analyzes how organizational conditions and resource constraints work against such substantive engagement with research.

In chapter 11, Lea Hubbard profiles a unique and long-standing partnership between the Boston Public Schools, a local intermediary organization called the Boston Plan for Excellence, and a local research organization called Education Matters. This partnership focuses on a much more targeted element of the research–practice relationship: the district's use of formative evaluation research on their own initiatives. In investigating this kind of research use, Hubbard hones in on the features of the relationship between the school district and their external partners. She argues that the intermediary organization played a crucial role in helping the school district use the evaluation findings in productive ways because it was able to facilitate communication between the researchers and the district, framed findings in the context of shared understandings, and had the capacity to work with the district to design programmatic responses to the evidence contained in the evaluation. The intermediary organization was able to play this role because of relations of trust and a shared vision of high-quality instruction among the leaders of the three organizations.

10

⚜️

The Partnership for District Change: Challenges of Evidence Use in a Major Urban District

Cynthia E. Coburn

School district central offices play a pivotal role in efforts to increase research and evidence use in U.S. public schools. In recent years, advocates have promoted a number of recommendations to support school districts in using research and other forms of evidence more systematically in their decision making. These include the development of more sophisticated data systems so that districts can access their own local data (Sharkey and Murnane 2006; Wayman 2007), lists of research-based practices to assist districts and others in choosing curricular materials and interventions (Curriculum Review Panel 2004; What Works Clearinghouse 2007; Weiss, Murphy-Graham, and Birkeland 2005), and partnerships to broker and translate research in ways that are usable for districts (Bickel and Cooley 1985; Corcoran and Rouk 1985; Kerr et al. 2006). Indeed, a number of efforts have been launched to put these recommendations into place (Kerr et al. 2006; Supovitz 2008).

In this chapter, I draw on data from a three-year study of one district's experience with an initiative that incorporated many of these elements.[1] The Partnership for District Reform (PDR)[2] brought together members of a university research center and a midsize urban school district in an effort to foster evidence-based decision making to support continuous instructional improvement at scale. While PDR was successful in its efforts to bring research into the district and in helping the district evaluate the degree to which instructional approaches under consideration were research based, district decision makers ultimately only rarely drew on these resources as they made instructional decisions. In this chapter, I draw on an in-depth analysis of twenty-three decisions about instruction that the district made during the three years of the partnership to argue that the limited success of PDR's strategies was due, in part, to the social and organizational conditions of decision making that are present in most major urban school districts. I further argue that absent attention to these underlying conditions, efforts to support districts in using research and other forms of evidence are likely to be partial at best.

PDR

The PDR was a foundation-funded initiative that brought together an external research organization with the district in question to foster the development of the district as a learning organization.[3] At the time of the study, the district served approximately 50,000 students, the majority of whom were low-income students of color and one-fourth of whom were classified as English-language learners. The partnership was driven by the theory that by working in partnership, the district and the external research organization could create the conditions for evidence-based practice in support of districtwide instructional improvement. According to the tenets of PDR, the collaborative work in the initiative was guided by the principle of coconstruction, which called for district and external partners to collaboratively identify problems and develop and implement solutions that would be informed by research but adapted to local conditions and capacities. This approach emphasized the importance of both research knowledge and clinical knowledge for solving the problems the district faced, and it was to be a partnership where diverse forms of knowledge were valued and differences of opinion were adjudicated with reference to evidence.

The outside research center coordinated a large number of external partners who came to the district to participate in this endeavor, including researchers from the research center, professors from several local universities, and experienced practitioners who were working as national consultants. In the second year of PDR, a second organization—a national organization devoted to district systemic change—was brought on board to provide additional capacity to support the initiative. On the district side, PDR involved district personnel at multiple levels of the district, including the superintendent, assistant superintendents, directors of key divisions, and professional development providers in the division of curriculum and instruction.

The external organization and the district worked to identify key areas of need for the district, focusing initially on redesigning the district's professional development offerings in mathematics and literacy, creating instructional frameworks in literacy and mathematics, developing a new approach to leadership development, and working to strengthen connections between the research office and the office of curriculum and instruction. The external partners also acted as advisers for many of the instructional decisions that emerged in the course of everyday district business. Through this work, the external partners brokered access to research on issues that were pressing in the district, constructed research reviews on approaches the district was considering, worked with the district research office to ensure that all divisions had access to the district's rich data resources, and attempted to build new approaches to decision making that were more inclusive, more systematic, and, most of all, rooted in data and research evidence.

ACCESS TO RESEARCH AND RESEARCH-BASED PRACTICES

Perhaps the most striking feature of the PDR experience is the degree to which the partnership brought access to research and research-based practices that district personnel drew on as they deliberated about instructional decisions. To investigate the pathways by which research and other forms of evidence became a part of deliberation around instructional issues, I conducted a social network analysis for the district leaders involved in each of the twenty-three decisions we analyzed. That is, I created a map of the network of colleagues that each district leader worked with on a given issue, taking care to include those inside the district as well as those outside the district. I then investigated what kinds of information, research, advice, and approaches came into the deliberations from these connections.

District leaders were much more likely to engage with research and research-based approaches when decisions involved their external partners. Of the twenty-three decisions related to instruction that we analyzed, twelve involved PDR external partners. Of these twelve, research or research-based practices were invoked as part of the deliberation in eleven, with external partners as the main or only source of these research ideas in eight of the eleven. In contrast, research and research-based practices were invoked in only four of the eleven decisions made without participation of external partners. The remaining seven decisions that did not involve external partners also did not involve direct engagement with research at all.

PDR facilitated access to research and research-based ideas and approaches in two ways. First, PDR external partners directly brought research or research-based approaches into the deliberations themselves. For example, one of the projects that PDR worked on was designing and developing a coaching initiative. External partners brought relevant research on school-site coaching and information about different models of school-site coaching that were in use in other parts of the country to the attention of district leaders. They also conducted their own meta-analysis of research on the effects of coaching on student outcomes. Research and research-based ideas brought to the table by PDR external partners became central to the discussion and debate on coaching in the district.

Second, external partners increased access to research and research-based practices by brokering connections to individuals in the field who then brought new ideas and approaches into the district central office. The social network analysis provides evidence that there were only a few key district leaders that had robust ties to external sources of knowledge independent of PDR during the time of the study. Of the thirty-two district personnel involved in the decisions we analyzed, only twelve had ties that brought access to research or research-based practices apart from that brokered by PDR, and only three had more than three ties to external sources of research or research-based practices.[4]

By brokering connections between key district leaders and researchers, national figures, and consultants in the field, PDR external partners created new pathways through which research ideas flowed into the district directly into decision contexts. For example, one of the major foci of the partnership during the first two years was the design and development of districtwide professional development in literacy. PDR external partners played a direct role in working with district literacy personnel to design a series of summer institutes that served hundreds of district teachers each summer and bringing in relevant studies and research-based approaches to support that work. But they also brokered connection with a range of literacy experts both locally and nationally who played pivotal roles as well. In the first year, PDR external partners connected district personnel with four literacy experts who brought research-based approaches to professional development to design the institutes themselves, models of instruction that were rooted in research, and research articles that district personnel read together as they made decisions about the focus of the institute. In the second year, the presence of external sources was even more pronounced. By this point, there were eight national and local literacy experts involved in various ways in the planning, none of whom heretofore had connections to the district.[5] In this and other decisions, research and research-based approaches brokered by external partners represented the main ideas and approaches that were considered in the deliberation. Thus, PDR external partners and the connections to others they brokered played a key role of getting research and research-based approaches into the hands of district decision makers as they were designing policies and programs to improve teaching and learning in the district.

ROLE OF RESEARCH IN DECISION MAKING

However, while the partnership clearly increased access to research and research-based approaches, these ideas did not always play a central role in the decision the district ultimately pursued. As mentioned earlier, there were eight decisions where research and other forms of evidence were not invoked at all during deliberations, and, even when research or research-based approaches did come up or even played a central role in the remaining fifteen decisions, district decision makers rarely used evidence in a manner that advocates of evidence use would expect.

When policymakers and others exhort districts to use evidence in their decision making, they often envision that evidence will play an instrumental role. That is, they imagine that district administrators will use evidence directly and centrally to make decisions related to policy or practice (Johnson 1999; Weiss 1980). Weiss (1980) describes the image of instrumental use in the following way: "A problem exists; information or understanding is lacking either to generate a solution to the problem or to select among alternative solutions; search [for other forms of evidence] provides the missing knowledge; a solution is reached" (11–12). Yet district personnel rarely used evidence instrumentally in this district. I determined that district personnel used evidence in an instrumental fashion if they used research or data centrally to select or generate solutions or weigh the costs and benefits of multiple, competing options. Key to this designation was that attention to data or research evidence came *before* advocacy for a particular solution. I saw evidence of instrumental use in only seven out of twenty-three decisions, three of which involved external partners. For example, during the first year of the study, the district decided to adopt a supplemental mathematics curriculum. While there were quite different viewpoints and much debate about whether or not the district needed a supplemental mathematics curriculum at all, once the decision was made to move forward with an adoption, members of the district collected research and other information about the different textbook options from their connections to the local university, from the textbook representatives, from local districts that used a particular textbook, and from national reform mathematics networks. Research findings were then central in discussion and deliberation about which package to select.

However, even when data were used instrumentally in one stage of the decision trajectory, such data were not always used in this manner at other stages. For example, after reviewing evaluation research on a project to improve reading instruction in eight district schools that showed increased student achievement, district leaders decided to model their professional development on the approach. According to our definition, this process is considered instrumental decision making. However, after setting the main priorities for the professional development, the decision making moved from the executive office to the professional development office that was charged with making further decisions about design and focus of the offerings. District leaders in the professional development office subsequently eschewed the model in question, opting for another approach without considering evidence of its effectiveness, undercutting the decisions made at the higher level that used research findings in an instrumental manner. This pattern was echoed in other decisions in the district as well. Even though the district considered evidence in an instrumental fashion in some aspect of seven decisions, the instrumental approach was marginal to the final outcome in nearly all these instances.

It was actually more common for district personnel to use research studies, data, or general claims that "research says" to justify, persuade, and bring legitimacy to potential solutions that were already favored or even enacted. Weiss and others (Feldman and March 1988; Weiss 1980) call this "symbolic use" of evidence. I determined that evidence was used in a symbolic manner if attention to research or data came *after* the emergence of a solution, if there was evidence of selective use of research or data, or if participants evoked evidence in very general terms (e.g., "research says") to generate legitimacy for a particular solution. Fourteen out of twenty-three decisions involved symbolic use of evidence, including nine decisions that involved participation of external partners. District decision makers were much more likely to use evidence symbolically when there were conflicts about the appropriate direction for district policy. In fact, district personnel invoked evidence in a symbolic manner in thirteen out of fourteen decisions that involved conflict but only one of the nine decisions where there were shared ideas about the appropriate direction to go.

Perhaps most significantly, invoking evidence in the course of policy discussions—instrumentally or symbolically—did little to shift decision makers' preexisting views. This was especially true when there were differences of opinion. Although research evidence appeared to strengthen commitment to solutions when there was shared agreement about its value and appropriateness, there were only two decisions (one of which involved PDR external partners) where drawing on research, evaluation evidence, or data in the course of deliberation caused decision makers to question their assumptions or consider alternative solutions.

Instead, when decision makers were unable to persuade one another of the merits of particular solutions using evidence or other means (twelve out of twenty-three decisions), they did one or more of the following three things. First, they narrowed the range of participants involved in decisions, including only those who agreed with their point of view (used in seven decisions). Second, they addressed conflicting ideas by building them into the structure of the program or policy, often creating contradictory policy and greater complexity. Structural elaboration, as I call it, was used in four decisions. Third, district leaders addressed disagreements by exercising authority. In these instances, individuals with positional authority selected the ultimate solution, often with little attention to the available research, a tactic that happened in seven decisions.[6]

While research was rarely used in ways anticipated by advocates of evidence use, engagement with research ideas did play an influential role in less direct ways. District personnel's engagement with the research outside the decision context at times influenced how they came to understand the nature of the problems in their district. Rather than using research directly to provide evidence for a solution, engagement with research outside of a decision context instead influenced the preexisting beliefs that district leaders brought to bear on understanding a situation and interpreting it as problematic. Weiss and her colleagues (Weiss 1980; Weiss and Bucuvalas 1980) call this phenomenon the "conceptual use of research." I determined that engagement with research informed how district decision makers saw the world when we observed district personnel reading or talking in-depth about research literature and then saw the language, conceptual categories, or ideas from the research play a role in how problems were defined or particular solutions were seen as appropriate, usually at a later date and sometimes without invoking the research explicitly.[7] I saw evidence of conceptual use in ten out of the twenty-three decisions.

PDR external partners played an especially important role in conceptual use of evidence. In the first year of the partnership, as part of a strategy to build trust and consensus, external partners engaged district decision makers in reading and discussing research literature about a range of topics related to issues of central concern to the partnership. These discussions often took place outside of the decision context, during study groups or during the initial period of time where external partners engaged district leaders in setting priorities for their work together. For example, at the start of the partnership, one PDR leader repeatedly spoke to district leaders and district professional development providers about the qualities of effective professional development and brought relevant research literature to their attention. External partners also ran study sessions for frontline professional development staff where they read and discussed research on professional development. The research that external partners promoted and discussed emphasized the importance of professional development that was situated at the school site and in the issues, questions, and curriculum that teachers were grappling with. When PDR external partners began their work with the district, there was virtually no professional development in the district that was situated at the school site. Our initial interviews with district staff about their vision of high-quality professional development suggested that it was not a concern for them, as not one district leader mentioned situated professional development as a key element of high-quality professional development. However, by the second year of the partnership, there was nearly consensus that it was problematic that district professional development was not situated at the school site.[8] This value for situated professional development subsequently became important in several decisions that happened in the second and third years of the project, including a decision to reconfigure the design of the school day districtwide to allow time for teachers to participate in professional development on site. All told, ideas, approaches, and ways of thinking that surfaced during external partner-facilitated conversations about research played a role in nine out of the ten decisions where we saw conceptual use of evidence. Interestingly, three of these decisions did not involve PDR external partners directly, suggesting that work with external partners had an impact with how district decision makers thought about instruction and professional development that informed its decision making even without direct involvement of external partners.

In summary, while collaboration with PDR external partners greatly increased the district's access to researchers, research literature, and research-based approaches and ideas, these ideas and approaches did not always play an influential role in instructional decisions made in the district. Few decisions involved use of evidence in an instrumental manner in a central way, and, even though evidence was used symbolically quite extensively—including some of the evidence brought into the district by PDR external partners—it was not always persuasive to district decision makers. There were only two occasions where invoking evidence—either instrumentally or symbolically—encouraged district decision makers to shift their point of view or led to the resolution of differences of opinion. PDR was most successful when the external partners worked with district leaders to create opportunities for conceptual use of research. However, this still occurred in only ten out of twenty-three decisions we analyzed.

Thus, the fact that PDR external partners brought lots of new research, ideas, and connections into the district did not always translate into evidence-based decision making by district leaders.

DISTRICT CONTEXT AND RESEARCH USE

Why didn't the access to research brokered by external partners result in more extensive and substantive use of evidence in instructional decisions? In this section, I argue that the limited role of research in decisions was related to the organizational and social conditions for decision making in the school district.

Deep Differences on Matters of Instruction

In this district, as in many, there were conflicting ideas about appropriate approaches to instruction. The district central office was especially divided on approaches to literacy instruction. While some in the district advocated direct instruction, others advocated a central focus on comprehension and meaning making, and still others focused on culturally responsive approaches to literacy instruction for students of color. There were also conflicts about appropriate assessments for early-grade students, approaches to mathematics education, approaches to professional development, and approaches to leadership development. One of the central intentions of the PDR project was to adjudicate these and other differences by bringing the district's own data and external research into the discussion. The idea was, in the words of one PDR leader, to "discipline the discussion" by holding each position up to the test of available research and district data.

However, when district administrators engaged with research and other forms of evidence in a decision setting, they tended to interpret it through the lens of these preexisting beliefs about instruction. For example, one of the central tasks of the partnership was to develop a framework for literacy to guide professional development and curriculum adoption. The development process was protracted and involved district staff, external partners, and as many as ten external experts in literacy who provided resources and feedback on the framework as it developed. However, how members of the district literacy staff viewed the draft framework depended on their preexisting views about literacy instruction. For example, members of the district who did not support the approaches to literacy contained in the framework argued against the draft document because they did not see it as sufficiently grounded in the research. As one said, "I don't think there was one expert on that thing who did that framework. It was a bunch of people who consider themselves to be experts. But I felt that it was a bunch of garbage." In contrast, those who favored the instructional approaches represented in the framework saw it as research based: "And it's such a research-based document. I mean, really a lot of the people writing about literacy now, we drew from that research." In this decision as in others, district administrators had a strong tendency to discount evidence when it did not support preexisting beliefs or actions (for other examples of this phenomenon, see Birkeland, Murphy-Graham, and Weiss 2005; David 1981; Kennedy 1982). Thus, research and other forms of evidence only rarely resolved differences of opinion when district administrators had contrasting interpretations of its meaning and implications. Instead, when research evidence was invoked instrumentally or symbolically during a discussion, debates about the appropriateness of a solution often shifted to become debates about the quality of the research or evidence.

Complex Organizational Structure

These different understandings of appropriate approaches to instruction were nurtured by the complex organizational structure of the district. Most school districts have highly complex, departmentalized, and multilevel organizational structures (Hannaway 1989; Meyer and Scott 1983; Spillane 1998). Responsibility for instruction is divided among multiple organizational subunits, each of which has distinct yet overlapping sets of responsibilities. As a result, decision making related to instruction is often stretched across multiple units and layers of the central office. In this district, the complex organizational structure tended to foster the development and sustenance of different views of appropriate instruction. For example, members of the special education division had quite different ideas about high-quality reading instruction than those in the curriculum office on the one hand and the English-language learners division on the other. Similarly, members of the research office had quite different views of high-quality assessment and valued outcomes to measure than those in the curriculum office. These differences originated in disciplinary background and training, as those in special education often learned very different things about high-quality instruction in their master's degree programs than those who were subject-matter specialists, for example (Coburn and Talbert 2006; Spillane 1998). The differences were also rooted in the nature of district personnel's work. Individuals in different parts of the district office paid attention to different aspects of schooling, resulting in a quite different assessment of what was going on and how to move the district forward (Coburn and Talbert 2006).

However, while the differences in understandings about appropriate approaches to instruction may have been rooted in disciplinary background and work roles, they were sustained by a lack of ongoing interaction across divisions in the district. Research on social sense making suggests that individuals develop shared understandings through social interaction and negotiation (Coburn 2001; Vaughan 1996; Weick 1995). In this district, as in many, most interaction happened within divisions rather than across divisions. There were few structured opportunities for anyone other than the directors of these divisions to meet and work with one another, even when they were working in the same schools. As such, there was limited opportunity to generate shared understandings across divisions. As a result of this state of affairs, decisions that implicated multiple divisions were much more likely to involve conflicting ideas about the direction to go than those located in a single division. Twelve out of the fifteen decisions that involved representatives from multiple divisions involved conflicting ideas of the problem or conflicting ideas about directions to pursue. In contrast, only three out of seven decisions made within a single division involved conflict. Engagement with the research brokered by PDR external partners and others in a decision context was not enough to shift deeply held views of instruction located in different parts of the district in the absence of substantive interaction across divisions that fostered conceptual use of research.

Resource Constraints

During the time frame of the study, this district experienced an acute contraction of resources. As a result of shrinking state funding and declining district enrollments, the district was forced to cut $20 million from their budget three years in a row. Over the course of the three years of our study, the central office became leaner, while the responsibilities remained the same or increased. The remaining central office personnel picked up more responsibilities, had less time to meet those responsibilities, and had less funding to bring in consultants to help with the work.

The vast decline in resources had a negative impact on efforts to engage substantively with research and other forms of evidence in decision making in two ways. First, resource constraints led to more conservative decision making. I determined that a decision took a conservative path if the solution borrowed heavily from preexisting district practices. In the crush of impending deadlines, district personnel tended to reach to the familiar as the basis for solutions. They were less likely to reach out to external resources from connections brokered by PDR or others, and they were less likely to embrace approaches that strayed too far from existing practice, even when they had research before them that supported those approaches. For example, in the third year of the initiative, district decision makers decided to simply repeat their approach to school-year professional development workshops from the previous year, even though they were aware that teachers and parents had been dissatisfied with the approach. Conservative decision making increased over the three years as resources to search for new and novel solutions became increasingly constrained. Twenty percent of decisions in the first year of our study involved conservative decision making, compared to 57 percent in the second year and 63 percent of decisions in the third year.

In addition, as resources got increasingly tight, there was a shift from more substantive to less substantive use of evidence. More specifically, when resources and time became more constrained, district personnel were less likely to use research in a conceptual manner, less likely to develop shared understandings, and more likely to use evidence symbolically.[9] As mentioned earlier, during early years of the project, district personnel spent time with external partners reading and discussing research literature on key topics under debate, resulting in conceptual use of research in multiple decisions. However, as resources became more constrained, district staff members felt that they had less time for these extended discussions informed by research and data. They had to make decisions at a pace that precluded in-depth conversation necessary to surface and examine underlying assumptions, and they were less able to parlay the discussions that did occur into shared understandings about the nature of the problem or appropriate solutions. Thus, while sustained engagement with research during the first year led to conceptual use in five decisions with shared understanding in four of the five, sustained engagement with research in the second year led to conceptual use in four decisions but shared understandings in only one. Finally, there were no instances of sustained engagement with research at all in the third year.

At the same time that there was a decrease in conceptual use of research, there was an increase in symbolic use as resources declined. During the first year, decision makers invoked research symbolically in 50 percent of the six decisions made that year. But that percentage increased to 57 percent of seven decisions in the second year of the study and 70 percent of ten decisions in the third year. Thus, as substantive use of evidence declined, political uses of evidence increased.

DISCUSSION

In the three years of the initiative, PDR external partners created greater access to research and research-based ideas for district leaders. They did so by bringing research directly into the decision context and encouraging district leaders to attend to it as they made crucial decisions about teaching and learning for the students in the district. They did so by connecting district leaders to individuals outside of the district who could provide expertise and resources on matters of pressing concern for the district, and, initially, external partners also did so by facilitating conversations and study sessions devoted to investigating the district's own data and reviewing and discussing research that offered new ways of thinking about instructional improvement in urban schools. These efforts infused research and research-based approaches into decision contexts, and district personnel reported that they were reading and consulting research to a much greater extent than before the partnership. But having access to research did not always mean that district personnel always drew on it in substantive ways when they made key instructional decisions.

This suggests that access to research, while important, is not enough. At root, research and evidence use is an interpretive process. Individuals bring preexisting beliefs and priorities to the decision setting and use those beliefs and priorities to make meaning of, evaluate, and respond to research and research-based approaches. They may draw different implications from research than that intended by the authors, or they may discount it altogether. Furthermore, district personnel may not always agree about appropriate instructional approaches and the appropriate direction for the district to go. In fact, organizational structures in districts often encourage the development of these multiple priorities and points of view. Absent opportunities to engage with one another and research in a substantive manner, it seems unlikely that the introduction of research findings and other evidence into a heated deliberation will shift deep assumptions about appropriate ways to teach and appropriate ways to improve public schooling.

Resources matter as well. Deliberation takes time. Including relevant decision makers at the table can involve a significant investment in human resources. Searching for, investigating, and working to understand new approaches require effort, access, and focus. As resources shrink in school districts, the conditions for engaging with new ideas and approaches in meaningful, planful, and strategic ways can diminish as well.

This suggests that programs and policies that seek to encourage district leaders to engage with and use research must go beyond access to focus on the conditions for decision making in school districts as well. This study points to potential avenues to explore in this regard. First, in the first year of work with the district, PDR external partners engaged district decision makers in a series of discussions where they read research and discussed instructional approaches and strategies for change. In part, this was an element of the external partners' strategy for building a relationship with the district and jointly identifying priorities for their work together. However, this work had much more lasting effects than anticipated. These conversations, which often occurred outside the context of a specific decision, influenced the beliefs and understandings that district leaders brought to bear on research and other forms of evidence that came up in debates about specific decisions. In some cases—as in the case of effective approaches to professional development—they generated shared understandings so that district leaders from multiple divisions came to the table with some shared ideas that enabled them to better work together toward shared solutions. Most interestingly, the discussions in this first year continued to influence decisions in the subsequent years, even when PDR external partners were not at the table. However, these kinds of conversations tapered off after the first year both because PDR external partners shifted priorities for how they spent their time in the district and because resource constraints made district leaders hesitant to devote time to discussion groups when they felt stretched in their ability to deal with immediate problems that required their attention. Given how important these conversations could be for the quality and deliberativeness of decisions, investing resources to enable district leaders to continue to participate in these discussions over time may go a long way toward encouraging conceptual use of research in district decision making.

Second, this study highlights the need to develop structures and processes to enable individuals in different divisions and different levels of the system to engage with one another on a more ongoing basis. Cross-divisional and cross-level engagement is likely necessary to develop sets of understandings about instructional issues that are truly shared. The presence of at least some shared understandings, rooted in research and evidence, can potentially serve as a base on which district leaders work through remaining differences of opinions on matters of strategy. It may enable continued dialogue rather than the tendency evinced in this district to sidestep debate through the use of such political tactics as narrowing participation, structural elaboration, and uses of authority to shut out opposing points of view. It might also work against the tendency for decisions at one level of the district to be overturned or undermined at another.

Finally, this study highlights the need for adequate resources to support the quantity and complexity of decision making in a given district at a given time. In this study, as resources to support decision making decreased (including time, adequate personnel, and external support), symbolic use of evidence increased and conceptual research decreased. Substantive evidence use requires adequate time and staffing resources to analyze data, to research solutions, and to engage deeply with the evidence and each other in the process of deliberation and debate. All of this suggests that initiatives designed to support districts in using research and other forms of evidence as a lever for improving the quality of policymaking in urban schools must not only address issues of the access and quality of research. They also must design and develop structures and processes to foster social and organizational conditions that enable substantive use of evidence by district leaders, and it suggests being realistic about the resources in time, money, and staffing that it may take to achieve this end.

NOTES

I would like to thank Joan Talbert, Kristin Crosland, Angie Eilers, and Judith Touré for help with data collection and Soung Bae, Judith Touré, Erica Turner, and Mika Yamashita for help with data analysis. Thanks also to the many members of the district and external research organization who gave generously of their time to help us understand their work.

1. I draw on data from a longitudinal case study of one midsize urban school district. From 2002 to 2005, we observed planning meetings and professional development, interviewed district personnel at multiple levels, and collected extensive internal and external documents. We conducted seventy-one interviews with thirty-eight members of the central office and three union officials. We also conducted thirty-one interviews with seventeen representatives from PDR and other external consultants who were working with the district in different capacities during the time of the study. We supplemented the interviews with observations of thirty-three planning meetings and thirty-one days of professional development for teachers and school leaders. Finally, we collected and analyzed numerous documents related to topics that were the focus of instructional decision making during the time of the study.

We identified forty-five decisions related to instruction made by the district during this time and conducted in-depth analysis of twenty-three for which we had at least three independent sources of information. For each decision, we conducted a social network analysis of each person involved in the decision-making process. First, we identified whom each person involved in a given decision was connected with, both inside the district and outside the district, and what flowed across that connection. We coded the degree to which research, instructional approaches, ideas, access to other individuals, or other resources flowed across a given tie. In this manner, we were able to see how decision makers' social networks were related to the kinds of ideas, approaches, and evidence that were considered in the course of each instructional decision. Second, we analyzed each decision for the degree to which research and other forms of evidence were used and how they were used, drawing on a typology of evidence use developed by Carol Weiss and her colleagues (Weiss 1980; Weiss and Bucuvalas 1980; Weiss et al. 2005). Finally, we analyzed each decision for the factors that influenced when and how evidence was used in the decision, using matrices to compare across decisions and to surface and investigate emerging patterns.

2. PDR is a pseudonym.

3. The foundation wishes to remain anonymous in order to protect the anonymity of the district in question.

4. Most (although not all) of the district personnel had ties to the external environment independent of PDR. However, while these ties brought new ideas or advice into the district, most ties did not yield information or advice that was rooted in research.

5. Two of these experts were brought in through the district's own ties.

6. For more details on this point, see Coburn, Touré, and Yamashita (2009).

7. This approach, which required that we actually observe engagement with research, was necessary to distinguish this phenomenon from symbolic use of research. However, it is a rather stringent criterion for determining conceptual use of research and likely underreports its prevalence.

8. It is important to note, however, that conceptual use of research did not always lead to shared understandings, even though it did in this example.

9. The pattern is less clear with instrumental use of evidence. During this same period, instrumental decision making initially decreased substantially from the first year to the second year but then increased again slightly in the third year.

11

⌒⌒

Research to Practice: A Case Study of Boston Public Schools, Boston Plan for Excellence, and Education Matters™

Lea Hubbard

The use of research by district central office leaders is emerging as a critical arena of educational leadership and administrative practice in part because of contemporary education policies that increasingly demand school district central offices to use evidence to ground their educational improvement efforts (Coburn, Honig, and Stein 2009). This case[1] examines one way in which leaders of urban public school systems can thoughtfully engage with research and the conditions that are needed to support such engagement. For more than a decade, reform in the Boston Public Schools (BPS) under the leadership of Superintendent Thomas Payzant was informed by the research efforts of Education Matters™ (EdMatters) a small, not-for-profit research firm led by founder Barbara Neufeld. Between 1996 and 2006 (the retirement of Payzant), EdMatters conducted numerous research studies aimed at providing "useful and usable" evidence to district leaders regarding how reform efforts were proceeding and/or ways in which district operations were facilitating or constraining those efforts.

This case study reveals that not every set of research findings was taken up and used by central office leaders to the same degree. While a study of the district's coaching model represents perhaps the best example of deep and broad use of research evidence for the purposes of refining and improving a key districtwide improvement strategy, other research findings did not appear to be accepted, taken up, and used to the same degree. Here, I take advantage of this variation to try to understand what might have caused the differences in degree of engagement by central office leaders. I do this by examining two in-depth examples of high uptake alongside two examples of more limited uptake. I argue that the difference between high and low uptake was the involvement of a strong and trusted intermediary organization—the Boston Plan for Excellence (heretofore referred to as the Plan) led by Executive Director Ellen Guiney— that functioned to facilitate the development of a shared knowledge base among the three partners (BPS, EdMatters, and the Plan)[2] and provided the capacity to interpret and act on research findings.

I begin by providing background on BPS and reform efforts during this time period. I then examine examples of high and low uptake of research by the district, followed by an analysis of what was different in those instances in which the district most benefited from the research. In the final section of the chapter, I explore the role of the Plan in more detail, including what enabled it to play the all-important role of fostering the uptake of research by BPS.

BACKGROUND

In 1996, Tom Payzant was hired as superintendent of BPS with the full support of the governing board, mayor, teachers' union, and the business community—an unusual congruence for a large urban district (Neufeld and Guiney 2003). From the beginning, Payzant cast his improvement efforts as a partnership between BPS and the Plan. One of the primary functions of the Plan was to act as "a catalyst and support" for Boston's school system and to secure outside funding from an array of private foundations (e.g., the Gates Foundation and the Annenberg Foundation) to help sustain BPS's reform initiatives.

The business community responded positively to the new superintendent, viewing him as a premier leader, mediator, and consensus builder (Nifong 1996). The year after Payzant was hired, a $10 million Annenberg Challenge grant was awarded to the district. The Annenberg monies were contingent on matching funds from the business community and the city. The business community raised $15 million (local and state agencies supplied another $10 million). According to Guiney, this strong business support reflected a new, positive attitude in the community: "It was a new superintendent, a new opportunity for starting over [for a district] that had been 'sleepy under the former superintendent'" (quoted in Vaishnav 2001). Payzant's collaborative style and his ability to attract large foundation-funded grants to improve test scores and to garner national acclaim for excellence in educational improvement reinforced the community's initial optimism. Boston increasingly saw itself as fortunate to have a leader of Payzant's caliber. These positive sentiments enhanced the superintendent's autonomy to make decisions he felt were right for BPS, including his decision to collaborate closely with the Plan.

Among the earliest initiatives undertaken by Payzant was a joint undertaking with the Plan to pilot the Collaborative Coaching and Learning (CCL) model in order to determine its efficacy and feasibility for district-wide implementation. To assess the implementation and efficacy of the pilot reform initiatives, Payzant and Guiney turned to EdMatters, a small, nearby research firm, for assistance.[3] EdMatters has been in existence since 1984. According to its founder, Barbara Neufeld, EdMatters is known for conducting the kind of applied research "that matters," that is, research that is helpful to educational practitioners who are trying to improve their practice. Typically, EdMatters designs and implements evaluations that are focused on ongoing improvement efforts aimed at helping leaders assess whether they are working as intended, redesign them when they are not, and identify challenges to their implementation. As such, our examination of the manner in which BPS used EdMatters's research provides a more focused look at a subset of the ways in which multiple kinds of research can be used by districts, as discussed by Coburn (chapter 10 in this volume). Specifically, this case sheds light on how and the conditions under which formative evaluation efforts that target school and district practices can be taken up and productively used to move improvement efforts forward.

RESEARCH ON BPS PROGRAMS

We turn now to an account of several research projects undertaken by EdMatters on behalf of BPS and the Plan, beginning with two cases that involved energetic district uptake and productive use of the findings, followed by a discussion of two studies that were not taken up and used in the same way. We show that, although EdMatters's reports always received a hearing by district leaders, there were distinct differences in how the district interpreted and acted (or failed to act) on the findings.

The CCL Model

EdMatters's evaluations of the CCL model can arguably be viewed as having the most widespread and deep impact on practice of any of the evaluations conducted by EdMatters. The CCL model had been developed by the Plan in collaboration with BPS educators "as a way to better support the improvement of teaching and learning and better spend the funds allocated to coaching (Neufeld et al. 2002). The model involves teachers working together in small groups with a coach over a six-week period. With support from their coach, the teachers analyze a particular instructional strategy through inquiry, demonstrate it in a lab site, and follow up with changes in their classroom practice. CCL was piloted in selected schools beginning with the 2001–2002 school year.

EdMatters wrote four evaluation reports about CCL. These evaluations examined the CCL process, highlighted its progress, and documented the challenges that accompanied use of the model. The first report (Neufeld et al. 2002), issued when the district decided to scale up CCL districtwide, identified challenges that the district would likely face in schools that did not yet have the organization, leadership, or professional culture that were needed to support the intense work associated with the CCL model.

The next two evaluations (Neufeld and Roper 2002; Neufeld, Roper, and Baldassari 2003) provided in-depth assessments of practitioners' use of the model in a sample of "effective practice" schools (i.e., schools that had been formally recognized as having achieved high levels of implementation of the district's "Six Essentials"). Through observations and interviews with coaches and teachers, EdMatters's researchers paid particular attention to the CCL's key components: the inquiry processes used to analyze instructional strategies and the classroom demonstration lesson. The last of the four evaluations (Neufeld and Roper 2003) focused on experiences with implementing CCL in a sample of schools that had not yet achieved "effective practice" status.[4]

Because of their involvement in the model's initial design, the Plan had a strong interest in EdMatters's findings—those that showed both the model's strengths and its weaknesses. Guiney immediately understood the significance and the helpfulness of the findings and responded to the reports enthusiastically. Her organization took responsibility for publicizing the research evidence widely. The studies were described on the Plan's website and highlighted in two major publications written by the Plan in collaboration with BPS: *Straight Talk about CCL: A Guide for School Leaders* (Boston Plan for Excellence 2003b) and *Plain Talk about CCL: Crafting a Course of Study* (Boston Plan for Excellence 2003a).

EdMatters's research on the CCL model not only made it into print but also directly impacted practice. According to Neufeld, EdMatters's evaluations of the early coaching model led to the complete redesign of the on-site coaching model, a redesign that increased its effectiveness (interview, February 2005). For example, based on the study's findings, a new series of workshops for coaches and other educators was designed and implemented. Another significant redesign element was the careful development of worksheets that served as useful guides for teachers and coaches as they negotiated the process of "crafting a course of study."

In addition, both *Straight Talk* and *Plain Talk* took advantage of the many quotes that EdMatters included in their evaluations to educate teachers about which aspects of CCL seemed to work best and least well. For example, these publications reported "what teachers say" about CCL:

> The CCL allows me to read and study with my colleagues. It puts teachers on the same playing field. . . . I think it's a very good support system for teachers, especially as we all . . . learn this new way of teaching. (quoted in Neufeld et al. 2003, 3, from Neufeld and Roper 2003, 42)

As Guiney noted, these quotes carried a lot of weight because teachers tend to place more confidence in what other teachers say than in administrators' decrees of how instruction should change. Additionally, the quotes helped ameliorate teachers' concerns that CCL was a top-down, district-driven mandate that they were expected to follow.

EdMatters's findings surrounding the CCL model were used in one final key way: to allow the district to make strong recommendations to school leaders regarding the conditions necessary for the effective implementation of the model. In the context of all the positive things teachers and coaches had noted about CCL, the Plan's publications cited findings that indicated the presence of challenges as well. EdMatters referred to these as "common breakdowns" that diminished CCL's effectiveness as a learning tool for teachers. Acknowledging these challenges made it possible to then make recommendations and suggest corrective actions to be taken by principals/headmasters who were charged with implementing CCL in their schools. After careful reading of the study's findings, the district—in consultation with the Plan—felt able to offer guidelines aimed at improving the likelihood that CCL components would all be implemented on a regularly scheduled basis and that they would be aligned with a specific instructional issue. Examples include the suggestion that principals or headmasters "make time [for CCL] and defend it; set clear expectations; and check in regularly, asking probing questions" (Boston Plan for Excellence 2003b, 11). Since EdMatters had found that some CCL courses were too general to be helpful, it was also recommended that schools invest in the planning stages of CCL; principals were urged to bring data to the table to help teachers shape a course of study that would be focused, relevant, and connected to the work of the school and to involve teachers regardless of their individual level of experience (Boston Plan for Excellence 2003b, 11).

To counter some fairly common teacher misunderstandings about CCL that were revealed by EdMatters's research, principals and coaches were advised to try to alleviate teachers' uncertainty by "giving [teachers] good information about the purpose of CCL, what they will get out of it, what it will ask of them and how schedules and lab-site groups will be organized (Boston Plan for Excellence 2003b, 4). Finally, again based on the evidence from EdMatters, it was suggested that coaches and principals/headmasters "practice talking together [with teachers] about instruction," and since "debriefs won't deepen until teachers feel able to talk about the teaching strategy separately from the teachers," principals/headmasters were urged to "seek input [directly] from teachers about how to make debriefs more comfortable and productive" (Boston Plan for Excellence 2003b, 13).

Overall, EdMatters's research on the CCL model had a highly influential impact on the premier reform strategy of BPS. Not only did the research lead to refinement of the model, but it also was used to educate teachers and building leaders about the program and how it could best be supported. Although EdMatters's evaluations of the CCL model may represent the broadest and deepest use of research findings by BPS, other reports were also used in important ways by the district. Another example of an evaluation that was useful to the district was EdMatters's report on the Making Meaning curriculum.[5]

Making Meaning Curriculum

Much of the research performed by EdMatters grew out of the fact that grant awards typically require the recipient to document how monies are used and to provide objective evidence of the effectiveness of the funded reforms. The impetus for the Making Meaning research (Neufeld and Sassi 2004) was different, however, in that it came out of practice. With BPS's approval, the Plan hired EdMatters to investigate how the integration of the Making Meaning curriculum into the district's workshop-based instructional approach could best provide support for improving reading comprehension. They were asked to do this by conducting an evaluation of a yearlong pilot implementation of the Making Meaning curriculum in a small group of classrooms.

Payzant recalled that initially (before the pilot) there were mixed views of whether the district should implement Making Meaning. Ultimately, there was such unanimous support for the program that "it was difficult for me to say no (to the pilot)" (personal communication, Tom Payzant, May 2007). But he also was adamant that an evaluation be conducted to help guide the effort. This district-initiated request illustrates the district's commitment to using systematically gathered evidence to support implementation of a new program.

EdMatters studied three schools, interviewing fourth- and fifth-grade elementary teachers, and found that Making Meaning "could be a valuable addition to teachers' repertoire of literacy strategies and could make a valuable contribution to students' opportunities to comprehend what they read" (Neufeld and Sassi 2004, 48). The report contained notes of caution as well. Quality implementation would require that the district provide teachers with supportive learning opportunities to enhance their ability to use both workshop instruction and Making Meaning materials effectively, and coaches and principals must understand and be able to help others understand how the Making Meaning curriculum could be integrated into the existing workshop model.

The presentation of findings to the Plan and to central office leaders went smoothly. Neufeld explained,

> We all met and we talked about the highlights of the report, and then the idea was "Okay, so what do they do next?" And there was a plan to create a day, a half-day, two half-days of professional development for principals to really give them the feedback—principals who were going to use this [Making Meaning curriculum at their sites]. (interview, February 2005)

In short, all parties agreed quickly that the recommendations made sense. Leaders in all three organizations shared an understanding of the goals and the strengths and weaknesses of the workshop program as it was being implemented prior to Making Meaning. This compatibility allowed them to initially agree on the problem (lack of comprehension instruction) and, once the findings were in, to push forward and decide next steps to determine how they could use the findings to integrate Making Meaning into the curriculum in a way that would strengthened the workshop program.

Soon afterward, the Making Meaning curriculum was adopted, and specific individuals were tasked with organizing the professional development sessions in order to begin to put into place the supports required for its effective implementation.

Other Evaluations and Their Influence

There were other instances of EdMatters's research that, although "heard" by the district, did not result in uptake followed by prominent changes. In these cases, district leaders listened to the findings; however, their responses were bounded. For example, for the "central office study," EdMatters was asked to evaluate the extent to which the central office was operating effectively and efficiently. Neufeld identified a key structural problem with the organization of central office—a problem that resulted in inconsistent messages being sent to principals. According to the deputy superintendent for teaching and learning, EdMatters's study produced findings about the administration's support of schools and brought to light "disconnects." EdMatters found places "where there are disconnects between either the deputies across the schools, or between the chief operating office and myself, and the deputies and that whole structure." The report noted that the central office was sending "mixed messages, depending on who was speaking to a school" (interview, September 2005).

In this case, the problem identified was an exceptionally challenging one, one that would require deep shifts in district organization to remedy. One concrete step that was taken immediately was the crafting of a letter that was sent to all principals about consistent expectations and nonnegotiables. To reinforce the message that central office leaders were on the same page, the letter was sent out over the signatures of all of the deputies. Although the deputy stated that they would be taking additional actions to "bring greater coherence across all the separate people whose work is related but distinct," no such actions were evident during the time period of our research.

In another example, EdMatters was asked to evaluate the initial stages of a high school reform effort (hereafter referred to as the HSR study). In 2003, BPS received a large grant from the Carnegie Corporation and additional funding from the Gates Foundation. The purpose of these grants was to fund high school renewal that would improve student literacy and reduce students' alienation from school. Much of the effort was to go toward restructuring high schools into smaller, more personalized environments for students. EdMatters was hired to evaluate a small sample of schools that had been selected to begin these restructuring efforts. In this case, EdMatters's evaluation reports (Neufeld, Levy, and Chrismer 2004, 2005) were the subject of prolonged negotiations about their content and findings, and, at the time of our data collection, their findings have not been used directly by the district.

However, while the district has been more reticent, the Plan has gone forward and disseminated the findings from the report. The Plan reported on the HSR evaluation in *School Clips* (March 1–31, 2006), a Plan publication with wide circulation inside and outside the Boston area, and also briefly summarized the findings on their website. Both steps had a significant impact on the awareness of people in the district as well as nondistrict educators and others.

The lack of uptake and, more important, remedial action by BPS did not go unnoticed. A *Boston Globe* editorial (May 18, 2006) singled out HSR as one of the most salient issues facing Boston's next superintendent (Payzant's retirement was effective June 2006). The editors noted that given the "uneven results" of HSR and EdMatters's recent findings showing that "students [are] not experiencing the expected benefits of smaller school settings," Payzant's successor would need to address the comprehensive reform of high schools, a task that "remains undone." While the Plan's coverage of the HSR evaluation apparently had succeeded in creating some awareness at the community level, the research had not yet affected practice.

CONDITIONS ASSOCIATED WITH MORE OR LESS UPTAKE

What accounts for the very different receptions received by each of these evaluations? Even more important, why were some successful in impacting practice while others were not? My analysis suggests that research was taken up and used in significant ways when 1) there was a shared knowledge base among the three leaders that could be used to frame the studies and interpret their results and 2) the capacity to act on the findings was ready, available, and willing. These conditions are discussed further next.

Shared Knowledge Base

The CCL and Making Meaning studies met with the highest degrees of success. Not only were their findings easily understood and accepted by district leaders, but they were also able to quickly assess the implications of those findings for practice. We argue that this "easy uptake" of research findings was the product of a high degree of common understanding around instructional matters that was shared by the BPS leadership, the Plan, and EdMatters. This shared knowledge base, we argue, came into play—however discreetly—in how the studies were framed, how they were carried out, and how their findings were interpreted and communicated. In contrast, the three leaders did not share a knowledge base for framing or making sense of the findings produced in the central office study and the HSR study.

In the cases of CCL and the Making Meaning evaluations, the shared underlying knowledge base that both framed and provided a context for understanding EdMatters's research findings centered on the importance of instructional improvement to districtwide reform. Our interviews provide evidence that all three leaders privileged instructional improvement as *the* key vehicle for transforming the district. When it came to setting goals and objectives and interpreting what needed to be done to improve teaching and learning in the district, Payzant and Guiney, in particular, were "on the same page." Guiney summed up their shared views this way:

> First of all, he [Payzant] knows we're in sync and that the key to all of this is instruction. People will learn more if they are taught better, period. You got to do a whole bunch of other things too, and he knows that, but at the heart of it is that belief [in instruction] and he knows we share it . . . he uses us (the Plan) sort of to test things out, you know, to work it out. He has a lot of trust in us. (interview, February 2005)

Guiney emphasized the importance of this kind of shared understanding. "We (the Plan) don't work with people who don't agree with our theory that this is how kids learn more," she stated. And, in describing what she valued most about the work that EdMatters undertakes, Guiney noted that Neufeld "knows what she's seeing, and I think there is a lot of agreement between us—what constitutes a high level of instruction and, you know, the high cognitive demands . . . what do [teachers] accept as evidence from kids? She [Neufeld] seems to really get it" (interview, Guiney, February 2005). The two women also agreed on good practice—what it is, how to support it, what changes are required, and how to change beliefs in order to prevent teachers from slipping back into their old practices. According to Guiney, another strength that Neufeld brought to the table was that she fully understood that if progress is to be achieved, practitioners must have a voice, and researchers must value or at least understand practice. Guiney noted that "[Barbara] very often hones in on the right things . . . she quotes teachers a lot" (interview, February 2005).

Capacity

As much as district leaders may understand research findings, those findings will not significantly impact practice absent district capacity to refine a poorly performing program or to design and implement additional programs. In the case of the central office study, capacity appeared to be lacking to design creative alternatives to the current managerial structure (B. Neufeld, personal communication). Despite the recognition that the current structure was causing difficulties, district leaders either lacked the know-how, the time, or the willingness to confront the situation and change it. Similarly, the HSR study findings were argued (by Payzant) to be an artifact of the particular schools that were studied and thus were dismissed as not indicative of the real problems that needed to be solved, thereby putting off an action plan for high school reform. According to the *Boston Globe* editorial (May 18, 2006), the development of a plan for dealing with the problem of high school reform was left undone by the Payzant administration.

In the two successful examples of uptake, the capacity to digest, understand, and act on CCL and the Making Meaning findings was evident in the quickness with which new and/or improved processes were put into place. In both cases, a large share of this capacity came from the Plan. The Plan not only instigated EdMatters's evaluations of the CCL model and the Making Meaning curriculum but also was an important partner in interpreting and acting on the results. With CCL, their intimate involvement can be traced to the fact that the evaluation was focused squarely on an innovation that they had helped to create and that they had the capacity to improve. Moreover, their belief in and affinity for the CCL model meant that using EdMatters's research for its promotion and its support (by addressing some of the common implementation breakdowns identified in the EdMatters's reports) was viewed as a logical and positive step in the right direction. Although not involved with Making Meaning in the same intimate way, the Plan nevertheless was on familiar instructional ground and understood how the adoption of Making Meaning by the district would improve the workshop model of instruction in the area of reading comprehension and that the Making Meaning curriculum would intersect productively with the CCL model. They were able and eager to set into motion professional development related to the districtwide rollout of Making Meaning.

In summary, the successful instances of research uptake were associated with a high degree of shared understanding among the three partners. We have argued that this understanding provided a conducive context for a fair hearing of EdMatters's research results by framing the results within a common framework of the kind of ambitious instructional practice the district wished to see in its classrooms. In addition, we have argued that strong uptake resulted when there was the requisite capacity to respond productively to the report's findings. Without the expertise and resources required to address problems uncovered by evaluations—or the time to learn what they needed to know—evaluations did not have their intended impact.

The Plan

Interestingly, the presence of a shared knowledge base among the three partners and the capacity to act on findings coincided with those instances in which the Plan was more centrally involved in the setup and use of the research findings. When they were not centrally involved—as in the central office study and the HSR study—EdMatters's findings were more susceptible to dispute, alternative framings, or dismissal. Here we argue that the key feature of the Plan's involvement was its capacity to act as a "boundary spanner" between BPS and EdMatters; that capacity, in turn, was directly related to the degree of trust that Guiney had engendered with both Payzant and Neufeld.

The Plan as Boundary Spanner

As studies were being designed and carried out, frequent, purposeful discussions helped keep all three parties informed, although the discussions did not always involve all three leaders simultaneously. The Plan often channeled information from BPS to EdMatters and from EdMatters back to BPS.

According to Neufeld, at different points in the process of designing and conducting an evaluation, she and Guiney held telephone conversations that basically were off the record but that offered very important opportunities to exchange views and avoid missteps. Periodically, when both leaders found themselves "terribly frustrated about something," they would talk out the problems. Conversations between Neufeld and Guiney could have far-reaching implications because, as Neufeld put it, "there is a way in which that organization is her and this organization is me." Their autonomous decision-making authority made each "key to what [our organizations] do" (interview, February 2005).

At the same time, Guiney and Payzant met regularly at a standing monthly meeting. Although these meetings covered a range of issues, at times, Guiney carried information regarding how the EdMatters's research was progressing. This is not to say that the three leaders never met together. Tom Payzant described his understanding of the three organizations' collaboration this way:

> There's involvement in terms of "what do we want to look at? What do we want the evaluation to do?" And then Ellen and Barbara and I usually have a conversation together about that, and getting agreement on the "what." And then we often have a conversation about the sampling of schools—which schools will be the focus and where the researchers will go, and then I'm pretty much out of it until a draft report shows up. (interview, February 2005)

Neufeld drew attention to the many negotiations that occurred as the three leaders worked to identify topics for investigation, to design appropriate studies, and to craft final reports: "There was a lot of negotiation. . . .

So from the beginning . . . there's been, I guess, call it a collaborative process of negotiations around different things" (interview, February 2005). The "different things" open to negotiation included the purpose and design of an evaluation, including agreement on the pertinent questions and the methods to be employed such that there would be no controversy around whether what EdMatters produced had validity and merit.

Neufeld pointed out that, over time, many more people were "at the table," and Payzant became somewhat less involved. Similarly, at certain times, such as when Neufeld reported the findings from her study of the district's high school renewal project directly to Payzant and his deputies, Guiney was out of the loop (phone conversation with Barbara Neufeld, May 2007).

When the Plan was less centrally involved, the use of research findings was more limited. A case in point was the HSR study that was undertaken under the auspices of the HSR committee comprised of BPS and four external partners, one of which was the Plan.[6] Working through such a complicated set of partners made agreement difficult and caused Payzant to push back against any attempt to generalize from EdMatters's findings from a small sample of schools. These schools, he argued, were plagued with problems from the start. Thus, he contended that EdMatters's findings, although valid for those schools, were not a fair reflection on the soundness of the reform efforts. He worried that EdMatters's reports could jeopardize a second round of funding and cause pressure from some of the HSR group's partners to back away from the systemic policies for high school renewal.

It is impossible to know if the course of events would have been different had the Plan been more centrally involved in mediating between the district, the external partners, and EdMatters in the HSR study. In this case, the presence of additional partners appeared to have further complicated the direct uptake of research findings. Nevertheless, as I argue next, there was a deep reservoir of trust between the Plan and the district and between the Plan and EdMatters. I contend that this trust enabled the Plan to be an effective boundary spanner in the first two cases of high uptake, while its absence in the latter two cases was associated with less commonality between BPS and EdMatters with respect to the definition of the problem and fewer shared ideas about potential remedies.

Trust

The unusual degree of trust between Payzant and Guiney was of long standing. Before coming to Boston, both had worked in Washington, D.C. (Guiney as Senator Ted Kennedy's "education person" and Payzant as President Clinton's assistant secretary of elementary and secondary education). Their jobs created and deepened a shared knowledge base about school reform, professional development, and instructional practice. Later, while serving as members of the Pew Forum on Education Reform, they became further aware of each other's perspectives and developed an effective working relationship. As Mary Ann Cohen of the Plan explained, even before Guiney and Payzant had left Washington, the two had envisioned a close partnership between BPS and the Plan. Their two organizations would be formally independent, but they would embody their leaders' shared vision, loyalty, and trust. Cohen put it this way: "It all has to do with . . . improved student performance. So, we [the Plan staff] are not going to go on a tangent and suddenly decide to take on [something different]." Moreover, she continued, since the two leaders were able to anticipate each other's actions and perspectives with a high degree of accuracy, the superintendent could be confident that Guiney would "never spring anything on him, or go off in a different direction or take on, particularly an issue with the schools that he didn't think was the right way to go" (interview, September 2005). Guiney's and Payzant's mutually predictable behaviors and their shared understandings further strengthened their already strong bond of trust.

A similar confidence-inspiring overlap in perspectives grew between the Plan and EdMatters. Guiney, who was a firm believer in independent evaluation, first began working with Barbara Neufeld when she hired EdMatters in the winter of 1997 to assess their earliest efforts in the Boston schools. Guiney knew that EdMatters was widely considered to be a trustworthy and reliable organization, but before making her final decision, she was careful to confirm that Neufeld's experiences, perspectives, and priorities were compatible with her own and with the superintendent's.

Interestingly, the trust between Guiney and Payzant and between Guiney and Neufeld appeared to have engendered trust between Payzant and Neufeld as well. In our interviews, Payzant, who described Neufeld as a "known quantity," echoed Guiney in emphasizing how much he trusted her and the work produced by EdMatters. Throughout the interviews we conducted for this case study, Payzant, Guiney, and Neufeld each repeatedly emphasized the importance of keeping people informed and of respecting boundaries. Since the superintendent could be reasonably confident that Neufeld would not intentionally jeopardize their productive working relationship by "surprising" him, he was comfortable with the repeated use of EdMatters as an outside evaluator.

The importance of Payzant's trust in the Plan and in EdMatters cannot be underestimated. In the first years of the reform, some individuals within BPS's central administration questioned the relationship between BPS and the Plan. The superintendent intervened swiftly. He successfully quieted concerns by making it clear that he valued the Plan's work, a strong testament to his commitment to an ongoing relationship with the Plan. Moreover, he demonstrated his trust in Guiney by also supporting the work of EdMatters when she hired the firm to evaluate the Plan's efforts to assist with the BPS reform. Because of Payzant's strong endorsements, the work with the Plan continued without interruption, EdMatters was able to conduct on-site research and evaluations, and support from key constituents in the Boston community was sustained.

SUMMARY AND CONCLUSION

In a climate in which evidence-based decision making is put forth as the treatment du jour, district leaders feel obligated to justify their practices based on data, the assumption being that data-based practices are superior to practices based on intuition or conventional wisdom. Yet, as a field, we know little about how and under what conditions districts can productively use research findings to improve their practices. The present case provides a focused look at when and how findings from evaluations of improvement efforts did and did not positively impact the trajectory of a large urban district's improvement efforts.

Research evidence does not speak for itself; it must be interpreted in order to be understood and acted on (Coburn, Touré, and Yamashita 2009; Kennedy 1982). This study reinforces and extends earlier work that established the role of interpretive frames in data use by illustrating that the interpretative frames must be shared among independent partners in order to lead to the productive uptake of findings. In this case of a three-way partnership, uptake was found to be more successful when the frameworks that the partner brought to the interpretation of findings were shared. When the district leader, the director of the intermediary, and the head of the research firm shared an understanding of instruction and its role in districtwide improvement, they were able to frame, interpret, and act on the research findings with much greater effectiveness than when they were operating on less articulated and less shared understandings of the problem and potential solutions.

Research findings can still fail to influence practice, however, when, despite agreement regarding what the findings mean, there is a lack of capacity for learning from the evaluation. Neufeld, in her more recent writings, has identified several possible reasons for the lack of use of research findings by district leaders:

> Districts generally lack a formal process by which high level administrators learn from their school improvement efforts . . . philosophy and deeply held beliefs are valued more than evidence in district-level discussions . . . central

office administrators may have competing views about what constitutes
good instruction . . . [the] superintendent and other central office administrators may believe that hiring the right person is the way to succeed with
instructional improvement . . . [they], too often, have little opportunity to
learn what they need to know . . . and there are structural, time-related factors that stand in the way of their use. (Neufeld 2007)

In this statement, Neufeld is referring to capacity very broadly—the
capacity to learn from evidence. Research is largely silent on what successful district leaders do when they productively frame and learn from
research conducted on their behalf.

In the present case, the positive instances of research uptake involved
active participation by a third party, in this case, a local education fund.
The Plan drew on a deep reservoir of trust between its director and the
district superintendent to act as a boundary spanner between the district
and EdMatters. This trust appeared to "spill over" into the relationship
between the superintendent and the director of EdMatters. No doubt, the
trust was instrumental in setting into motion a self-reinforcing cycle in
which the district supplied transparency and access that, in turn, allowed
EdMatters to gain better data from practitioners that, in turn, led to more
valid and useful findings.

While previous studies have illustrated the positive functions that intermediaries like the Plan can and do perform (Datnow and Honig 2008),
the epilogue to this case also reveals potential limitations to three-way
relationships: When the vast majority of communication and trust resides
primarily in the upper layers of management, the arrangement becomes
susceptible to leader turnover. After Payzant retired in 2006 and a new
superintendent was hired, the Plan no longer enjoyed the access that it
had under Payzant. The standing meetings were off, and the taken-for-
granted shared goals for district improvement no longer existed. Pres-
ently, Guiney is in the process of rebuilding trust and shared understandings with the new superintendent. At the same time, EdMatters, no longer
the first evaluator of choice, is in the process of reestablishing a reputation
with the new superintendent. Had bridges been formed at middle layers
of management, perhaps the positive relationship could have continued
unabated.

NOTES

1. Data for this case study were collected during January 2005 and October
2005. Using a case study approach (Yin 2003), we conducted interviews of key
stakeholders in Boston Public Schools (BPS), the Boston Plan for Excellence (the
Plan), and Education Matters™ (EdMatters) in order to learn about the work of

each organization and about their interactions. At the Plan, we interviewed Executive Director Ellen Guiney, the assistant director for instructional improvement, the communications director, as well as staff researchers. At BPS, we interviewed Superintendent Dr. Thomas Payzant, the deputy superintendent, the superintendent for teaching and learning, the assistant superintendent for teaching and learning, the School Leadership Institute director, and an elementary school headmaster. We also interviewed the Boston Teachers Union president. At EdMatters, we interviewed President and Executive Director Barbara Neufeld and several staff researchers. A total of fifteen interviews were conducted; all were taped and transcribed verbatim.

We also consulted the organizations' websites for background information and analyzed numerous documents detailing the work of EdMatters, the Plan, and BPS. We triangulated the data from these sources (i.e., from the interviews, observation, documents, and websites) and then coded and analyzed these data (Miles and Huberman 1994). We also engaged in a process of member checking (Creswell 2009; Patton 2002) with the primary participants to ensure that our findings were consistent with their understandings. Data were collected with the assistance of Virginia Loh and Tricia Gallant.

2. For a complete text of the mission statements of the Plan and EdMatters, see http://www.bpe.org and http://www.edmatters.org.

3. EdMatters conducted its first evaluation for the Plan during the 1996–1997 school year when it was asked to evaluate some of the Plan's early work in BPS, including an initial coaching effort. EdMatters was also hired to do the initial evaluative work for the Boston Annenberg Challenge in 1999.

4. For further details and the complete text of each of these reports, see http://www.edmatters.org/reports.html.

5. Making Meaning was created by the Developmental Studies Center, a private firm based in Oakland, California.

6. There was pressure from some of the HSR group's partners to back away from the systemic policies for high school renewal. Abandoning the reform work would have undermined the district's efforts to improve high schools.

12

✺

Key Lessons about the Relationship between Research and Practice

Cynthia E. Coburn and Mary Kay Stein

In the past two decades, researchers and practitioners have worked to forge new ways to bring research and practice together in the service of school improvement. University researchers, national nonprofits, and school and district leaders have crafted new models for developing research-based innovations and creating conditions in schools and districts that are more conducive to ongoing learning and improvement. However, much of the work of these endeavors has been private. We hear about the products but not about the process by which the new approaches and innovations are created and sustained. At the same time, there is a vigorous debate at the policy level about the best way to improve the quality and reach of educational research. Yet this debate happens largely in the absence of evidence from existing initiatives that are already doing this work.

This book remedies this problem. By studying the work of ten nationally known research-and-development projects, this book moves past the rhetoric to examine what it means to bring research and practice together in productive ways. We focus on the reality and complexity of how research and practice actually interact with one another. It is only by understanding the potential and the possibility of how things work that we can identify new systems, structures, and policies that can help make the initiatives profiled here the norm rather than the exception.

In this chapter, we look across the ten individual case studies to surface key lessons about bringing research and practice together for school improvement. The lessons are organized according to the sections of the book, beginning with lessons about productive collaboration, followed by lessons about the role of tools in bringing research-based practices to scale. We then move to the practice side of the equation. We discuss ways to create conditions in schools that are conducive to engagement with research-based ideas and the ongoing challenges of using research in decision making at the school district level. We close this chapter with implications of these lessons for designers, school and district leaders, funders, and universities.

PARTNERSHIP FOR EDUCATIONAL INNOVATION

This book provides much-needed examples of the ways in which researchers, practitioners, and others can interact productively to support educational improvement. Despite the many challenges to joint work, researchers and practitioners in the Middle-School Mathematics through Applications Project (MMAP; chapter 2), the Center for Learning Technologies in Urban Schools (LeTUS; chapter 3), and the Information Infrastructure System Project (IIS; chapter 4) were able to manage and use diverse resources, build trust for collaborative work, and develop shared understandings of the meaning of their work together.

For decades, research on collaboration has pointed to the importance of trust (Bryk and Schneider 2002) and shared frameworks for joint work (Gorman 2004). And we have known for some time now that complex tasks require input from individuals with diverse knowledge and skills (Derry, DuRussel, and O'Donnell 1998). The research on MMAP, LeTUS, and IIS extends these findings in at least three ways. It demonstrates the need for participants to stake out new identities if research and practice are to be bridged in more than a temporary manner. It teaches us about the dividends paid by early investments in the development of trust once pressures mount to scale up. And these cases show that work on mutually valued products can foster the development of shared mental models that can guide the work.

The Opportunities and Challenges of Diverse Partners

Researcher–practitioner collaborations are a key strategy for developing educational approaches that are rooted in research but also can work in the complex world of the school and classroom. Such collaborations gain their strength because they tap differing forms of expertise and diverse perspectives. To quote an oft-cited sentiment, "People can help each other learn when they use their differences" (Bredo 1992, 35). Nevertheless, if participants have goals, identities, and incentive structures that are too dissimilar, it can be difficult to find common ground, relevant problems for mutually engaging joint work, or enough commitment to sustain work toward an agreed-on goal. MMAP, LeTUS, and IIS had different strategies for balancing multiple perspectives and diverse forms of expertise with enough overlap in participants' goals. Ultimately, those projects that required participants to forge new professional identities were better able to sustain long-lasting collaborative work that stretched beyond the bounds of a single project to become a new way of interacting to support educational reform.

In the case of MMAP, intense and productive researcher–practitioner collaboration occurred early in the partnership, producing lasting goodwill, but did not produce a foundation for work beyond the project. As Engle demonstrates in chapter 2, the inclusion and good use of diverse partners was the centerpiece of the MMAP project. MMAP actively sought out and managed diversity by recruiting individuals who possessed varying viewpoints and expertise but, at the same time, had enough overlap in goals with other project participants to be able to find mutually engaging problems on which to work. However, when pressures to scale up their work occurred, MMAP participants became less intent on problematizing the work and returned to an organizational arrangement in which less diverse sets of individuals assumed responsibilities for meeting deadlines and producing a product. In the end, although their intellectual lives had been greatly enriched by the cross-institutional work, the MMAP participants retained their identities as practitioners or particular kinds of researchers or curriculum developers. The earlier, more integrated phase of MMAP can be viewed as an intense but time-bounded "boundary encounter" (Wenger 1998), that is, as a foray of researchers and practitioners into the practices of each others' communities that required the temporary crossing of boundaries that typically differentiate those who belong to a community and those who do not. While perhaps leaving the individuals open to future such encounters, it did not create a forum for ongoing mutual engagement beyond the bounds of the project among this particular group of researchers and practitioners.

In LeTUS, by contrast, joint work led to lasting changes in the identities of both researchers and practitioners—changes that sowed the seeds for work that continues to this day. In chapter 3, D'Amico explains how researchers entered the collaboration with a commitment to focus on practitioners' problems of practice but perhaps an incomplete idea of what that would entail. Early on, when their district partners insisted that the project focus on the design of curriculum units (not stand-alone activities, as initially envisioned by the researchers), the researchers, none of whom considered themselves to be experts in curriculum, were forced to reconsider their identities as researchers in their respective fields of expertise. In the long run, participation in the LeTUS project changed the career trajectories of LeTUS researchers as they moved toward more of a focus on curriculum design and professional development. Many LeTUS researchers are now viewed as pioneers in creating a new kind of work that represents a "boundary practice" (Wenger 1998). That is, they have created a novel set of work habits and routines that are located between the conventional practices of the researcher and practitioner communities, reflecting more than a temporary crossing of boundaries between the two. Perhaps as a result, the legacy of the LeTUS project is an ongoing set of relationships between university-based researchers and district-based individuals in Detroit and Chicago that enables a continuing set of joint projects that builds off and extends their earlier work together (MacArthur Network meeting, January 2006).

Finally, the IIS case teaches us that boundaries between diverse practices do matter and that, absent attention to managing diverse talents and perspectives, individuals may retreat to their own ways of viewing the work and have difficulty negotiating new, mutually productive solutions. Because its partners were the most diverse, the IIS project represents the greatest challenge to managing diversity. As Rosen explains in chapter 4, IIS appeared to have assembled an ideal mix of differential expertise (the IIS project team had the academic know-how, the Literacy Collaborative had the clinical know-how, and Teachscape had the scale-up know-how) and overlapping goals (all partners aspired to a long-term collaboration that would result in getting more useful, evidence-based tools into the hands of more educators and also generate revenue). Yet tensions emerged that were related to the differential expertise and diverse perspectives held by the various partners. For example, because of its business interests and scaling-up expertise, Teachscape wanted to move quickly to widespread use of the new tool. Because of its long-standing concern for quality and the privacy rights of teachers, on the other hand, the Literacy Collaborative insisted on moving slowly and "getting it right" before moving to scale.

This dynamic was illustrated by the Area 15 incident, where the Literacy Collaborative and Teachscape joined forces to create professional development for much larger numbers of participants than had heretofore been involved in the project. At that point, a joint solution appeared distant because of tensions between Teachscape's commitment to scale and the Literacy Collaborative's identity as careful, up-close researchers and developers. Because the Literacy Collaborative partners—indeed most design-based partners—typically have not conducted research or designed at scale, constructing the frameworks or models that would allow them to do so would constitute a transformative shift in how they view themselves as educational designers and researchers. At the same time, a joint solution would also have required a shift for Teachscape's identity inasmuch as the Literacy Collaborative approach demanded a focus on close-in work to a degree that challenged Teachscape's modal way of working. Both parties had important and worthwhile concerns, but neither could afford to hold on to their old worldviews completely if this new product was indeed going to be unique and successful. When this chapter was written, the jury was still out on whether the Literacy Collaborative and Teachscape found a common space in which to move forward.

Development of Trust

Although the virtues of trust have been noted for small-scale collaborations, there is less research on how trust develops and is used over time as well as the challenge of sustaining trust when expanding to larger and increasingly diverse groups. All three cases suggest that time spent early in a project's life span building trust pays off in the long term.

For example, Engle shows how the early attention to establishing group norms and collaborative processes in the initial phase of the MMAP project led to the development of a reservoir of goodwill and trust. When the work later became deadline driven and more constraining, that reservoir paid huge dividends. Similarly, in LeTUS, the trust that was developed during the early phase of curriculum development work laid the groundwork not only for the expansion to joint work around professional development but also for the development of a long-lasting cross-institutional partnership.

The IIS case points to the difficulty of establishing trust in alliances between academic and commercial entities, each with their own, very different traditions of how to accomplish work and some degree of mutual suspicion. Moreover, it teaches us about the complexities introduced when trust must be built across three rather than two entities. Indeed, in chapter 4, Rosen shows us that trust was established between the IIS project team and each of the other two partners (the Literacy Collaborative and Teachscape), but there appeared to be less attention to the development of trust between the Literacy Collaborative and Teachscape. The case vividly illustrates the importance of three-way relationship building in the early stages of such complex partnerships.

Development of Shared Mental Models

In order to work productively across different institutional settings, the participants in all three cases had to establish some common understandings of the purpose and meaning of their work. In each case, codevelopment of joint products played a critical role in building shared mental models across participants from diverse backgrounds. Joint products provided a common focal point for discussions during early critical phases. For example, D'Amico illustrates how LeTUS participants' early curriculum development work focused on "curriculum seeds," or partially completed instructional designs from earlier projects. Similarly, MMAP participants' earliest work sessions focused on a broad map of the proposed unit along with sample activities or prototypes of software. Because these initial artifacts were only partially completed, there was ample room for negotiations over how they might be further developed. In both projects, teachers were encouraged to create that which did not already fully exist, providing space for multiple people to make contributions, leading to feelings of mutual understanding and joint ownership.

Artifacts also played a critical role in the development of shared mental models between Teachscape and IIS leaders early in the project. The leaders began with a vision of a technological tool that would be used by literacy coaches in their professional development work with teachers. Rosen argues that it was not until mock-ups of the tools were designed and discussed, however, that IIS and Teachscape participants could gauge the extent to which they had a shared vision of what the tool might look like and be able to do from the user's perspective. Successive iterations of the tool during the initial design phase provided a concrete focus for a series of conversations that were critical to their codevelopment of shared mental models.

The design of joint products also served to reveal differences in goals or ideas about how to reach goals during the beta phase of the IIS project. After working on parallel but separate tracks for a period of time, the Learning Collaborative and Teachscape joined forces to codevelop an implementation curriculum to be used in the Area 15 trial. Their attempted collaboration revealed a distinct lack of a shared understanding about the work.

All this highlights challenges that those engaged in collaborative work must be prepared to encounter and also suggests ways to overcome those challenges. First, extended collaborative work that breaks new ground often demands that individuals rethink past practices and entertain new identities. Relinquishing old, comfortable ways of approaching work—

ways that are sanctioned by one's community—represents a loss. Engaging in collaborative practice can test individuals' willingness to experience that loss and create something new but untested. These cases also illustrate the importance of shared frameworks for collaborative work and bring to light a novel method of establishing such frameworks: partially completed artifacts that necessitate participants to fill in the "blank spaces." Not only do such artifacts test whether individuals are on the same page, they also provide opportunities for the establishment of new, shared constructions of the meaning of the work before them.

ROLE OF TOOLS IN BRIDGING RESEARCH AND PRACTICE

This book also provides lessons about how tools can bridge research-based knowledge and educational practice on a large scale. Tools are curriculum materials, observation protocols, rubrics, and other materials that seek to embody research knowledge in ways that are usable in practice. Because research knowledge is embedded in the tool, tools are uniquely positioned to carry that knowledge to large numbers of teachers, schools, and districts.

Three cases—Success for All (SFA; chapter 5), the Institute for Learning (IFL; chapter 6), and the Quantitative Understanding: Amplifying Student Achievement and Reasoning project (QUASAR; chapter 7)—provide evidence that tools may be designed in substantially different ways, with implications for how they function to link research and practice at scale. In SFA, research was embedded in highly specified tools and used by teachers to deliver effective practice directly to students. In contrast, the IFL and QUASAR cases illustrate the use of tools that were designed to reach students indirectly, that is, tools that target teachers (and other professionals) and their understandings and beliefs about practice. As explained by Ikemoto and Honig in chapter 6, the IFL developed a set of tools that communicate the implications of a broad body of research (i.e., advances in cognitive science) for thinking about one's own practice. Unlike the SFA tools that embody a set of research-proven practices directly in the tools themselves, the IFL tools shape practitioners' thinking to align with research-derived principles. Similarly, QUASAR tools were designed to help teachers notice specific features of their own practice and to relate them to a larger set of research-based ideas about how to maintain the cognitive demands of instructional tasks. These different ways of embedding research in tools have implications for the manner in which tools influence teacher learning and professional development and for the trade-offs between specificity and adaptation in tool design.

Teacher Learning and Professional Development

Because the tools were designed in such different ways, the three cases broaden our understanding of how people learn from and with tools. In particular, they demonstrate how certain kinds of learning are constrained or afforded by different tool designs. In chapter 5, Datnow and Park describe how, in the first phase of SFA, teacher learning was primarily about how to use the tools with professional development focused on making sure that teachers used the tools "correctly." As SFA moved to "goal-focused implementation," however, the developers began to value principled adaptation of tool use as well. In order for teachers to be able to make principled adaptations, however, teachers needed to possess and use judgment and reasoned interpretation. Therefore, SFA revamped its professional development sessions so that they focused on making the research ideas embedded in tools more explicit and helping practitioners to understand how to maintain the integrity of those ideas when using the tool.

Honig and Ikemoto make the case that IFL used tools to help practitioners develop research-based understandings; to learn how to use those understandings to identify, label, and talk about key aspects of practice; and, ultimately, to construct new practices that align with the research-based understandings. As such, learning was not conceptualized as learning to use a tool that then closely guided one's practice. Instead, practitioners were assisted to develop conceptual understandings of research-based ideas through IFL-led tool-based professional development and then to create locally appropriate practices that instantiated those ideas. This creation of research-aligned practices occurred with the assistance of IFL-trained coaches.

The QUASAR tools represent a third approach to teacher learning. As Baxter argues in chapter 7, QUASAR tools were not intended to be used as research-proven models of "effective practice" as is the case with SFA or a template from which teachers learn to create a practice that is aligned with cognitive principles as with IFL. Rather, the QUASAR tools guided teacher learning by helping them reflect on their instructional practice. QUASAR used a research-based framework that highlights how students' opportunities to learn are dependent on the kinds of thinking and reasoning that their classroom-based experiences require of them. QUASAR tools assisted teachers to understand research-based patterns of practice that impact students' opportunities to learn, to critique their own practice with respect to those patterns, and to formulate ways to improve their own practice to be more helpful to student learning. Through traveling back and forth between the general patterns and specific instances of teaching and learning in their own classrooms, teachers learned to make sense of the particularities of their own practice with reference to a larger set of research-based ideas.

These contrasts suggest that tool designers have a broad range of choices with regard to how to design tools to promote teacher learning in ways that align with research. Equally important, however, is that professional developers need to be aware of the particular kinds of learning afforded by different tools so that they can design, adapt, or carry out professional development in ways that will be supported by the tool. Thus, an important new design feature for tools might be explication of the kind of teacher learning supported by the tool along with how professional development might support that learning, something rarely made explicit in most tools.

Navigating Tensions between Tool Specificity and Adaptation

These cases also offer lessons regarding different approaches to navigating the tension between specificity and adaption when designing tools for use in practice. On the one hand, tools must have some degree of specificity and stability because they are meant to bridge research and practice across many sites and across time. On the other hand, specificity and stability can present problems because the kinds of practices that these tools are meant to impact are context dependent and interactive and, therefore, cannot be entirely specified in advance. Therefore, tools must be designed with some room for adaptation but not too much room lest the adaptations create a practice that is unmoored from the deeper meaning and structure of the tool. SFA and QUASAR, the two projects that focused primarily on instructional practice, placed their bets in very different places with regard to where on this continuum from specificity/stability to adaptation their tools would fall. Their respective "bets," in turn, appear to relate to their assumptions about how students learn in an instructional context.

Datnow and Park describe how SFA brings research to instructional practice using a specific and stable set of tools that guide teacher execution of instructional practices. The developers made this decision based on research that has shown that these instructional practices will—under a particular set of conditions—produce a desired set of student learning outcomes. Their decision also rests on the assumption that students learn from well-designed tools enacted by conscientious teachers who assure their proper use. QUASAR tools, on the other hand, help teachers to reflect on practice (their own and others') using a framework that makes salient that students' opportunities to learn are dependent on the kinds of thinking and reasoning in which they engage in the classroom. This approach to tool design rests on the assumption that students learn from their interactions with teachers and other students surrounding complex academic tasks and that instruction cannot be entirely prescribed in advance but rather must unfold based on the goals of the lesson and students' thinking. Instead of scripting a specific set of instructional practices, QUASAR researchers designed tools that provide frameworks within which teachers can think about and make sense of their practice in terms of how it impedes or facilitates students' learning.

There are also different consequences for scale associated with these different approaches to specificity versus adaptation. The highly specific SFA approach has resulted in a set of tools that tend to retain their integrity across time and sites. This approach, along with the intensive professional development that routinely accompanies the tools, leads to greater stability of enactment across sites. However, because of the interactive and context-dependent nature of instructional practice, it may not lead to the desired outcomes in all contexts. To address this concern, the SFA designers have targeted a specific context and population of teachers as places where their program should be implemented: high-poverty schools in which students are traditionally underserved by inexperienced teachers who turn over frequently (Slavin 1997). QUASAR tools, on the other hand, because they are based on the assumption that teaching is inherently complex, do not offer a specific set of teaching practices that will always work to produce student learning. Rather, they offer a way for teachers to make decisions while teaching and to reflect on their practice based on an understanding of how student learning occurs. While not leading to a singular, recognizable "QUASAR" enactment across sites, this approach is applicable across more teachers and sites.

All this highlights the tight connection between how tools are designed and their constraints and affordances for teacher and student learning. Tools that are designed to "reify" research findings demand a different kind of teacher learning than tools that are designed to be an object for discussion or a framework for reflection. Finally, the design of tools reflects designers' views of how learning occurs and what stands the best chance for increasing the odds of improved student learning in particular settings. More highly specified tools place their bets on student learning from proven materials in specified kinds of settings, whereas less specified tools place their bets on teacher learning of how to interpret and improve their practice through engagement with a research-based framework.

CONDITIONS TO FOSTER
KNOWLEDGE DEVELOPMENT IN SCHOOLS

While the development of new tools can assist teachers in engaging with new research-based ideas and practices, tools alone may not be sufficient for sustained involvement with research-based practices absent attention to the conditions for learning and change in teachers' workplaces. The cases of Lesson Study in Bay Area School District (LS; chapter 8) and the National Writing Project (NWP; chapter 9) provide insight into strategies for addressing and improving conditions for teachers to engage in ongoing learning. More specifically, both of these initiatives developed structures and processes to foster knowledge development and, at the same time, created pathways for research ideas to feed into these processes.

At the core of both initiatives is the opportunity for teachers to engage with each other and knowledgeable others about problems of practice that are central to their work. Although they use somewhat different approaches, both LS and the NWP have developed what Laura Stokes in chapter 9 calls generative processes for knowledge development through which teachers come together to develop new approaches to instruction in a dialogue between research ideas and classroom experience.

These processes of knowledge development share several key features. First, both LS and the NWP involve iterative experimentation where teachers get together to plan or develop new approaches, experiment with them in their classrooms, and then reconvene to reflect on their experience, adjust, and experiment again. This cycle of experimentation and reflection challenges the norm of privacy in teaching that is endemic in public schools by putting teachers' practice on the table for observation, discussion, and critique. Further, because the learning opportunities are situated in teachers' classrooms, the approaches promoted in both LS and the NWP provide a concrete mechanism to literally bridge the gap between research and practice. For example, in chapter 8, Perry and Lewis argue that the public lesson structure of LS rendered research more accessible because it connected research ideas to specific instructional moves or classroom environments. Stokes argues that the norms of critical inquiry in the NWP enabled teachers to work together to interrogate new ideas and approaches, fit them together, and create new approaches that bring research and practice together in useful and usable ways. In this way, both projects enabled teachers to integrate new approaches into real classrooms in all their complexity.

Equally important, both initiatives created mechanisms for verifying the effectiveness of new ideas and approaches teachers developed and modified in the interrogation and experimentation process. As Hiebert, Gallimore, and Stigler (2002) caution,

> Professional knowledge . . . must be accurate, verifiable, and continually improving. There is no guarantee that the knowledge generated at local sites is correct or even useful. Teachers working together or a teacher working with his or her students might generate knowledge that turns out to undermine rather than improve teaching effectiveness. (8)

Both LS and NWP use evidence of student learning as a central mechanism for testing and verifying instructional modifications. In Lesson Study, participants, aided by well-crafted tools, collect systematic evidence of student learning during the observation of the research lesson. During the debrief, teachers and other participants draw on these data to assess the impact of the lesson on student learning and revise the lesson in response. Perry and Lewis provide evidence that, over time, this practice created what they call "a new currency" for evaluating research ideas in practice in the school: observational data on students. Similarly, Stokes shows how evidence from student work is the ultimate arbiter of successful practice in the NWP. Both chapters argue that the knowledge developed from these processes is more robust because any new approach—whether emerging from research, practice, or some combination of the two—is held to the standards of student learning in real classrooms. Furthermore, in the case of the NWP, the structure of regional networks that bring individuals together from diverse sites means that new approaches are held to standards of student learning in multiple classrooms that span across many diverse contexts. This increases the likelihood that new practices will be suitable for diverse classrooms, in turn increasing the scalability of the new instructional approaches.

Third, both chapters make the case that these structures of interaction created cultures of critique that differ substantially from those present in most schools. Stokes documents how the NWP fosters a culture of questioning and critique. At every level of the system, teachers and others learn to critically interrogate and question ideas and approaches. Perry and Lewis document an increased openness for new ideas and approaches. They argue that the publicness of practice in LS surfaces competing assumptions about mathematics teaching and learning as teachers are exposed to alternative points of view, gaps in their own knowledge, and compelling new ideas. Interaction with others raised questions about mathematics instruction that teachers did not know that they had and motivated them to reach out to others, sometimes beyond their school walls, for answers. Perry and Lewis document a modest but steady increase in the requests for external sources of information, including research, among teachers over the six years of their study.

Finally, one of the most important features of knowledge development activities in LS and the NWP is that the knowledge development did not happen in isolation among a group of teachers or a single school. Rather, both initiatives created pathways to support the flow of ideas and resources into local knowledge development activities. In Lesson Study, teacher leaders fostered connections to university researchers and a local foundation that provided sustained access to research, curriculum materials, and other resources for doing lesson study. The structure of the public lesson itself also fosters the flow of ideas into design and development activities. The tradition of public lessons in Japan is to bring together guests from inside and outside a school to participate. In the Bay Area School District, teacher leaders replicated this tradition, inviting local researchers and mathematics educators, and even used grant funding to bring lesson study practitioners from Japan to participate in public research lessons. In this way, public lessons brought a range of perspectives, ideas, and expertise to the investigation of classroom practice and student learning that were not readily available in the school itself. These new ideas helped teachers see new possibilities and think about their problems in new and different ways.

In the NWP, these pathways were institutionalized to a much greater extent and at a much greater scale than LS. The NWP has an infrastructure that links local sites to each other, to regional and subject-specific networks, and to the national office. This infrastructure allows resources from NWP sites across the country to flow into local and regional design and development activities. But it also provides pathways for knowledge developed locally or regionally to flow out and be shared with NWP sites across the country. For example, the rubric developed by the Improving Students' Academic Writing (ISAW) network charting the development of students' academic writing flowed up to the national office, where it was shared with NWP sites across the country. Teacher leaders used the rubric as well as some of the instructional approaches developed by ISAW participants as they provided professional development to schools in their areas, providing teachers across the country with access to the new instructional approaches developed by the ISAW participants. Stokes argues that it is this feature of the NWP that "enable[s] the building of cumulative leadership and knowledge capacity for the improvement of teaching."

By putting these structures in place, both LS and the NWP have created conditions for learning and knowledge generation that are unlike those that exist for most teachers in public schools. They have created conditions for collaborative problem solving where new ideas are discussed, debated, tried out, and scrutinized for their impact on student learning. They have created pathways to feed this design and development work with ideas, research, and research-based approaches. And, in the case of the NWP, they have created systematic mechanisms for sharing the fruits of this knowledge development activity with others. In this way, both of these initiatives have created a fertile environment for research–practice exchange—an environment that perhaps makes it more possible that teachers and others bring research ideas into their classrooms and sustain them in ways that support learning for their students.

RESEARCH USE AT THE DISTRICT LEVEL

Finally, we turn to an arena that has received less attention in the debates about the relationship between research and practice: the use of research in school district policymaking and practice. Most efforts to increase research at the district level to date have focused on increasing access to research and data. However, the Partnership for District Reform (PDR; chapter 10) and the partnership between Boston Public Schools, Boston Plan for Excellence, and Education Matters (EdMatters; chapter 11) help us see that access to research is a necessary but not sufficient condition for substantive use of research by school district central offices.

In both of these cases, the partnership between districts and research-based intermediary organizations went a long way toward increasing access to research and research-based approaches for school district decision makers. In her discussion of PDR in chapter 10, for example, Coburn shows that decisions involving representatives of the external research organization were three times as likely to involve research and research-based ideas as those decisions involving district personnel alone. The strength of the PDR approach was that external partners were able to bring research right into decision makers' hands in a timely and targeted manner and work side by side with district leaders as they engaged with it. Similarly, in the Boston case, EdMatters was able to present research findings directly related to the district's own practices at moments that decisions about how to improve or continue them needed to be made.

Yet both of the cases also provide evidence that decision makers tended to discount evidence that they did not agree with. In chapter 11, Hubbard shows that researchers and district personnel in Boston disagreed with the analysis when they lacked a shared framework for evaluating the evidence. Coburn shows that research almost never changed the mind of district leaders in the course of deliberation when they had conflicting views of the action to take. Further, even when district leaders carefully considered research at one stage of the decision trajectory, other individuals at different stages or in different parts of the system could and did disregard research or undercut the decision.

The partnerships profiled here were most successful at facilitating productive engagement with research when they created opportunities for district leaders to engage with research and research-based ideas in ways that enabled all involved to question their assumptions and challenge their frames. For example, Coburn illustrates how the external research organization's efforts to create study groups and discussion sessions outside the decision context in PDR enabled a very different kind of research use. Rather than drawing on research directly to make decisions, this kind of engagement enabled district leaders to work with one another to think about their problem and solutions in different ways. This conceptual use of research, as Carol Weiss (Weiss and Bucuvalas 1980) calls it, had a much greater impact on district decision making than attempts to integrate attention to research findings into the actual deliberations in cabinet meetings and other decision settings. And its impact was felt for several years after the initial study groups as shared ideas built together continued to play a role in decision making, even when the external partners who facilitated the conversations were no longer involved in the district.

Ikemoto and Honig's discussion of the IFL's work with school districts (chapter 6) also speaks to this point. These authors show how engagement with well-crafted tools, coupled with assistance from IFL providers and adequate time for district leaders to discuss the implication of research for their work, shifted and deepened district personnel's understandings of research-based ideas related to teaching and learning in ways that influenced district policy and practice.

Opportunities such as those afforded by IFL and PDR are rare in contemporary school districts and, as Coburn shows, are likely to decrease as budgets tighten. Yet engagement with research outside the time-bound context of deliberation and debate appears to be crucial if district personnel are to integrate new ideas and approaches into their work in substantive ways.

The partnerships between districts and research intermediary organizations were also most successful when they attended to the social aspects of research use. These cases suggest that district leaders' responses to research depended not only on the nature and quality of the research itself but also on the social interactions that accompany the research. This is highlighted most clearly in Hubbard's account. Strong relations of trust and frequent opportunities for communication between the leadership in the Boston Public Schools and the leadership at the Boston Plan for Excellence and EdMatters enabled the district to open itself up for scrutiny and enabled the partners to have hard conversations about research findings on the district work. Having some shared understandings also enables productive exchange. Hubbard argues that shared vision of high-quality instruction was the foundation for the productive research–practice partnership. This vision of instruction shaped what researchers from EdMatters attended to and made the findings more believable and actionable for leaders from the district and the Boston Plan for Excellence.

However, Coburn's account illustrates the difficulty of attaining these shared understandings in school districts. She argues that the complex organizational structure of the district tends to foster the development of different points of view as those in different parts of the district have different disciplinary backgrounds, different work roles, and different ways that they focus their attention. In some ways, the Boston partnership circumvented these difficulties by focusing primarily on the top leadership level of the district. But this strategy is risky. In the Boston case, it led the partnership to be vulnerable when the superintendent eventually stepped down one year after this study was completed (Neufeld and Guiney, MacArthur Network meeting, January 2008).

Finally, these cases highlight the role of district capacity. Prior studies of research use have focused on the need to develop a district's capacity to analyze data and critically evaluate research findings (Burch and Thiem 2004; Corcoran, Fuhrman, and Belcher 2001; Mac Iver and Farley 2003). The cases profiled here suggest a different point. Even when the districts profiled in these studies engaged with research in a substantive manner and it informed their design work, they did not always have the human and other resources and infrastructure to orchestrate and support new designs or new initiatives that emerge. As Hubbard's case illustrates, the district was most able to leverage formative evaluation findings to make changes in the design of initiatives when they had the capacity to do so. In the Boston example, the capacity was enhanced by the presence of a local intermediary organization that acted in partnership with the district. But, as Ikemoto and Honig caution in their chapter on the IFL, not all local intermediaries have the capacity to work with districts in this way.

All this suggests the need to design systems in districts that take into account what we know about how people engage with new research-based ideas and approaches. And it suggests renewed attention to district capacity—not only the capacity to access, interpret, and bring research to bear on specific local problems but also the capacity to orchestrate systemwide responses as well.

Taken together, the ten cases profiled here help us move beyond the linear model of the relationship between research and practice. First, while the linear model assumes that the source of innovation is the research community, the cases in this book illustrate that there is a much broader range of possibilities for bringing research and practice together for school improvement. Innovation can emerge from practice, as the cases of QUASAR, LS, and the NWP illustrate. Here, research and researchers learn from innovative practice and create conditions to feed research ideas and approaches into practitioner experimentation in systematic ways. In still other instances, innovation is initiated by intermediary organizations collaborating with schools and districts on one hand and with researchers and universities on the other, as illustrated by the Boston Plan for Excellence and IFL. Finally, research *can* be a powerful source of educational innovation, as in the case of SFA and other projects not profiled in the book, but it is only one among several pathways to meet this goal.

These cases also highlight the fact that a broad range of actors not only may be involved but may play critical roles as well. While the linear model focuses attention primarily on researchers and practitioners, the research-to-practice equation does not implicate these actors alone. The cases profiled in this book also involve commercial partners, nonprofit intermediary organizations, and funders. These actors play crucial roles in the research–practice interchange, from being the agent that brings research and practice together to inform district decision making (as was the case with the Boston Plan for Excellence and IFL) to being the main vehicle for bringing research-based tools and curricula to scale (in the cases of IIS, MMAP, QUASAR, and LeTUS). Solutions to address the problem of research in public education must pay attention to these actors and institutions as well.

Third, these cases highlight the importance of attention to how people in schools learn with and from research-based innovations. Attention to the dynamics of learning and the organizational contexts that shape that learning can lead to a better match between tools that carry research and the learning needs of practitioners, stronger coordination between innovation and professional development to support its use, and intentional efforts to foster conditions that are more conducive to deeper enactments of new approaches and greater likelihood of sustaining new approaches over time. This suggests the need to move beyond the metaphor of "dissemination" to pay close attention to the conditions and practices of learning.

IMPLICATIONS FOR RESEARCH AND PRACTICE

The case studies profiled in the book provide a vision of the possible. But they are exceptions rather than the norm. Here, we draw on the lessons from the book to suggest actions that can be taken by key actors to enable these types of projects to be more widespread and more sustained and thus to touch more teachers, schools, and children. We start by discussing implications for those who design curricula, frameworks, and processes that bring research and practice together. Next, we turn our attention to school and district leaders who seek to create conditions in schools for engagement with research and research-based practices. We then discuss implications for funders concerned with leveraging research to support instructional improvement. Finally, we talk about the implications of these cases for new ways of training researchers and designers and supporting research faculty as they become engaged with this work.

Implications for Designers

The cases profiled here suggest that designers should place renewed attention on teacher learning and organizational change. Typically, research-and-development efforts are focused primarily on creating classroom approaches or materials that promote student learning. This is, of course, critical. If the ultimate goal is to promote student learning, then designers must focus attention on how instructional approaches meet that goal. However, our cases suggest that an intentional focus on teacher learning may also be critical if teachers are expected to integrate new, research-based instructional approaches in ways that support their student learning goals. New approaches may not be used or may be used in partial or superficial ways absent attention to how teachers learn to use an instructional approach and integrate it into their classroom practice. To add complexity, our cases suggest that different kinds of instructional tools may require different approaches to teacher learning, depending on the designers' conceptions of student learning and their vision of how the teacher will interact with the tool.

Yet designers are rarely explicit about the demands that new approaches place on teachers or the ways to link approaches to professional development to the specific learning demands of their tools. When designers do focus on teachers, they tend to focus on how teachers should teach rather than how teachers might *learn how to teach* in ways that their research suggests would be beneficial for students (Fishman and Davis 2006). Our cases suggest that explicit attention to how teachers learn—and how they learn differently to use different tools—is an important piece of ensuring that research-based approaches actually make it into classroom practice.

Issues of organizational or systemic change to support teacher learning are even further marginal in most design efforts. Yet the cases profiled here suggest that the practice side of the research–practice equation matters for research-and-development activities, and it matters significantly. Most designers of educational innovations—research based or otherwise—have had the experience of struggling with implementation because of contextual conditions in schools or districts. Indeed, there are legions of studies that document the challenges of implementing new instructional approaches in schools (Berends, Kirby, Naftel, and McKelvey 2001; Datnow, Hubbard, and Mehan 2002; Gurthrie 1990; Spillane, Reiser, and Reimer 2002; Tyack and Cuban 1995). To address this concern, many designers—including those involved with several of the projects profiled here—involve practitioners in the design effort. The rationale is that practitioners bring knowledge about what is feasible and practical in the real world of schools and that this knowledge can increase the likelihood that research-based designs will be "usable" in practice. This strategy focuses on the tool itself, using practitioner knowledge to try to create a better match between the tool and the contexts in which the tool will be used.

But this study suggests that designers can create designs that address the context of schools and classrooms as well. The cases of NWP and

LS suggest that it is possible to foster contexts for teachers that enable them to engage more substantively with new tools and approaches and use them to make changes in classroom practice that support student learning. The conditions in NWP sites and LS sites did not happen by accident. Through a combination of well-designed tools to foster particular kinds of interaction among teachers, participation structures that linked experimentation to student outcomes, and intentional pathways to bring research and research-based ideas into local deliberations, these two projects created fertile environments for teachers to engage with, come to understand, and enact new research-based ideas and approaches. Designers should not only pay attention to the instructional tool but also consider ways to foster environments in schools that are more conducive for teachers to learn new approaches carried by the tools.

Implications for School and District Leaders

School and district leaders are also in a position to influence the conditions for learning new approaches and practices. Districts and others have spent an enormous amount of time and effort creating better access to information and data as a way to bring research and data to bear on improvement efforts. They have purchased data systems and trained school and district administrators to use these data systems. But these cases show that access to data, high-quality research, and research-based innovation may be insufficient for transforming teaching and learning in schools and decision making in districts. At the school level, teachers and school leaders need opportunities to learn new approaches, to experiment and reflect, and to adjust approaches in response to evidence of student learning. At the district level, having access to evidence does not mean that district leaders will use it.

This suggests that district leaders place renewed attention on the conditions for engagement with research and data. At the district level, this means creating opportunities for district administrators to learn about research related to its issues and needs outside the decision context. Research presented during the decision context has little likelihood of influencing preexisting beliefs, given limited time and the high-pressure setting. Instead, districts can create seminars, working groups, or opportunities to engage directly with researchers so that district leaders can work with one another to interpret research findings and discuss implications for district work in more depth and in a less politicized setting. Occasions such as these may be tough to prioritize given the fast pace and limited resources at the district central office, but they may be critical if district staff want to use research and evidence in more than a superficial or symbolic manner. District leaders should also consider creating opportunities for cross-unit discussions of key issues involved in instructional improvement outside the decision context. The cross-divisional engagement enables district leaders to develop shared understandings of the problem to solve and appropriate coordinated action.

At the school level, the cases profiled here suggest the importance of structures at the school site that foster teachers' ability to experiment with new approaches in their classroom, discuss that experience with their colleagues, and adjust their practice in dialogue with evidence of student learning. The work of both LS and NWP also suggests the benefit of linking school-based communities to one another and to knowledge resources outside of schools. Districts might consider developing networks of teacher leaders that link schools to each other and the district. These teacher networks can serve as intentional pathways for carrying new ideas into schools to inform teachers' local deliberation. At the same time, these networks can provide a mechanism for sharing local knowledge development efforts that show promise at improving student learning beyond the school.

Second, the cases in this book suggest that school districts consider partnering with intermediary organizations to support the development of local capacity. Not all districts have the human resources or infrastructure to support new designs or new initiatives. Even if district personnel draw on research or data to diagnose problems and identify solutions, they may not have the capacity to orchestrate these solutions systemwide. Studies of research-based intermediaries suggest that these organizations often have credibility with school and district personnel because they are able to integrate research knowledge with an awareness of local needs and conditions, thus supporting its effective use (Corcoran and Rouk 1985; Spillane and Thompson 1997). The case studies in this book provide examples of partnerships between intermediary organizations and district central offices that aimed to orchestrate systemwide improvement efforts, including providing professional development to schools (Boston Plan for Excellence) and using research-based tools to directly build the capacity of district personnel to support instructional change (IFL). Districts should use caution with this approach, however, as not all intermediary organizations support research-based solutions. And the lesson of the Boston case is that it is important to build connections with local intermediaries at both the top level and the middle level of the district. Connections at the middle level of the district alone may result in projects that are disconnected from or marginal to the district's main priorities. Yet connections to the top level alone may make it difficult to sustain agendas and relationships in the face of leadership turnover.

Implications for Funders

Foundations have become increasingly interested in supporting educational improvement efforts by funding the development of instructional approaches, tools, and curricula designed to carry research and research-based approaches into schools. However, this funding is often focused on the development of a specific project or tool. In these instances, researchers, practitioners, and others come together to develop this tool, approach, or curriculum. When the resources run their course, partners go their separate ways, on to new projects or the busywork of their everyday jobs.

The cases in this book suggest rethinking this approach to funding research-and-development efforts. These cases show that it takes time and energy to create and sustain the collaborative relationships necessary for productive partnerships. Trust is difficult to build. It takes time to negotiate common agreements about appropriate work roles and to develop shared mental models. Doing this kind of collaborative work requires individuals to extend themselves in ways that challenge typical roles and identities. Yet in the project-by-project model of funding, these relationships and roles must be developed anew for each and every project, and this is ultimately very resource intensive. Furthermore, this approach to funding design and development can result in a fragmented approach to educational improvement if the individual projects are not well coordinated. This approach thus can limit long-term, focused work where initiatives build on each other over time.

The LeTUS case suggests the importance of funding the development of an infrastructure to support long-term collaboration across individual projects and partners. The LeTUS project built on prior relationships between Northwestern University and the Chicago Public Schools on the one hand and the University of Michigan and the Detroit Public Schools on the other. The relationships, capacity, and ways of working fostered in the LeTUS project have since been tapped repeatedly for a series of grants to support research-and-development work that takes up where the LeTUS project left off (D'Amico 2005). To this day, several projects that could be considered "grandchildren" of LeTUS continue to extend the partnership and the work. Because the LeTUS participants built a network of ongoing relationships and linked projects together over time, they were able to produce a stream of high-quality products and to continue to build the capacity of the district to provide high-quality instructional guidance in science education to teachers. Yet this long-term relationship has been possible only because the team has been successful at attaining and knitting together a series of individual grants (MacArthur Network meeting, January 19–21, 2006). This work shows the benefits from sustained partnership, but it is rare to find in practice because it is so challenging to achieve the sustained funding to enable it to occur.

Rather than fund individual projects, funders could support more coordinated work and deeper partnerships by funding efforts to create institutional infrastructures that support partnerships between researchers and practitioners. The Strategic Education Research Partnership (SERP) provides one model of what this might look like. SERP has a mission to build sustained collaboration between researchers, educators, and designers as a way to encourage innovative research and development. It does this by developing and supporting long-term collaborative relationships between select major urban districts (so far, Boston and San Francisco) and their local research universities. These partnerships are focused on joint research-and-development around problems of practice identified by the local district. SERP's role is to convene the partnership, foster relationship building, and create parameters for joint work. This coordination helps ensure that individual research-and-development projects that happen under the auspices of SERP build on each other and work toward district-identified goals, resisting the inevitable pull of fragmentation. Furthermore, these individual research-and-development efforts do not have to forge working partnerships anew.

Funding the development and maintenance of the sort of infrastructure that SERP and LeTUS have achieved represents a shift in strategy from the more typical approach of funding individual projects. Yet this approach may ultimately lead to a more efficient, more coordinated approach to leveraging partnerships for high-quality educational research and development.

Second, funders should also attend to the multiple pathways by which research and practice interact in productive ways. The largest funder of educational research in the United States is the Institute for Education Sciences of the U.S. Department of Education. Since 2002, this agency has structured its grant giving in a manner that implicitly follows the linear model—that is, as a one-way pipeline of research into practice. Applicants are instructed to locate their proposed research into one of a series of phases of research to practice. Those phases portray a unidirectional flow from basic laboratory studies intended to uncover new principles of learning, to studies that aim to design interventions based on those principles, to small-scale studies of the efficacy of the research-based intervention, and, finally, to large-scale studies that test the effectiveness of the design at scale. Applicants who step into the flow at any point upstream from basic research are required to substantiate that their work builds on proven or promising research findings.

This book suggests limitations with this approach. As our case studies illustrate, basic research does not always flow to practice in the way imagined by the linear model of research to practice. Basic research is often not picked up and used in more applied settings; practitioners are often not aware of the latest advances. Similarly, knowledge and insight can also emerge from practice. In recent years, some federal funding agencies involved in medical research and the social and behavioral sciences have begun to recognize the limitations of the linear model as well. This recognition has led to the identification and funding of a new form of research—translational research—which focuses on encouraging a two-way flow of activity: from research to practice but also from practice to research. Translational research emphasizes the development of in-depth knowledge of the practice side of the research–practice equation. Its advocates argue that bringing research and practice together requires an understanding of the practitioners and practice-based settings that might benefit from research knowledge.

Our study suggests that the structure of federal funding for education should be adjusted to acknowledge and indeed encourage the two-way flow of activity. That is, applicants should be able to propose work that is inspired by practice-based observation as well as work that builds on fundamental research. We have also argued that equal attention needs to be paid to the conditions in schools and district that actually work against practitioners picking up and using research. Funding structures must acknowledge this, too, and direct funds for understanding and leveraging the practice side of the equation as well.

Implications for Research Universities

Finally, this study has important implications for schools of education and other institutions that train researchers and designers. First, these cases show how this kind of work requires researchers to play new roles. Researchers in the projects profiled here chose problems to work on not based on disciplinary specialty or their potential contribution to theory but rather to address real-world problems. The world of practice is not carved into disciplinary slices, so doing research for and with practitioners often requires researchers to move beyond their disciplinary training or to collaborate with others across disciplines.

Similarly, the work of partnership requires human relations skills. As MMAP, LeTUS, IIS, and the Boston case vividly illustrate, working together across institutions requires trust and the development of shared understandings to guide the work. Yet researchers typically are trained as if their work will be individual work. Students in many universities lack sufficient opportunities to learn how to partner, build trust, and work with people with diverse expertise and statuses, yet it is exactly these skills that may make the difference between successful partnerships or not.

Universities could rectify these problems by providing a range of training experiences to enable aspiring researchers and designers to build their knowledge of the real work of schools and districts and to learn how to work on the problems of practice in cross-disciplinary collaborative teams. These training experiences could start with course work that emphasizes field experiences to help researchers and designers become more intimately familiar with issues facing schools and districts. This approach to instruction could combine participation in educational settings with theoretical and empirical research that contextualizes and illuminates the issues observed and final projects that require students to develop research or design plans that address problems or challenges observed. Universities could also design courses that enable students to learn how scholarship in different disciplines might be productively combined to address various issues in public schools. Such courses could be cotaught by faculty with different disciplinary backgrounds and emphasize how theoretical approaches and methodologies from different disciplines might inform a problem that crosses disciplinary boundaries.

Course work could be paired with opportunities to apprentice with researchers or designers who are engaged in collaborative work with local schools. Ideally, student apprentices would be able to participate or observe all phases of the research or design process. The specific approaches may vary depending on the kind of research or design involved. But, regardless of the approach, students should have access to the processes of negotiating the parameters of joint work, building trust, using artifacts to facilitate the development of shared mental models between research collaborators and practitioners, and other activities that support sustained collaborative work. It is important to note that the framework for training we advocate here, which emphasizes collaboration with practitioners and across disciplines, does not preclude the development of disciplinary expertise. Rather, it involves developing future researchers and designers who have disciplinary grounding or depth of focus in a specific area but also have enough breadth of experience and knowledge to be able to engage, communicate, and productively work with others in improvement efforts that may stretch beyond the bounds of disciplinary expertise.[1]

Beyond training for novice researchers, universities also create a series of disincentives for their research faculty to do this kind of research and design work. Promotion criteria in many research universities work against collaboration, valuing single-authored publications beyond all others and struggling to find metrics for assessing the degree of individual contribution to a joint or collaborative product. Universities also tend not to have agreed-on ways to assess the quality of or to take into account the contribution of tools, curricula, or other educational designs (Burkhardt and Schoenfeld 2003). Applied research in general and applied research that crosses disciplinary boundaries in particular are seen as low status in the university context (Schoenfeld 2009). Yet being responsive to the nature of problems of practice may require researchers to move beyond their disciplinary specialties, taking on new foci and identities. Perhaps because design research and collaborative work more broadly with schools and districts challenge traditional university promotion and review practices, across the case studies in the book, it was much more common to find researchers involved in these collaborations who were non–tenure-line or very senior tenured faculty. Early career tenure-line faculty were few and far between.

In order to support the kinds of research-and-development efforts profiled in this book, universities may need to develop ways to acknowledge and reward design work as part of tenure and promotion policies. This may include developing a set of criteria for assessing the quality of tools, curriculum, and other products so that they may be counted as part of scholarly output. Universities could place a stronger emphasis on collaborative work by valuing coauthored publications in review and promotion decisions. Practices could be developed to assess individual contributions to collaborative work for universities that are concerned about the difficulties of assessing individual contributions. Absent this sort of reorientation in the procedures for assessing and evaluating faculty productivity, it seems unlikely that collaborative work will become more than the occasional boundary encounter between senior tenure-line faculty and public school educators.

Universities could also support faculty in pursuing this kind of work by funding research centers that are problem focused, that is, centers that focus on bringing research to bear on problems that public schools identify as pressing needs. These centers could draw faculty from schools of education and as well as related disciplines in configurations that address the needs of schools. Centers of this sort would have the added benefit of serving as training grounds for a new generation of researchers in training. Universities could also offer internal seed grants to foster interdisciplinary collaboration. Finally, universities can develop and support long-term partnerships with local school systems. These partnerships can take different forms, but the goal is to encourage faculty of multiple ranks to work with each other and local educators on research projects that respond to local needs. Universities could take these and other steps to value ongoing generation of knowledge that sits at the boundaries of the world of research and the world of practice.

Bringing research and practice together for school improvement is a complex process precisely because it implicates multiple actors and institutions. Yet the projects profiled here have found ways to work across institutional differences and coordinate the work of multiple, disparate actors to promote instructional improvement. By taking seriously the challenges these projects faced and the strategies they developed to overcome them, the field can begin to take steps to develop policies and practices that are more supportive of productive research–practice exchanges.

NOTE

1. We are grateful to Alan Schoenfeld for helping us to articulate this last point.

Appendix:
Research Methodology

This study took place under the auspices of the MacArthur Network on Teaching and Learning. In 2000, the John D. and Catherine T. MacArthur Foundation provided funding for a distinguished panel of scholars and practitioners to investigate ways to bring research and evidence to bear on educational improvement efforts.[1] After careful investigation, the Network determined that there were many programs and initiatives that were successfully bringing research and practice together for school improvement but that little was known about what these initiatives were doing or the conditions that supported their work. They decided to make investigation of these efforts one of several initiatives of the Network's work. The editors of this book were then asked to direct this research effort, which was dubbed by the Network as the "metastudy." From 2002 to 2006, we directed the study of ten projects and programs that were rethinking the relationship between research and practice for school improvement, with support and guidance from the Network.

CASE SELECTION

Our aim was to select cases that spanned a multitude of ways in which research and practice might be organized. Thus, to guide our case selection, we did a scan of existing efforts to reconfigure the relationship between research and practice and used this scan to develop a typology. We developed this typology both deductively and inductively. We began by reviewing relevant literature on the relationship between research and practice in school improvement. Because this research provided little guidance, we shifted to an inductive approach, identifying six national projects that represented different strategies.[2] We then conducted a thorough review of the published and unpublished literature on the projects, using the constant comparative method (Glaser and Strauss 1967) to identify key contrasts in the ways the projects drew on and contributed to research knowledge, development knowledge, and practitioner knowledge as they did their work. Drawing on both sources of data, we identified four classes of activities: design research, designing for scale, the development of accounts of educational improvement, and the development of systems for documentation, codification, and sharing of practitioner knowledge. We summarize each class of activity here.

Design Research

Researchers in this tradition seek to work collaboratively with practitioners to design a learning environment or innovation and then study the impact of this environment or innovation on learning (Brown 1992; Cobb et al. 2003; Collins 1992). This class of activities is viewed as both pulling from and contributing to both research and practitioner knowledge. Design researchers purposefully work in the complex setting of real classrooms, schools, and districts, drawing on both preexisting research and practitioners' knowledge of the complexity of the setting to coconstruct a design. In many cases, the design is in response to problems as defined in and by that setting (Brown et al. 1999). Projects in this tradition purposefully structure iterative cycles of design and redesign based on careful analysis of process and outcomes. These endeavors seek to contribute to both practice and research. They seek to develop innovations (or designs) that will improve instruction and, through careful study, contribute to research and theory.

Designing for Scale

This class of activities seeks to bring research knowledge to multiple local sites in the form of tools, materials, processes, or principles. Scalable improvement is the main aim. Contribution to research knowledge is less important as a goal. As is the case with design research, development occurs through an iterative cycle of design and redesign. Although researchers and developers may initially work in interaction with practitioners, unlike design research, they are developed not for one particular site or context but rather for many sites and contexts. For this reason, the tools, materials, or processes may be experienced as "external" by practitioners in local settings, raising challenges for attempts to move them to scale.

Development of Accounts of Educational Improvement

In this class of activities, researchers identify and document exemplary practices or locally defined improvement efforts. Thus, rather than drawing on research knowledge to design or develop an approach to improve practice, researchers learn from practice about innovation and improvement, situating practitioner-developed approaches in a larger body of research knowledge and sharing it with a broader audience. Projects in this vein are rooted firmly in practitioner knowledge but also seek to connect that knowledge with research literature as they develop accounts. The principal goal of these accounts is to increase knowledge concerning the improvement of practice. Local sites receive fresh insights and critique of their work; the educational field more broadly benefits from improved understanding, especially when researchers are able to do multiple studies in varying contexts.

Development of Systems for Documentation, Codification, and Sharing of Practitioner Knowledge

Rather than changing the way that research is done, this class of activities seeks to create conditions for practitioners to engage with and critically evaluate research knowledge in the situated context of their school or district. Practitioners learn a great deal through their own iterative experimentation. Yet, more often than not, this knowledge—often referred to as "craft" knowledge or clinical expertise—is private, with few opportunities to capture, share, verify, and improve it (Hiebert, Gallimore, and Stigler 2002). Furthermore, this ongoing experimentation rarely engages research knowledge. Projects in this class seek to alter these conditions of ongoing, private experimentation by creating mechanisms to capture, codify, and share clinical knowledge and foster dialogue between this clinical knowledge and research knowledge in schools and school systems. In this way, projects in this emerging genre seek to improve the knowledge base for teaching by drawing on both practitioner and research knowledge.

We identified several nationally visible research-and-development projects in each category of the typology. To make our selections, we conducted literature reviews and site visits with leaders of more than fifteen of these projects. From these initial fifteen projects, we selected eight established projects that represented the full range of ways of configuring research and practice that we identified in our typology. These eight projects had been in existence for at least five years, that afforded adequate access to key staff and documents, and, taken together, provided key contrasts with one another from which we could learn.

We then supplemented these "established" cases with longitudinal studies of two projects that were just starting at the time of the metastudy: the Information Infrastructure Study and the Partnership for District Reform.[3] We selected these cases because we were able to gain access to the work from the very early days of their work, which was a key criteria for our study, and because they complemented well our existing "established" case studies.

TRAINING OF RESEARCHERS

We worked with a team of researchers from across the country to study these ten projects. We convened a series of five meetings with the researchers over a thirty-one-month time period to develop shared frameworks and to learn about emerging findings from each other's studies. Because the cases were completed on a staggered schedule, some authors were able to benefit from the advice of others who had already completed the main portion of their work. All authors had the opportunity to present their emerging findings and receive feedback from the group. Often, authors were able to discern common themes across the cases; this, in turn, led to the development of new insights about their own case.

DATA COLLECTION

Each of the established cases was studied over the course of a calendar year through interviews, observations, and review of key documents. We began by interviewing project leaders to gain insight into the project goals and strategies, paying particular attention to the nature and sources of expertise brought to bear on project work, mechanisms that were established for ongoing learning from the work, and the ways in which the work was influenced by the larger context. Interviews were supplemented (when possible) by observations of key project activities (e.g., design retreats, professional development, and visits to project sites) to understand the project strategy in greater depth and to ascertain the roles and relationships between key participants (researchers, practitioners, and developers) in project activities. To understand how projects evolved over time, we identified and interviewed individuals who played important roles at different stages of the initiative, including former project leaders, developers, and site liaisons or professional developers. We also tried to identify and visit two or three schools that participated in the initiative at different stages to capture practitioners' perspectives on the experience at different times in the initiative's history. We were particularly interested in understanding the ways in which goals, strategies, and the nature of expertise changed over time. These historical accounts provided insights into the ways in which the project shaped and was shaped by the social and political contexts of research and practice.

The emergent projects were studied through interviews and observations that were conducted as the projects unfolded over the course of four years. We conducted regular interviews of key individuals from both the research and the practice sides of the projects. We also identified key moments in the project's trajectory to observe and/or interview around, thereby capturing interactions and individuals' knowledge and beliefs at critical junctures.

INTERVIEW AND OBSERVATION PROTOCOLS

Interview and observation protocols were both general enough to allow for comparisons across sites and tailored to the opportunities afforded by individual sites. All researchers were urged to gather data that illuminated the expertise that was brought to bear on the work, how the work was organized, how various contexts enabled and constrained the project's efforts, and the consequences of the project's efforts. However, they were also instructed to follow up on important leads and events associated specifically with their project.

The following key questions guided the data collection:

1. What is the relevant knowledge/expertise for school improvement in this project and according to whom?
2. How is the work organized to bring this knowledge to bear on particular problems of practice? What roles, processes, structures, and norms are established?
3. How do various contexts—and the relationships between them—enable and constrain projects' efforts (e.g., institutional contexts, policy contexts, professional contexts, and so on)?

4. What are the consequences of the project's efforts in terms of changes in practice and changes in research as well as changes in paradigms for organizing relationships between research and practice?

DATA ANALYSIS AND REVIEW PROCESS

Each researcher produced a technical report (most were more than 100 pages) that covered the territory of our research questions. The editors and a team of graduate students on the project reviewed the technical reports. Authors revised the reports based on our feedback and then sent them to the leaders of the projects about whom they had been written who provided information about accuracy of facts and sometimes commentary on interpretations. At that point, cases were sent to members of the MacArthur Network on Teaching and Learning for final review. Each case was discussed for a minimum of one-half day at a Network meeting, beginning with a brief presentation by the author followed by comments from project leaders. Afterward, members of the Network asked questions of both the author and the project leaders and made recommendations for strengthening the case. After review by the Network, authors engaged in one more round of revision, culminating in a technical report that is posted on our project's website.[4]

The editors then engaged in a preliminary cross-case analysis using such techniques as matrices and conceptually oriented displays (Miles and Huberman 1994). After surfacing an initial set of themes, we engaged the authors in discussions regarding how to focus their technical reports into chapters for this volume. Finally, Network members played a key role in drawing on findings to craft recommendations for research, policy, and practice.

NOTES

1. Network members included Deborah Stipek (chair), Tony Bryk, John Bransford, Cynthia Coburn, Tom Corcoran, Tom Glennan, Louis Gomez, Diana Lam, Fritz Mosher, Nancy Owen, Charla Rolland, Mary Kay Stein, and Janet Weiss.

2. These projects included Success for All (Robert Slavin and Nancy Madden), Fostering a Community of Learners (Ann Brown and Joe Campione), Cognitively Guided Instruction (Thomas Carpenter and Elizabeth Fennema), High Performance Learning Communities (Lauren Resnick, Richard Elmore, and Mary Kay Stein), The Learning Partnership (Thomas Corcoran), and the Information Infrastructure Study (Anthony Bryk and Louis Gomez).

3. Partnership for District Reform is a pseudonym that we adopted to protect the identity of the district involved.

4. http://www.lrdc.pitt.edu/metastudy/pub.htm.

References

Academy for Educational Development. *National Writing Project: Findings from a Three-Year Evaluation.* New York: Academy for Educational Development, 2002.

Austin, James E. *The Collaboration Challenge.* San Francisco: Jossey-Bass, 2000.

Ball, Deborah L., and David K. Cohen. "Reform by the Book: What Is—or Might Be—the Role of Curriculum Materials in Teacher Learning and Instructional Reform." *Educational Researcher* 25, no. 9 (December 1996): 6–8, 14.

Berends, Mark, Sheila N. Kirby, Scott Naftel, and Christopher McKelvey. *Implementation and Performance in New American Schools: Three Years into Scale-Up.* Santa Monica: Rand Education, 2001.

Berliner, David. "Educational Research: The Hardest Science of All." *Educational Researcher* 31, no. 8 (November 2002): 18–20.

Bickel, William E., and William W. Cooley. "Decision-Oriented Educational Research in School Districts: The Role of Dissemination Processes." *Studies in Educational Evaluation* 11, no. 2 (1985): 183–203.

Birkeland, Sarah, Erin Murphy-Graham, and Carol Weiss. "Good Reasons for Ignoring Good Evaluation: The Case of the Drug Abuse Resistance Education (D.A.R.E.) Program." *Evaluation and Program Planning* 28, no. 3 (2005): 247–56.

Borko, Hilda. "Professional Development and Teacher Learning: Mapping the Terrain." *Educational Researcher* 33, no. 8 (November 2004): 3–15.

Borman, Geoffrey D., Gina Hewes, Laura T. Overman, and Shelly Brown. "Comprehensive School Reform and Student Achievement: A Meta-Analysis." *Review of Educational Research* 73, no. 2 (November 2003): 125–230.

Borman, Geoffrey, Robert E. Slavin, Alan Cheung, Anne Chamberlain, Nancy A. Madden, and Bette Chambers. "The National Randomized Field Trial of Success for All: Second-Year Outcomes." *American Educational Research Journal* 42, no. 4 (2005): 673–96.

Boston Plan for Excellence. *Plain Talk about CCL: Crafting a Course of Study.* Boston: Boston Plan for Excellence, 2003a.

———. *Straight Talk about CCL: A Guide for School Leaders.* Boston: Boston Plan for Excellence, 2003b.

Brandt, Deborah. "Sponsors of Literacy." *College Composition and Communication* 49, no. 2 (May 1998): 165–185.

Bredo, Eric. "Teaching, Relating, and Learning (Book review of *The Construction Zone* and *Rousing Minds to Life*)." *Educational Researcher* 21, no. 5 (June–July 1992): 31–35.

Brown, Ann L. "Design Experiments: Theoretical and Methodological Challenges in Creating Complex Interventions in Classroom Settings." *Journal of Learning Sciences* 2, no. 2 (1992): 141–78.

Brown, Ann, James Greeno, Magdalene Lampert, Hugh Mehan, and Lauren B. Resnick. "Recommendations Regarding Research Priorities: An Advisory Report to the National Educational Research Policy and Priorities Board." Washington, DC: National Academy of Education, 1999.

Brown, John S., and Paul Duguid. "Organizational Learning and Communities-of-Practice: Toward a Unified View of Working, Learning, and Innovation." *Organization Science* 2, no. 1 (February 1991): 40–57.

Bryk, Anthony S., and Barbara Schneider. *Trust in Schools: A Core Resource for Improvement.* New York: Russell Sage Foundation, 2002.

Burch, Patricia E. "Constraints and Opportunities in Changing Policy Environments: Intermediary Organizations' Response to Complex District Contexts." Pp. 111–26 in *School Districts and Instructional Renewal*, edited by Amy M. Hightower, Michael S. Knapp, Julie A. Marsh, and Milbrey W. McLaughlin. New York: Teachers College Press, 2002.

Burch, Patricia E., and C. H. Thiem. "Private Organizations, School Districts, and the Enterprise of High Stakes Accountability." Unpublished manuscript, 2004.

Burkhardt, Hugh, and Alan H. Schoenfeld. "Improving Educational Research: Toward a More Useful, More Influential, and Better Funded Enterprise." *Educational Researcher* 32, no. 9 (December 2003): 3–14.

Carpenter, Thomas P., Elizabeth Fennema, Megan L. Franke, Linda Levi, and Susan Empson. *Children's Mathematics: Cognitively Guided Instruction.* Portsmouth, NH: Heinemann, 1999.

Clifford, Geraldine. "A History of the Impact of Research on Teaching." Pp. 1–46 in *Second Handbook of Research on Teaching*, edited by Robert Travers. Thousand Oaks, CA: Sage, 1973.

Cobb, Paul, Jere Confrey, Andrea diSessa, Richard Lesh, and Leona Schauble. "Design Experiments in Educational Research." *Educational Researcher* 32, no. 1 (January–February 2003): 9–13.

Cobb, Paul, Terry Wood, and Erna Yackel. "Classrooms as Learning Environments for Teachers and Researchers." Pp. 125–46 in *Constructivist Views on Teaching and Learning Mathematics*, edited by Robert B. Davis, Carolyn A. Maher, and Nel Noddings. Reston, VA: National Council of Teachers of Mathematics, 1990.

Coburn, Cynthia E. "Collective Sensemaking about Reading: How Teachers Mediate Reading Policy in Their Professional Communities." *Educational Evaluation and Policy Analysis* 23, no. 2 (Summer 2001): 145–70.

———. "Rethinking Scale: Moving beyond Numbers to Deep and Lasting Change." *Educational Researcher* 32, no. 6 (August–September 2003): 3–12.

———. "Shaping Teacher Sensemaking: School Leaders and the Enactment of Reading Policy." *Educational Policy* 19, no. 3 (July 2005): 476–509.

Coburn, Cynthia E., Meredith I. Honig, and Mary Kay Stein. "What Is the Evidence on Districts' Use on Evidence?" Pp. 67–86 in *The Role of Research in Educational Improvement*, edited by John D. Bransford, Deborah J. Stipek, Nancy J. Vye, Louis M. Gomez, and Diana Lam. Cambridge, MA: Harvard Education Press, 2009.

Coburn, Cynthia E., and Joan E. Talbert. "Conceptions of Evidence-Based Practice in School Districts: Mapping the Terrain." *American Journal of Education* 112, no. 4 (Winter 2006): 469–95.

Coburn, Cynthia E., Judith Touré, and Mika Yamashita. "Evidence, Interpretation, and Persuasion: Instructional Decision Making in the District Central Office." *Teachers College Record* 111, no. 4 (2009): 1115–61.

Cochran-Smith, Marilyn, and Susan Lytle. "Relationships of Knowledge and Practice: Teacher Learning in Communities." *Review of Research in Education* 24 (1999): 249–305.

Cohen, David K., and Carol A. Barnes. "Pedagogy and Policy." Pp. 207–39 in *Teaching for Understanding: Challenges for Policy and Practice*, edited by David K. Cohen, Milbrey W. McLaughlin, and Joan E. Talbert. San Francisco: Jossey-Bass, 1993.

———. "Research and the Purposes of Education." Pp. 17–44 in *Issues in Educational Research: Problems and Possibilities*, edited by Ellen Lagemann and Lee Shulman. San Francisco: Jossey-Bass, 1999.

Collins, Allan M. "Toward a Design Science of Education." Pp. 15–22 in *New Directions in Educational Technology*, edited by Eileen Scanlon and Tim O'Shea. New York: Springer-Verlag, 1992.

Collins, Allan M., John S. Brown, and Ann Holum. "Cognitive Apprenticeship: Making Thinking Visible." *American Educator* 12, no. 6 (Winter 1991): 38–47.

Collins, Allan M., J. S. Brown, and A. Holum. "Cognitive Apprenticeship: Making Thinking Visible." Pp. 1–18 in *The Principles of Learning: Study Tools for Educators*. Pittsburgh, PA: University of Pittsburgh Press, 2003.

Collins, Allan M., Diana Joseph, and Katherine Bielaczyc. "Design Research: Theoretical and Methodological Issues." *Journal of the Learning Sciences* 13, no. 1 (January 2004): 15–42.

Cook, Thomas D. "Randomized Experiments in Educational Policy Research: A Critical Examination of the Reasons the Educational Evaluation Community Has Offered for Not Doing Them." *Educational Evaluation and Policy Analysis* 24, no. 3 (Fall 2002): 175–99.

Corcoran, Thomas, Susan H. Fuhrman, and Catherine L. Belcher. "The District Role in Instructional Improvement." *Phi Delta Kappan* 83, no. 1 (September 2001): 78–84.

Corcoran, Thomas B., and Ullik Rouk. *Using Natural Channels for School Improvement: A Report on Four Years of the Urban Development Program.* Philadelphia: Research for Better Schools, Inc., 1985.

Creswell, James. *Research Design.* 3rd ed. Thousand Oaks, CA: Sage, 2009.

Curriculum Review Panel. *Review of Comprehensive Programs.* University of Oregon: Oregon Reading First Center, 2004.

D'Amico, Laura. *Final Due Diligence Report on the Center for Learning Technologies in Urban Schools (LeTUS).* Pittsburgh, PA: Learning Research and Development Center, University of Pittsburgh, 2003.

———. *The Center for Learning Technologies in Urban Schools: A Case of Design-Based Research in Education.* Pittsburgh, PA: Learning Research and Development Center, University of Pittsburgh, 2005.

Datnow, Amanda, and Marisa Castellano. "Teachers' Responses to Success for All: How Beliefs, Experiences, and Adaptations Shape Implementation." *American Educational Research Journal* 37, no. 3 (Fall 2000): 775–99.

Datnow, Amanda, and Meredith I. Honig. "Introduction to the Special Issue on Scaling Up Teaching and Learning Improvement in Urban Districts: The Promises and Pitfalls of External Assistance Providers." *Peabody Journal of Education* 83, no. 3 (July 2008): 323-27.

Datnow, Amanda, Lea Hubbard, and Hugh Mehan. *Extending Educational Reform: From One to Many.* New York: Routledge, 2002.

David, Jane L. "Local Uses of Title I Evaluations." *Educational Evaluation and Policy Analysis* 3, no. 1 (January 1981): 27–39.

Derry, Sharon J., Lori A. DuRussel, and Angela M. O'Donnell. "Individual and Distributed Cognitions in Interdisciplinary Teamwork: A Developing Case Study and Emerging Theory." *Educational Psychology Review* 10, no. 1 (August 1998): 25–56.

Dickey, Kathleen, Judy Hirabayashi, Mark St. John, and Laura Stokes. "Client Satisfaction and Program Impact: Results from a Satisfaction Survey and Follow-Up Survey of Participants at 2002 Invitational Institutes." Inverness Research Associates, 2003. http://www.inverness-research.org (accessed October 28, 2009).

———. "Client Satisfaction and Program Impact: Results from a Satisfaction Survey and Follow-Up Survey of Participants at 2003 Invitational Institutes." Inverness Research Associates, 2004. http://www.inverness-research.org (accessed October 28, 2009).

Elmore, Richard F. "Getting to Scale with Good Education Practice." *Harvard Educational Review* 66, no. 1 (Spring 1996): 1–26.

Elmore, Richard F., and Deanna Burney. "Investing in Teacher Learning: Staff Development and Instructional Improvement." Pp. 263–92 in *Teaching as the*

Learning Profession, edited by Linda Darling-Hammond and Gary Sykes. San Francisco: Jossey-Bass, 1999.

Engelbart, Douglas C. "Toward High-Performance Organizations: A Strategic Role for Groupware." The Bootstrap Institute, 1992. http://www.bootstrap.org (accessed October 28, 2009).

Engle, Randi A. "Engaging Diverse Stakeholders in Innovative Curriculum Design and Research: The Case of the Middle-School Mathematics through Applications Project (1990–2002)." Pittsburgh, PA: Learning Research and Development Center, University of Pittsburgh, 2006. http://www.lrdc.pitt.edu/metastudy/PDF/MMAPCase0706.pdf (accessed October 28, 2009).

Engle, Randi A., and Faith R. Conant. "Guiding Principles for Fostering Productive Disciplinary Engagement: Explaining an Emergent Argument in a Community of Learners Classroom." *Cognition and Instruction* 20, no. 4 (2002): 399–483.

Engle, Randi A., and Robert B. Faux. "Towards Productive Disciplinary Engagement of Prospective Teachers in Educational Psychology: Comparing Two Methods of Case-Based Instruction." *Teaching Educational Psychology* 2, no. 1 (June 2006): 1–22.

Englert, Richard M., Michael H. Kean, and Jay D. Scribner. "Politics of Program Evaluation in Large City School Districts." *Education and Urban Society* 9, no. 4 (August 1977): 429–50.

Erickson, Frederick, and Kris Gutierrez. "Culture, Rigor, and Science in Educational Research." *Educational Researcher* 31, no. 8 (November 2002): 21–24.

Feldman, Martha S., and James G. March. "Information in Organizations as Signal and Symbol." Pp. 409–28 in *Decisions and Organizations,* edited by James G. March. Oxford: Basil Blackwell, 1988.

Fernandez, Clea, and Makoto Yoshida. *Lesson Study: A Case of a Japanese Approach to Improving Instruction through School-Based Teacher Development.* Mahwah, NJ: Lawrence Erlbaum Associates, 2004.

Feuer, Michael, Lisa Towne, and Richard Shavelson. "Scientific Culture and Educational Research." *Educational Researcher* 31, no. 8 (November 2002b): 4–14.

———. "Reply." *Educational Researcher* 31, no. 8 (November 2002a): 28–29.

Fink, Elaine, and Laura B. Resnick. "Developing Principals as Instructional Leaders." *Phi Delta Kappan* 82, no. 8 (April 2001): 598–606.

Fishman, Barry J., and Elizabeth A. Davis. "Teacher Learning Research and the Learning Sciences." Pp. 535–50 in *The Cambridge Handbook of the Learning Sciences,* edited by R. Keith Sawyer. Cambridge: Cambridge University Press, 2006.

Fishman, Barry J., Jay Fogleman, Beth Kubitskey, Ron Marx, Jon Margerum-Leys, and Deborah Peek-Brown. "Taking Charge of Innovations: Shifting Ownership of Professional Development within a District University Partnership to Sustain Reform." Paper presented at the annual meeting of the National Association for Research on Science Teaching, Philadelphia, 2003.

Gallison, Peter. "Trading Zone: Coordinating Action and Belief." Pp. 137–60 in *The Science Studies Reader,* edited by Mario Biagioli. New York: Routledge, 1999.

Gallucci, Chysan, Beth Boatright, Dan Lysne, and Juli Anna Swinnerton. "District Reform as Teaching and Learning: How the System 'Learns' to Improve

Instruction." Paper presented at the annual meeting of the American Educational Research Association, San Francisco, April 2006.

Glaser, Barney, and Anselm Strauss. *The Discovery of Grounded Theory: Strategies for Qualitative Research*. Chicago: Aldine, 1967.

Goffman, Erving. *Frame Analysis: An Essay on the Organization of Experience*. Boston: Northeastern University Press, 1986.

Goldman, Shelley. "Instructional Design: Learning through Design." Pp. 1163–69 in *Encyclopedia of Education*, 2nd ed., edited by James Guthrie. New York: Macmillan, 2002.

Gomez, Louis M., R. Marx, E. Soloway, J. Clay-Chambers, C. Burgess, and R. Schank. "Center for Learning Technologies in Urban Schools (Centers for Research on Learning and Teaching (CRLT))." Proposal to the Directorate for Educational and Human Resources. Washington, DC: National Science Foundation, 1997.

Gonzalez, Jennifer S. *The 21st Century Intranet*. Centreville, VA: Prentice Hall, 1998.

Gorman, Michael E. "Collaborating on Convergent Technologies: Education and Practice." *Annals of the New York Academy of Sciences* 1013, no. 1 (May 2004): 25–37.

———. "Levels of Expertise and Trading Zones: Combining Cognitive and Social Approaches to Technology Studies." Pp. 287–302 in *Scientific and Technological Thinking*, edited by David C. Gooding, Michael E. Gorman, Alexandra P. Kincannon, and Ryan D. Tweney. Mahwah, NJ: Lawrence Erlbaum Associates, 2005.

Gray, James. *Teachers at the Center: A Memoir of the Early Years of the National Writing Project*. Berkeley, CA: National Writing Project, 2000.

Greeno, James G., Ray McDermott, Karen Cole, Randi A. Engle, Shelley Goldman, Jennifer Knudsen, Beatrice Lauman, and Charlotte Linde. "Research, Reform, and Aims in Education: Modes of Action in Search of Each Other." Pp. 299–335 in *Issues in Education Research: Problems and Possibilities*, edited by Ellen Lagemann and Lee Shulman. San Francisco: Jossey-Bass, 1999.

Grier, Robert, Phyllis Blumenfeld, Ronald Marx, Joseph Krajcik, Barry Fishman, and Elliot Soloway. "Standardized Test Outcomes of Urban Students Participating in Standards and Project-Based Science Curricula." Paper presented at the Sixth International Conference on the Learning Sciences, Santa Monica, CA, June 22–26, 2004.

Grossman, Pamela L., Peter Smagorinsky, and Sheila Valencia. "Appropriating Tools for Teaching English: A Theoretical Framework for Research on Learning to Teach." *American Journal of Education* 108, no. 1 (November 1999): 1–29.

Grossman, Pamela, Samuel Wineburg, and Stephen Woolworth. "Toward a Theory of Teacher Community." *Teachers College Record* 103, no. 6 (December 2001): 942–1012.

Guthrie, J. W., ed. *Educational Evaluation and Policy Analysis* 12, no. 3 (special issue, 1990).

Hannaway, Jane. *Managers Managing: The Workings of an Administrative System*. New York: Oxford University Press, 1989.

———. "Political Pressure and Decentralization in Institutional Organizations: The Case of School Districts." *Sociology of Education* 66, no. 3 (July 1993): 147–63.

Hargreaves, Andy. "Experience Counts, Theory Doesn't: How Teachers Talk about Their Work." *Sociology of Education* 57, no. 4 (October 1984): 244–54.

Hargreaves, Andy, and Corrie Stone-Johnson. "Evidence-Informed Change and the Practice of Teaching." Pp. 89–109 in *The Role of Research in Educational Improvement*, edited by John D. Bransford, Deborah J. Stipek, Nancy J. Vye, Louis M. Gomez, and Diana Lam. Cambridge, MA: Harvard Education Press, 2009.

Hatch, Thomas, and Noel White. "The Raw Materials of Reform: Rethinking the Knowledge of School." *Journal of Educational Change* 3, no. 2 (June 2002): 117–34.

Havelock, Ronald. *Planning for Innovation through Dissemination and Utilization of Knowledge*. Ann Arbor, MI: Institute for Social Research, 1969.

Henningsen, Margaret, and Mary Kay Stein. "Mathematical Tasks and Student Cognition: Classroom-Based Factors That Support and Inhibit High-Level Mathematical Thinking and Reasoning." *Journal for Research in Mathematics Education* 29, no. 5 (1997): 524–49.

Herman, Phillip, Scott Mackenzie, Brian Reiser, and Bruce Sherin. "Student Learning in the Earth Structures Unit." Paper presented at the annual meeting of the American Educational Research Association, Chicago, 2003.

Herman, Phillip, Scott Mackenzie, Bruce Sherin, and Brian Reiser. "Assessing Student Learning in Project-Based Science Classrooms: Development and Administration of Written Assessments." Paper presented at the internal conference of the Learning Sciences, Seattle, 2002.

Hiebert, James, Ronald Gallimore, and James Stigler. "A Knowledge Base for the Teaching Profession: What Would It Look Like and How Can We Get One?" *Educational Researcher* 31, no. 5 (June–July 2002): 3–15.

Hindin, Alisa, Catherine C. Morocco, Emily A. Mott, and Cynthia M. Aguilar. "More Than Just a Group: Teacher Collaboration and Learning in the Workplace." *Teachers and Teaching: Theory and Practice* 13, no. 4 (August 2007): 349–76.

Honig, Meredith I. "Building Policy from Practice: District Central Office Administrators' Roles and Capacity for Implementing Collaborative Education Policy." *Educational Administration Quarterly* 39, no. 3 (August 2003): 292–338.

———. "The New Middle Management: Intermediary Organizations in Education Policy Implementation." *Educational Evaluation and Policy Analysis*, 26, no. 1 (Spring 2004): 65–87.

Honig, Meredith I., and Cynthia E. Coburn. "Evidence-Based Decision Making in School District Central Offices: Toward a Research Agenda." *Educational Policy* 22, no. 4 (2008): 578–608.

Honig, Meredith I., and Gina S. Ikemoto. *Making and Re-Making the Link between Research and Practice: The Case of the Institute for Learning*. College Park: University of Maryland, 2007.

Hood, Paul. *The Role of Linking Agents in Education: A Review, Analysis, and Synthesis of Recent Major Studies*. San Francisco: Far West Laboratory, 1982.

———. *Perspectives on Knowledge Utilization in Education*. San Francisco: West Ed, 2002. http://www.WestEd.org/online_pubs/perspectives.pdf (accessed October 5, 2005).

Huberman, M. "What Knowledge Is of Most Worth to Teachers? A Knowledge-Use Perspective." *Teaching and Teacher Education* 1, no. 3 (1985): 251–62.

Ikemoto, Gina S. "Supports for Principals' Sensemaking: Lessons from the Institute for Learning's Instructional Leadership Program." Doctoral diss., University of Maryland, 2007.

Institute for Learning. *Tools for Developing Instructional Leaders: A Preliminary Proposal to the Wallace-Readers Digest Funds*. Pittsburgh, PA: Learning Research and Development Center, University of Pittsburgh, 2003.

Johnson, Bob L., Jr. "The Politics of Research-Information Use in the Education Policy Arena." *Educational Policy* 13, no. 1 (January–March 1999): 23–36.

Kaestle, Carl F. "The Awful Reputation of Education Research." *Educational Researcher* 22, no. 1 (January–February 1993): 23, 26–31.

Kanter, Rosabeth Moss. "Collaborative Advantage: The Art of Alliances." *Harvard Business Review* (July–August 1994): 96–108.

Kennedy, Mary M. *Working Knowledge and Other Essays*. Cambridge, MA: Huron Institute, 1982.

———. "The Connection between Research and Practice." *Educational Researcher* 26, no. 7 (October 1997): 4–12.

———. *Inside Teaching: How Classroom Life Undermines Reform*. Cambridge, MA: Harvard University Press, 2005.

Kerr, Kerri, Julie Marsh, Gina S. Ikemoto, Hilary Darilek, and Heather Barney. "Strategies to Promote Data Use for Instructional Improvement: Actions, Outcomes, and Lessons from Three Urban Districts." *American Journal of Education* 112, no. 4 (August 2006): 496–520.

Kittle, Peter. "Walking in Our Students' Shoes: Reading Teachers and the Writing Project Model." *Quarterly of the National Writing Project* 26, no. 1 (2004): 35–41.

Krajcik, Joseph. "Middle School Science Curriculum Materials: Meeting Standards and Fostering Inquiry through Learning Technologies." Proposal for an instructional materials development grant, Division of Research on Learning in Formal and Informal Settings (DRL) of the Directorate for Education and Human Resources of the National Science Foundation, Washington, DC, 2001.

Lagemann, Ellen C., and Lee S. Shulman. *Issues in Educational Research: Problems and Possibilities*. San Francisco: Jossey-Bass, 1999.

Lane, Suzanne. "The Conceptual Framework for the Development of a Mathematics Performance Assessment." *Educational Measurement: Issues and Practice* 12, no. 2 (June 1993): 16–23.

Lane, Suzanne, and Edward A. Silver. "Fairness and Equity in Measuring Student Learning Using a Mathematics Performance Assessment: Results from the QUASAR Project." Pp. 97–120 in *Measuring Up: Challenges Minorities Face in Educational Assessment*, edited by A. L. Nettles and T. Nettles. Boston: Kluwer, 1999.

Lane, Suzanne, Clement A. Stone, Robert D. Ankenmann, and Mei Liu. "Examination of the Assumptions and Properties of the Graded Item Response Model: An Example Using Mathematics Performance Assessment." *Applied Measurement in Education* 8, no. 4 (1995): 313–40.

Lave, Jean, and Etienne Wenger. *Situated Learning: Legitimate Peripheral Participation*. Cambridge: Cambridge University Press, 1991.

Lehming, R., and M. Kane, eds. *Improving Schools: Using What We Know*. Beverly Hills, CA: Sage, 1981.

Lesson Study Research Group. [Database]. Teachers College, Columbia University, 2004 (accessed July 19, 2004).

Lewis, Catherine. "Does LS Have a Future in the United States?" *Nagoya Journal of Education and Human Development* 1, no. 1 (January 2002a): 1–23.

———. *LS: A Handbook of Teacher-Led Instructional Change*. Philadelphia: Research for Better Schools, 2002b.

Lewis, Catherine, Rebecca Perry, and Aki Murata. "How Should Research Contribute to Instructional Improvement? The Case of Lesson Study." *Educational Researcher* 35, no. 3 (April 2006): 3–14.

Lewis, Catherine, and I. Tsuchida. "Planned Educational Change in Japan: The Shift to Student-Centered Elementary Science." *Journal of Education Policy* 12, no. 5 (1997): 313–31.

———. "A Lesson Is Like a Swiftly Flowing River: Research Lessons and the Improvement of Japanese Education." *American Educator* 22, no. 4 (Winter 1998): 14–17, 50–52.

Lichtenstein, G., J. Weissglass, and K. Ercikan-Alper. *Final Evaluation Report: Middle School Mathematics through Applications Project, MMAP II (1994–1998)*. Denver: Quality Evaluation Designs, 1998.

Lieberman, Ann, and Maureen Grolnick. "Networks and Reform in American Education." *Teachers College Record* 98, no. 1 (Fall 1996): 7–45.

Lieberman, Ann, and Diane R. Wood. *Inside the National Writing Project: Connecting Network Learning and Classroom Teaching*. New York: Teachers College Press, 2003.

Linde, Charlotte. *Life Stories: The Creation of Coherence*. New York: Oxford University Press, 1993.

Little, Judith W. "The Persistence of Privacy: Autonomy and Initiative in Teachers' Professional Relations." *Teachers College Record* 91, no. 4 (Summer 1990): 509–36.

Lord, Brian, Hillary D. Burns, and Johanna Nikula. *Preliminary Research Status Report: LS Communities in Secondary Mathematics Research Component*. Newton, MA: Education Development Center, Inc., 2003.

Lord, Brian, and Jane Gorman. "'Publicness' in Lesson Study." Paper presented at the annual meeting of the American Educational Research Association, San Diego, CA, 2004.

Lortie, Dan C. *Schoolteacher: A Sociological Study*. Chicago: University of Chicago Press, 1975.

Luria, Aleksandr R. *The Working Brain*. Harmondsworth: Penguin, 1973.

Ma, Liping. *Knowing and Teaching Elementary School Mathematics*. Mahwah, NJ: Lawrence Erlbaum Associates, 1999.

Mac Iver, Martha A., and Elizabeth Farley. *Bringing the District Back In: The Role of the Central Office in Improving Instruction and Student Achievement*. CRESPAR Report No. 65. Baltimore: Johns Hopkins University Press, 2003.

Madden, Nancy, M. Livingston, and N. Cummings. *Success for All/Roots and Wings Principal's and Facilitator's Manual*. Baltimore: Johns Hopkins University Press, 1998.

Magone, Maria, Jinfa Cai, Edward A. Silver, and Ning Wang. "Validating the Cognitive Complexity and Content Quality of a Mathematics Performance Assessment." *International Journal of Educational Research* 21, no. 3 (1994): 317–40.

Marsh, Julie A., Kerri A. Kerr, Gina S. Ikemoto, and Hilary Darilek. *The Role of an Intermediary Organization in District Instructional Improvement: Early Experiences and Lessons about the Institute for Learning*. Santa Monica, CA: RAND Corporation, 2004.

Marsh, Julie A., Kerri A. Kerr, Gina S. Ikemoto, and Hilary Darilek. "Developing District Intermediary Partnerships to Promote Instructional Improvement: Early Experiences and Lessons about the Institute for Learning." Pp. 241–70 in *System-Wide Efforts to Improve Student Achievement*, edited by Kenneth K. Wong and Stacey Rutledge. Greenwich, CT: Information Age Publishing, 2006.

Marsh, Julie A., Kerri A. Kerr, Gina S. Ikemoto, Hilary Darilek, Marika J. Suttorp, Ron Zimmer, et al. *The Role of Districts in Fostering Instructional Improvement: Lessons from Three Urban Districts Partnered with the Institute for Learning*. Santa Monica, CA: RAND Corporation, 2005.

Marx, Ronald W., Phyllis C. Blumenfeld, Joseph S. Krajcik, Barry J. Fishman, Elliot Soloway, Robert Geier, et al. "Inquiry-Based Science in the Middle Grades: Assessment of Learning in Urban Systemic Reform." *Journal of Research in Science Teaching* 41, no. 10 (December 2004): 1063–80.

McDonald, Joseph P., Judy Buchanan, and Richard Sterling. "The National Writing Project: Scaling Up and Scaling Down." Pp. 81–106 in *Expanding the Reach of Education Reforms: Perspectives from Leaders in the Scale-Up of Educational Interventions*, edited by Thomas K. Glennan, Susan Bodilly, Jolene Galegher, and Kerri A. Kerr. Santa Monica, CA: RAND Corporation, 2004.

McDonald, Joseph P., and Emily J. Klein. "Networking for Teacher Learning: Toward a Theory of Effective Design." *Teachers College Record* 105, no. 8 (October 2003): 1606–21.

McDonald, Sarah-Kathryn, Venessa A. Keesler, Nils J. Kauffman, and Barbara Schneider. "Scaling-Up Exemplary Interventions." *Educational Researcher* 35, no. 3 (April 2006): 15–24.

Meyer, John W., and W. Richard Scott. *Organizational Environments: Ritual and Rationality*. Beverly Hills, CA: Sage, 1983.

Miles, Matthew B., and A. Michael Huberman. *Qualitative Data Analysis: An Expanded Sourcebook*. 2nd ed. Thousand Oaks, CA: Sage, 1994.

Mills College Lessson Study Group. *How Many Seats?* (DVD). Oakland, CA: Mills College, 2005. http://www.lessonresearch.net (accessed October 28, 2009).

Mosteller, Frederick, and Robert Boruch. *Evidence Matters: Randomized Trials in Education Research*. Washington, DC: Brookings Institution Press, 2002.

National Academy of Education. *Recommendations regarding Research Priorities: An Advisory Report to the National Educational Research Policy and Priorities Board*. Washington, DC: Office of Educational Research and Improvement, 1999.

Nelson, Richard R., Merton Peck, and Edward D. Kalachek. *Technology, Economic Growth, and Public Policy*. Washington, DC: Brookings Institution, 1987.

Neufeld, Barbara. "Learning, Teaching and Keeping the Conversation Going: The Links between Research, Policy, and Practice." Pp. 243–60 in *The State of Education Policy Research*, edited by Susan H. Furhman, David K. Cohen, and Fritz Mosher. Mahwah, NJ: Lawrence Erlbaum Associates, 2007.

Neufeld, Barbara, Carol Baldassari, Claudia Johnson, Robin Parker, and Dana Roper. *Using What We Know: Implications for Scaling-Up Implementation of the CCL Model*. Cambridge, MA: Education Matters, Inc., 2002.

Neufeld, Barbara, and Ellen Guiney. "Transforming Events: A Local Education Fund's Efforts to Promote Large-Scale Urban Reform." Pp. 51–68 in *Research Perspectives on School Reform: Lessons from the Annenberg Challenge*, edited by Brenda Turnbull. Los Angeles: Annenberg Institute for School Reform, 2003.

Neufeld, Barbara, Anne Levy, and Sara Schwartz Chrismer. *Baseline Report: High School Renewal in Boston*. Cambridge, MA: Education Matters, Inc., 2004.

———. *High School Renewal in the Boston Public Schools: Focus on Organization and Leadership*. Cambridge, MA: Education Matters, Inc., 2005.

Neufeld, Barbara, and Dana Roper. *Off to a Good Start: Year I of Collaborative Coaching and Learning in the Effective Practice Schools*. Cambridge, MA: Education Matters, Inc., 2002.

———. *Year II of Collaborative Coaching and Learning in the Effective Practice Schools: Expanding the Work*. Cambridge, MA: Education Matters, Inc., 2003.

Neufeld, Barbara, Dana Roper, and Carol Baldassari. *Year I of Collaborative Coaching and Learning in the Boston Public Schools: Accounts from the School*. Cambridge, MA: Education Matters, Inc., 2003.

Neufeld, Barbara, and Annette Sassi. *Getting Our Feet Wet: Using "Making Meaning"™ for the First Time*. Cambridge, MA: Education Matters, Inc., 2004.

Nifong, Christina. "'Power to the Schools' Is Credo of Boston's New Chief." *Christian Science Monitor*, June 17, 1996, 1.

Olson, Carol B., and Robert Land. "Teaching Strategic Reading and Analytical Writing to English Language Learners in Secondary School: Curricular Approaches from the Pathway Project." Draft research report, available from the UCI Writing Project, University of California, Irvine, 2003.

Palincsar, AnnMarie, Shirley J. Magnussen, Nancy Marano, Danielle Ford, and Nancy Brown. "Designing a Community of Practice: Principles and Practices of the GIsML Community." *Teaching and Teacher Education* 14, no. 1 (January 1998): 5–19.

Parke, Carol, and Suzanne Lane. "Learning from Performance Assessments in Math." *Educational Leadership* 54, no. 4 (January 1997): 26–29.

Parke, Carol, Suzanne Lane, Edward A. Silver, and Maria Magone. *Using Assessment to Improve Middle-Grades Mathematics Teaching and Learning*. Reston, VA: National Council of Teachers of Mathematics, 2003.

Patton, Michael Q. *Qualitative Research and Evaluation Methods*. 3rd ed. Thousand Oaks, CA: Sage, 2002.

Perry, Rebecca, and Catherine Lewis. "A Perfect Storm: Using Lesson Study to Build and Share Professional Knowledge." Unpublished manuscript, 2006.

Pfeiffer, Lauren, and Helen Featherstone. *"Toto, I Don't Think We're in Kansas Anymore": Entering the Land of Public Disagreement in Learning to Teach*. Research Report 97-3. East Lansing: National Center for Research on Teacher Learning, Michigan State University, 1997. http://ncrtl.msu.edu/full.htm (accessed October 28, 2009).

Powell, Walter W. "Inter-Organizational Collaboration in the Biotechnology Industry." *Journal of Institutional and Theoretical Economics* 120, no. 1 (1996): 197–215.

Reichardt, Robert E. *The State's Role in Supporting Data-driven Decision-Making: A View of Wyoming.* Aurora, CO: Mid-Continent Research for Education and Learning, 2000.

Roberts, Jane M. E., and Shirley C. Smith. *Instructional Improvement: A System-Wide Approach.* Philadelphia: Research for Better Schools, Inc., 1982.

Robertson, Peter J. "Interorganizational Relationships: Key Issues for Integrated Services." Pp. 67–87 in *Universities and Communities: Remaking Professional and Interprofessional Education for the Next Century*, edited by J. McCroskey and S. D. Einbinder. Westport, CT: Praeger, 1998.

Sawyers, LeAnne, Irene Fountas, Gay Su Pinnell, Patricia L. Scharer, and Lisa Walker. "Transforming Teacher Learning through Design Activity: Creating a Web-Based Professional Development Support System for Video Case-Based Professional Learning." Paper presented at the annual meeting of the American Educational Research Association, Chicago, 2007.

Schoenfeld., A. H. "The Math Wars." *Educational Policy* 18, no. 1 (January–March 2004): 253–86.

———. "Instructional Research and the Improvement of Practice." Pp. 161–88 in *The Role of Research in Educational Improvement*, edited by John D. Bransford, Deborah J. Stipek, Nancy J. Vye, Louis M. Gomez, and Diana Lam. Cambridge, MA: Harvard Educational Press, 2009.

Sharkey, Nancy S., and Richard J. Murnane. "Tough Choices in Designing a Formative Assessment System." *American Journal of Education* 112, no. 4 (August 2006): 572–88.

Shavelson, Richard J., and Lisa Towne. *Scientific Research in Education.* Committee on Scientific Principles for Education Research, Center for Education, Division of Behavioral and Social Sciences and Education. Washington, DC: National Academies Press, 2002.

Shrader, Greg W., Kimberly P. Williams, Louis M. Gomez, Judy Lachance-Whitcomb, and Lou-Ellen Finn. "Participatory Design of Science Curricula: The Case for Research for Practice." Unpublished manuscript, 2003.

Silver, Edward A., Margaret Smith, and Barbara S. Nelson. "The QUASAR Project: Equity Concerns Meet Mathematics Education Reform in the Middle School." Pp. 9–56 in *New Directions for Equity in Mathematics Education*, edited by Walter Secada, Elizabeth Fennema, and Lisa Byrd Adajian. New York: Cambridge University Press, 1995.

Silver, Edward A., and Mary Kay Stein. "The QUASAR Project: The 'Revolution of the Possible' in Mathematics Instructional Reform in Urban Middle Schools." *Urban Education* 30 (January 1996): 476–521.

Slavin, Robert E. "PET and the Pendulum: Faddism in Education and How to Stop It." *Phi Delta Kappan* 70, no. 10 (June 1989): 752–58.

———. "Sands, Bricks, and Seeds: School Change Strategies and Readiness for Reform." Baltimore: Center for Research on the Education of Students Placed at Risk, Johns Hopkins University, 1997.

———. "Evidence-Based Education Policies: Transforming Educational Practice and Research." *Educational Researcher* 31, no. 7 (October 2002): 15–21.

———. "A Reader's Guide to Scientifically Based Research." *Educational Leadership* 60, no. 5 (February 2003): 12–16.

———. "Education Research Can and Must Address 'What Works' Questions." *Educational Researcher* 33, no 1 (January–February 2004): 27–28.

Slavin, Robert E., Nancy A. Madden, and Amanda Datnow. *Research In, Research Out: The Role of Research in the Development and Scale-up of Success for All*. Baltimore: Johns Hopkins University Press, 2005.

Sloane, Finbarr C. "Randomized Trials in Mathematics Education: Recalibrating the Proposed High Watermark." *Educational Researcher* 37, no. 9 (2008): 624–30.

Smith, Margaret, Edward A. Silver, and Mary Kay Stein. *Improving Instruction in Algebra*. Vol. 2 of *Using Cases to Transform Mathematics Teaching and Learning*. New York: Teachers College Press, 2005a.

———. *Improving Instruction in Geometry and Measurement*. Vol. 3 of *Using Cases to Transform Mathematics Teaching and Learning*. New York: Teachers College Press, 2005b.

———. *Improving Instruction in Rational Numbers and Proportionality*. Vol. 1 of *Using Cases to Transform Mathematics Teaching and Learning*. New York: Teachers College Press, 2005c.

Smylie, Mark A., and Thomas B. Corcoran. "Nonprofit Organizations and the Promotion of Evidence-Based Practice." Paper presented at the annual meeting of the American Educational Research Association, San Francisco, 2006.

Smylie, Mark A., and Thomas B. Corcoran. "Nonprofit Organizations and the Promotion of Evidence-Based Practice." Pp. 111–36 in *The Role of Research in Educational Improvement*, edited by John D. Bransford, Deborah J. Stipek, Nancy J. Vye, Louis M. Gomez, and Diana Lam. Cambridge, MA: Harvard Educational Press, 2009.

Spillane, James P. "State Policy and the Non-Monolithic Nature of the Local School District: Organizational and Professional Considerations." *American Educational Research Journal* 35, no. 1 (1998): 33–63.

Spillane, James P., Brian J. Reiser, and Todd Reimer. "Policy Implementation and Cognition: Reframing and Refocusing Implementation Research." *Review of Educational Research* 72, no. 3 (Fall 2002): 387–431.

Spillane, James P., and Charles L. Thompson. "Reconstructing Conceptions of Local Capacity: The Local Education Agency's Capacity for Ambitious Instructional Reform." *Educational Evaluation and Policy Analysis* 19, no. 2 (Summer 1997): 185–203.

St. John, Mark. *The National Writing Project Model: A Five-Year Retrospective on Findings from the Annual Site Survey*. Inverness, CA: Inverness Research, 1999.

Star, Susan L., and James R. Griesemer. "Institutional Ecology, 'Translations,' and Boundary Objects: Amateurs and Professionals in Berkeley's Museum of Vertebrate Zoology, 1907–39." *Social Studies of Science* 19, no. 3 (August 1989): 387–420.

Stein, Mary Kay, and Laura D'Amico. "Inquiry at the Crossroads of Policy and Learning: A Study of a District-Wide Literacy Initiative." *Teachers College Record* 104, no. 7 (October 2002): 1313–44.

Stein, Mary Kay, Barbara Grover, and Marjorie Henningsen. "Building Student Capacity for Mathematical Thinking and Reasoning: An Analysis of Mathematical Tasks Used in Reform Classrooms." *American Educational Research Journal* 33, no. 2 (Summer 1996): 455–88.

Stein, Mary Kay, and Suzanne Lane. "Instructional Tasks and the Development of Student Capacity to Think and Reason: An Analysis of the Relationship between Teaching and Learning in a Reform Mathematics Project." *Educational Research and Evaluation* 2, no. 1 (1996): 50–80.

Stein, Mary Kay, Edward A. Silver, and Margaret S. Smith. "Mathematics Reform and Teacher Development: A Community of Practice Perspective." Pp. 17–52 in *Thinking Practices in Mathematics and Science Learning*, edited by James G. Greeno and Shelley V. Goldman. Mahwah, NJ: Lawrence Erlbaum Associates, 1998.

Stein, Mary Kay, and Margaret S. Smith. "Mathematical Tasks as a Framework for Reflection: From Research to Practice." *Mathematics Teaching in the Middle School* 3, no. 4 (January 1998): 268–75.

Stein, Mary Kay, Margaret S. Smith, Margaret Henningsen, and Edward A. Silver. *Implementing Standards-Based Mathematics Instruction: A Casebook for Professional Development*. New York: Teachers College Press, 2000.

Stein, Mary Kay, Margaret S. Smith, Margaret Henningsen, and Edward A. Silver. *Implementing Standards-Based Mathematics Instruction: A Casebook for Professional Development*. 2nd ed. New York: Teachers College Press, 2009.

Stigler, James W., and James Hiebert. *The Teaching Gap: Best Ideas from the World's Teachers for Improving Education in the Classroom*. New York: Summit Books, 1999.

Stokes, Donald E. *Pasteur's Quadrant: Basic Science and Technological Innovation*. Washington DC: Brookings Institution Press, 1997.

Stokes, Laura. "Short-Term Policy Support for Long-Term School Change: A Dilemma for Reform-Minded Practitioners." *Journal of Education Policy* 12, no. 5 (1997): 371–84.

———. "California Writing Project Partnerships with Schools: A Study of Benefits to Teachers and Students." Inverness Research Associates, 2003. http://www.inverness-research.org (accessed October 28, 2009).

Success for All Foundation. "About SFAF-Mission, Vision, and Values." Success for All Foundation, 2005. http://www.successforall.net/about/index.htm (accessed October 28, 2009).

Supovitz, Jonathan. "Melding Internal and External Support for School Improvement: How the District Role Changes When Working Closely with External Instructional Support Providers." *Peabody Journal of Education* 83, no. 3 (August 2008): 459–78.

Tharp, Roland G., and Ronald Gallimore. *Rousing Minds to Life: Teaching, Learning, and Schooling in Social Context*. Cambridge: Cambridge University Press, 1988.

Thomas, Guy, Sam Wineburg, Pam Grossman, Oddmund Myhre, and Stephen Woolworth. "In the Company of Colleagues: An Interim Report on the Development of a Community of Teacher Learners." *Teaching and Teacher Education* 14, no. 1 (June 1998): 21–32.

Tyack, David, and Larry Cuban. *Tinkering toward Utopia: A Century of Public School Reform*. Cambridge, MA: Harvard University Press, 1995.

Vaishnav, Anand. "Business Partnership Yields Major Gains for Boston Schools." *Boston Globe*, November 18, 2001.

Vaughan, Diane. *The Challenger Launch Decision: Risky Technology, Culture, and Deviance at NASA*. Chicago: University of Chicago Press, 1996.

Vygotsky, L. S. *Mind in Society: The Development of Higher Psychological Processes*. Cambridge, MA: Harvard University Press, 1978.

Waddock, Sandra A. "Understanding Social Partnerships: An Evolutionary Model of Partnership Organizations." *Administration and Society* 21, no. 1 (May 1989): 78–100.

Waide, Patrick J., Jr. 1999. "Principles of Effective Collaboration." Pp. 243–50 in *Leading beyond the Walls*, edited by Iain Sommerville. San Francisco: Jossey-Bass, 1999.

Wayman, Jeffrey C. "Student Data Systems for School Improvement: The State of the Field." Pp. 156–62 in *TCEA Educational Technology Research Symposium*. Lancaster, PA: ProActive Publications, 2007.

Weick, Karl E. *Sensemaking in Organizations*. Thousand Oaks, CA: Sage, 1995.

Weiss, Carol H. "Knowledge Creep and Decision Accretion." *Knowledge: Creation, Diffusion, Utilization* 1, no. 3 (1980): 381–404.

Weiss, Carol H., and Michael J. Bucuvalas. *Social Science Research and Decision-Making*. New York: Columbia University Press, 1980.

Weiss, Carol H., Erin Murphy-Graham, and Sarah Birkeland. "An Alternate Route to Policy Influence: How Evaluations Affect D.A.R.E." *American Journal of Evaluation* 26, no. 1 (March 2005): 12–30.

Wenger, Etienne. *Communities of Practice: Learning, Meaning, and Identity*. Cambridge: Cambridge University Press, 1998.

Wertsch, James V. *Voices of the Mind: A Sociocultural Approach to Mediated Action*. Cambridge, MA: Harvard University Press, 1991.

———. *Mind as Action*. New York: Oxford University Press, 1998.

West, Russell F., and Cheryl Rhoton. "School District Administrators' Perceptions of Educational Research and Barriers to Research Utilization." *ERS Spectrum* 12, no. 1 (Winter 1994): 23–30.

What Works Clearinghouse. *WWC Topic Report: Beginning Reading*. Washington, DC: Institute for Education Science, 2007.

Wilson, Suzanne. *California Dreaming: Reforming Mathematics Education*. New Haven, CT: Yale University Press, 2003.

Wohlstetter, Priscilla, Joanna Smith, and Courtney L. Malloy. "Strategic Alliances in Action: Toward a Theory of Evolution." *Policy Studies Journal* 33, no. 3 (August 2005): 419–42.

Wood, Diane. "Teachers' Learning Communities: Catalyst for Change or a New Infrastructure for the Status Quo?" *Teachers College Record* 109, no. 3 (March 2007): 699–739.

Yin, Robert K. *Case Study Research*. 3rd ed. Thousand Oaks, CA: Sage, 2003.

Index

problematizing: and collaboration, 22; in MMAP, 24–26; narrowing, 31; in NWP, 157, 158*f*

professional development: LeTUS and, 38, 40, 46–50; LS and, 131–45; NWP and, 147–62; PDR and, 167–82; SFA and, 84; tools and, 97–99, 208–9

Professional Development Support System (PDS2), 55–71; stages of, 58–69

QUASAR, 9, 109–25, 207–10; generations of tools in, 113–22, 114*t*; organization of, 111–13; overview of, 110–13; term, 109

QUASAR Cognitive Assessment Instrument (QCAI), 111, 113–22; generations of, features of, 114*t*

rapid prototyper role, 60–61

recruiting, issues in, 24–25

redesign, collaboration and, 23–30

relational trust, 56–57, 71n3. *See also* trust issues

research: access to, PDR and, 169–71; demand for, building, 131–45; expectations for, 1; PDS2 and, 62–66; QUASAR tools and, 114–17, 121–22; recommendations for, 217–26; SFA and, 81–83; timeframe of, 7–8, 8*f*, 32, 71n4. *See also* use of research

researchers: and accountability, 28–29; and authority, 26–27; on collaboration, 21; NWP and, 158–59; QUASAR and, 109–25; recommendations for, 223–26; training of, 230. *See also* collaboration

research-practice relationship, xiii; alternative model of, 7–8, 8*f*; historical context of, 4–7; linear model of, 4–6, 5*f*; recommendations on, 201–26; reframing, 1–13; tools and, 80–81, 94–96

Resnick, Lauren, 107

resources: and collaboration, 22–23; in MMAP, 29–30; and research use, 177–78

revenue agreements, and scale-up, 67, 69

Rosen, Lisa, 55–71

royalties, scale-up and, 67

rubric, improvement, 155, 213

St. John, Mark, 162n5

Sawyers, LeAnne, 61–62

scaffolding, tools and, 95, 97

scale-up: collaboration and, 56, 59, 68–69; issues in, 37, 63–64, 66–68

Scharer, Patricia, 62, 66

school conditions, 12, 127–62, 210–13; LS and, 131–45; NWP and, 147–62

science, LeTUS and, 37–53

Scorski, Mike, 63

SERP. *See* Strategic Educational Research Partnership

SFA. *See* Success for All

shared mental models, 60–61, 206–7; lack of, effects of, 63–64; need for, 69–70; trading zone, 57

shared understandings: and collaboration, 57; lack of, 63; and use of research, 177, 191–92

Silver, Ed, 111, 120

Slavin, Robert, 78, 81–83, 86–88, 90

Smith, Margaret S., 112

social learning, tools and, 101–3

sociocultural learning theory, on tools, 94–96, 107

staff. *See* researchers

standardized tests, in Michigan, 39–40

status, and research, 26–28

Stein, Mary Kay, 1–13, 112, 201–26

stereotypes, expectations and, 65

Sterling, Richard, 148

Stokes, Donald, 7

Stokes, Laura, 147–62

Strategic Educational Research Partnership (SERP), 4, 222

Success for All Foundation, 78, 83

About the Contributors

Juliet A. Baxter is associate professor at the University of Oregon. Her work focuses on teacher learning and the teaching of mathematics. Her current research, funded by the National Science Foundation, examines models of professional development that support the integration of mathematics and science.

Cynthia E. Coburn is associate professor in policy, organization, measurement, and evaluation at the University of California, Berkeley. Her research brings the tools of organizational sociology to understand the relationship between instructional policy and teachers' classroom practices in urban schools. She is particularly interested in the role of research and evidence in this process, which she has investigated in a series of studies involving large urban school districts throughout the United States.

Laura D'Amico is adjunct professor at Simon Fraser University in British Columbia, Canada. Her research revolves around the study of systems useful for supporting and implementing educational improvement and reform, including assessment infrastructures, learning technologies, and professional development systems for teachers and principals. She has been a researcher on several projects that use design-based research methods.

Amanda Datnow is professor and director of education studies at the University of California, San Diego. Her research focuses on the policies and politics of educational reform.

Randi A. Engle is assistant professor at the Graduate School of Education at the University of California, Berkeley. She studies principles and practices for fostering productive engagement, learning, and transfer by students and teachers alike.

Meredith I. Honig is associate professor of educational leadership and policy studies at the University of Washington and a senior fellow at the Center for Educational Leadership. Her research, teaching, and community partnerships focus on policy implementation, organizational change, and leadership in urban education systems. She is the author of various publications on evidence-use processes in school district central offices.

Lea Hubbard is professor at the University of San Diego in the School of Leadership and Education Sciences. Her work focuses on educational reform with particular attention to district and principal leadership.

Gina Schuyler Ikemoto is an education policy researcher for the RAND Corporation. Her research examines implementation of reform efforts aimed at building district and school capacity to improve teaching and learning with a particular focus on improving instructional leadership. She has conducted several studies of the Institute for Learning, including studies of how it assists principals and central office leaders in understanding and supporting the implementation of high-quality instruction.

Catherine Lewis is Distinguished Research Scholar at Mills College in Oakland, California. She studies the impact of educational change efforts on both student and teacher learning and development. Fluent in Japanese, she wrote the earliest English-language accounts of lesson study and has made many Japanese educational practices accessible on video at http://www.lessonresearch.net.

Vicki Park is assistant project scientist at the University of California, San Diego. Her research focuses on the impact of accountability policies on urban schools and students, how educators make sense of school reform, and the research-to-practice gap.

Rebecca Perry is senior research associate at Mills College in Oakland, California. Her current research (with Catherine Lewis) focuses on producing materials to support teachers' lesson study professional development and learning in mathematics and studying these lesson study efforts to produce knowledge for the field about teachers' learning. Past research efforts have emphasized implementation of innovative national reform movements in a wide range of educational settings (e.g., charter schools, teacher professional communities, and lesson study) and the ways in which educators' learning from implementation can be applied toward continuous education improvement.

Lisa Rosen is a research professional for the Urban Education Institute at the University of Chicago. Her research and writing bring the tools of cultural anthropology to bear on questions surrounding educational policy formation and implementation, urban school improvement, and organizational development. She is especially interested in efforts to strengthen the role of research universities in the improvement of public schools and to create new roles for teachers that include participation in improvement-oriented research.

Mary Kay Stein is professor in the School of Education and senior scientist at the Learning Research and Development Center at the University of Pittsburgh. Her research focuses on schools and districts as contexts for teacher learning and on the relationships among research, policy, and practice. Stein has served on several national panels that have examined the relationship between research and practice. She is also the founding director of the Learning Policy Center at the University of Pittsburgh.

Laura Stokes is senior researcher at Inverness Research, a private educational research and evaluation firm. Much of her research focuses on teacher leadership and professional development, including the design of large teacher development networks and centers and the multiple short- and long-term contributions that such organizations make to educational improvement from the classroom to the policy process.